EASY-LISTENING ACID TRIP

ISBN: 9781627310956

Feral House
1240 W Sims Way #124
Port Townsend WA 98368
www.feralhouse.com

10 9 8 7 6 5 4 3 2 1

Design: designSimple
Printed in Korea

EASY-LISTENING ACID TRIP

AN ELEVATOR RIDE THROUGH '60s PSYCHEDELIC POP

JOSEPH LANZA

6

For the late Vinnie Bell—
Champion of the Electric Sitar and the Water Guitar

8

ACKNOWLEDGMENTS

Special thanks to John Leon and Forrest Patten for going those extra miles with me in my music searches—and to my appreciative and patient editor Monica Rochester.

Thanks also to Dana Countryman, Jack Fetterman, Jarrett McGehee, Adam Parfrey, Jessica Parfrey, Todd Rutt, Jim Schlichting, Bill Smith, Marlin Taylor, and Christina Ward.

Additional gratitude goes to Easy-Listening greats who had granted past interviews and helped to inform this book. They include Les Baxter, Ray Charles (of the Ray Charles Singers), Ray Conniff, Ethel Gabriel, Morton Gould, Frank Hunter, Johnny Mann, Brad Miller, Tony Mottola, Nick Perito, Stu Phillips, Paul Weston, and Roger Williams.

CONTENTS

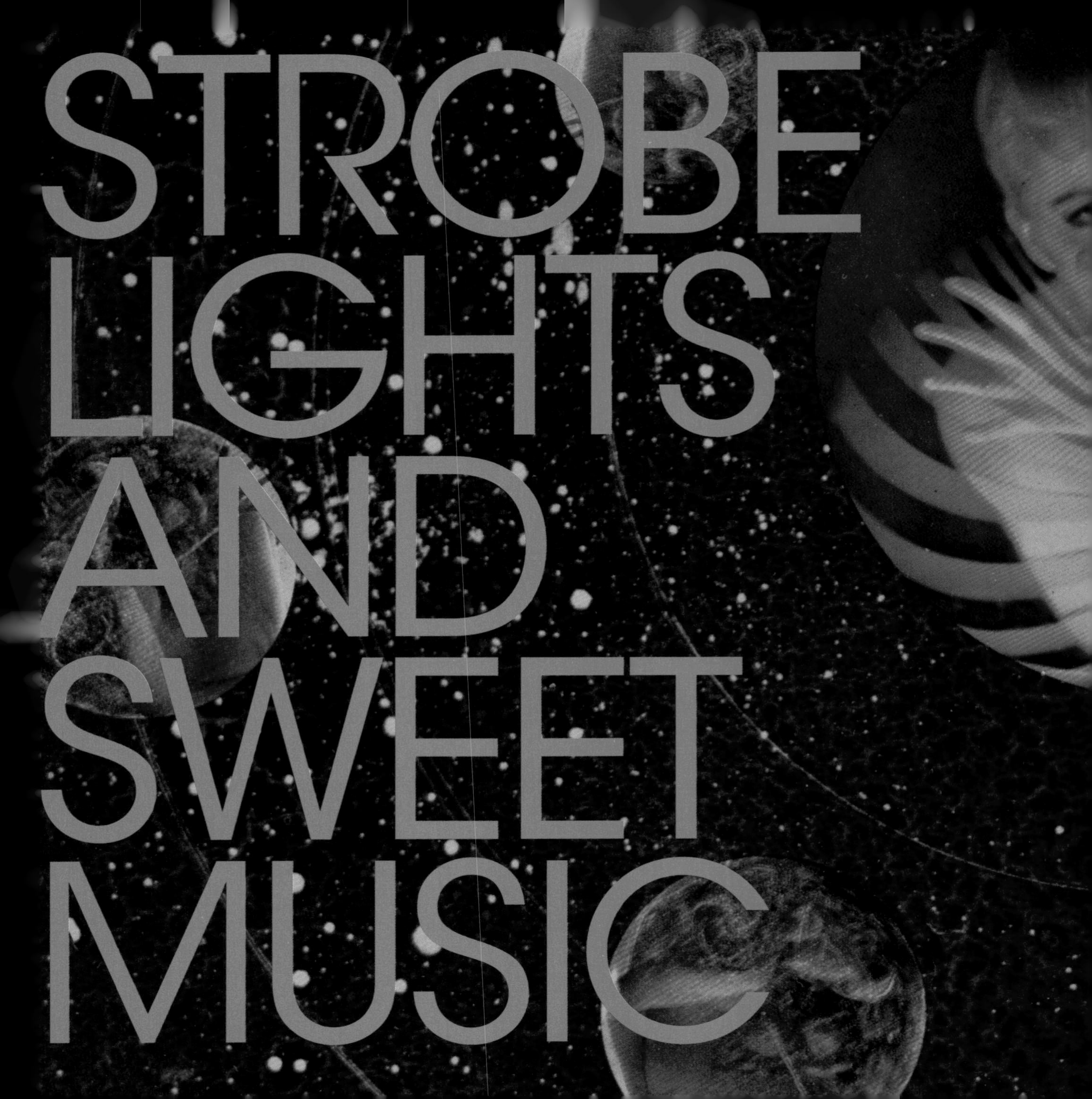
STROBE
LIGHTS
AND
SWEET
MUSIC

"THERE IS GEOMETRY IN THE HUMMING OF THE STRINGS; THERE IS MUSIC IN THE SPACING OF THE SPHERES."

—QUOTE ATTRIBUTED TO PYTHAGORAS

The psychedelic era from the mid- to late '60s offered fluorescent promises of love and expanded consciousness, but it also unleashed darker moments of uncertainty and even violence. For many, the strobe light's beam calculated to ignite cosmic energy also morphed into bleak, hypnotic triggers that prompted others to surrender to psycho messiahs or to self-destruct. The psychedelic music, a vital part of that era, also posed a paradox. The so-called "acid rock" by such acts as the 13th Floor Elevators, the Grateful Dead, and variations on Jimi Hendrix was loud, brash, distorted, and just plain scary in its all-out war on the established order, both musically and socially. A healthy portion of psychedelic pop, however, offered a safety net for those who cherished the "trippy" production novelties but wanted to avoid oblivion, inspiring elevator-music maestros to extract more method out of the media-generated madness. These were songs full of dulcet melodies, ecstasy and insight, sadly romantic reflections, and nostalgic whimsy that cradled listeners in the face of chaos. In short, the weirdness of the psychedelic '60s also had a more harmonious angle, offering Easy-Listening arrangers and conductors a fresh supply of tunes to reinterpret and redistribute.

The scary side of John Lennon, for instance, could advise fans on "Tomorrow Never Knows" to "turn off your mind, relax, and float downstream," but even this most unruly Beatle gazed through Lewis Carroll's *Looking Glass* to conjure such lasting, tuneful creations as "Strawberry Fields Forever" and "Lucy in the Sky with Diamonds." These two 1967 entries alone, despite their hallucinatory lyrics, soon inspired crafty arrangers and performers to transpose them into pleasing instrumental versions that reached additional audiences whose idea of an altered state might have been a dose of Valium or a couple of dry martinis.

An Easy-Listening acid trip, however, is not quite like the instrumental interludes from the pre-psychedelic past. Pop and rock influences made elevator music more challenging and intricate as it combined otherwise conflicting instruments, styles, and time periods. Nevertheless, most of the output still included strings—a vital element that this book will also refer to as "acoustical glaze," "fluttering fiddles," "heavenly flutter," "luster," "massed violins," "shimmer," and other adjectives or nouns connoting the ear-pleasing wonders of Christmas music without the religious trappings. There are also the harps; celesta; harpsichord, Hammond and Wurlitzer organs; pianos and dual pianos; soft horns and woodwinds; acoustic and electric guitars; seductive percussion; vibraphone and xylophone; marimbas and steel drums; harmonicas, tambourines, dulcimers, Ondiolines, and Claviolines; the theremin and the Moog synthesizer; as well as the Hawaiian slack-key, the Japanese koto, and the East Indian sitar (both organic and electric).

Easy-Listening entered the mind-altering '60s by supplementing the conventional orchestras with sounds that in previous eras might have seemed out of place but became welcome confections as mainstream tastes also changed, albeit not at the counterculture's jackrabbit stride. In no other time in contemporary history had so many previously clashing musical attitudes merged to satisfy melody-starved consumers. As a result, the Percy Faiths, Paul Mauriats, David Roses, Lawrence Welks, and Hollyridge Strings of the world feasted on a fresh garden of sonic delights, offering an over-the-counter version of psychedelia's already synesthetic rapture.

How unfortunate then that "Easy-Listening"—a term meant to describe sweet and relaxing music—has elicited controversy and discord. For decades, the unappreciated art of playing soft or breezy instrumental salutes to old standards and pop favorites has been in the crosswinds of snobbery and prejudice from otherwise disparate and dysfunctional coteries of musicians, music critics, and others who fancy themselves gourmands of musical "taste." Be it classical, opera, country, swing, the blues, jazz (hard and smooth), rock (hard and soft), rap, "alternative," "new age," and music of the arty "ambient" variety, those who glom onto and advocate one or more of these contrasting modes can at least break bread over the shibboleth that Easy-Listening is beneath them, especially the lush, melodic, and string-laden

instrumentals that have entertained millions from the home stereo to the public elevator.

The definition of "Easy-Listening" has been especially troublesome through the decades: a category that the many musicians claim they had not chosen but that niche-minded marketers had imposed. This is not altogether true. To get a better grip on what this term meant at a time when popular music was blasting out in so many different directions, the narrative must (like many of the interludes that fill this book) travel back in time.

The term's origins, in America anyway, originate in the mid-1940s, when former big-band orchestrator Paul Weston realized that the close of World War II (and the gloom of Glenn Miller's 1944 disappearance over the English Channel) signaled a new direction. The jitterbug and bebop mutated with the rise of rock-and-roll, but swing bands were essentially over, as many new recordings with elaborate orchestra backings featured vocalists not as mere band components but as stars. Not content with being relegated to wallpaper for singers, Weston and others redirected their orchestras to make instrumental music that sounded more melodic, atmospheric, and ethereal. They blended with the logic of a postwar landscape that focused more on lifestyles, releasing records with lush arrangements to assist those in the mood for love, dining, dreaming, reading, and other domestic rituals.

Though others like Lawrence Welk, Guy Lombardo, Andre Kostelanetz, and Percy Faith had been providing sweet music long beforehand in hotel ballrooms and on radio shows, Weston helped to launch a new market of long-playing (10" and then 12") albums for pleasant backgrounds. Weston would use brief interludes of controlled improvisation on his tracks, but his main focus was on what he called his "creamy-on-the-melody" versions of popular hits and older standards. As early as 1944, he released a 10" EP on Capitol Records called *Music for Dreaming*. By 1950, Weston released his album *Music for Easy Listening*, and he appears to be the first to popularize the immortal term.

When Weston switched to Columbia Records, the Jackie Gleason Orchestra took over on such Capitol titles as *Music for Lovers Only*, *Music to Make You Misty*, and *Music, Martinis, and Memories*. Gleason, a comedian whose bigger cultural impact was as Ralph Kramden in *The Honeymooners*, compensated for his lack of technical skills by rallying the musicians to play what he called his "plain vanilla music." Like Weston, Gleason and his Orchestra used string-enhanced melodies but relied on moments of what Weston called "the jazz feel," particularly the trumpet of Bobby Hackett. The result was that many of the tracks got so repetitive that listeners tended to anticipate the exact timing of a Hackett eruption.

The Gleason "Mood" albums got more intriguing and creative when they started using

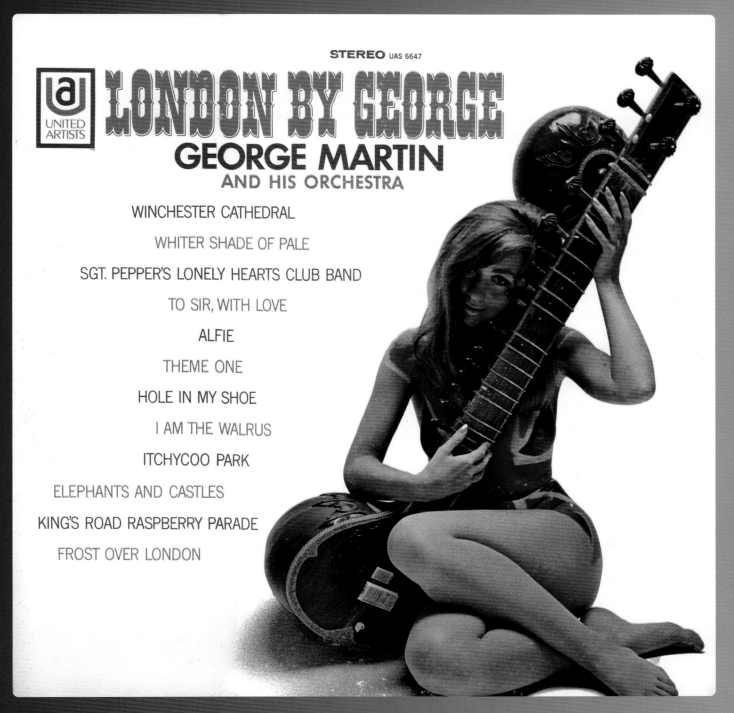

STEREO UAS 6647

LONDON BY GEORGE

GEORGE MARTIN
AND HIS ORCHESTRA

WINCHESTER CATHEDRAL

WHITER SHADE OF PALE

SGT. PEPPER'S LONELY HEARTS CLUB BAND

TO SIR, WITH LOVE

ALFIE

THEME ONE

HOLE IN MY SHOE

I AM THE WALRUS

ITCHYCOO PARK

ELEPHANTS AND CASTLES

KING'S ROAD RASPBERRY PARADE

FROST OVER LONDON

UNITED ARTISTS

different and less intrusive instruments. Among the first of these was the 1955 best-selling album *Lonesome Echo*—a "surrealistic" amalgam of cellos, guitars, mandolins, marimbas, and melancholy solo intervals from an "oboe d'amour." *Lonesome Echo* also included a back-cover picture of Gleason shaking hands with the album's cover designer Salvador Dali. Meanwhile on Columbia, Weston continued his soft-and-sultry instrumental ventures: what many American fans dubbed "mood music" (a term the British use for different purposes to denote the many moods offered in their vast production-music libraries).

With the advent of the long-playing record and the focus on music as an environmental contour, soft and appealing melodies were in higher demand. Both Capitol and Columbia followed up with a series of instrumental LPs, featuring various artists and written testimonials advising consumers to (as one Capitol album advised) enjoy "music arranged, played, and produced especially for your background use."

At the same time, another potent American force was applying Easy-Listening ideas in a more scientific manner. Muzak had to please casual listeners in public settings yet not put them in the same sensual or sleepy mood that Weston or Gleason had the freedom to do when fashioning their albums for quieter times away from the hubbub. As the leading providers of background music for business and government settings, Muzak had to keep the music "Easy" yet also stimulating enough for the workaday world. Their programmers also needed to vary their instruments and to schedule their songs to range from slower to faster in segmented blocks, without repeating any tracks for at least twenty-four hours. While abiding by more rules than Easy-Listening albums had to follow, Muzak still employed several of the same session musicians that played on many commercial "mood music" albums, and its recordings usually conformed to the formula of massed strings, pianos, harps, and horns, with more "exotic" instruments to follow.

Muzak's instrumental ventures evolved from the time it became a formal company in 1934. As the Second World War produced many foundries and other places where workers needed aural stimuli, both America and Britain sought to use music to combat the dangers of worker fatigue. Light orchestras were the usual fare, but foundries with lots of noise needed more up-tempo marching band recordings to get them through the toil and to keep the patriotic spirit. Britain had a radio program called *Music While You Work* and also released a 1937 study called *Fatigue and Boredom in Repetitive Work*, which inspired Muzak to focus on background music as a methodology.

An American arranger, conductor, and composer named Ben Selvin also helped set the Easy-Listening tone. The New York-born Selvin specialized in the violin, orchestrating sweet ballads and dance tunes to aid hotel patrons as they digested their bubblies and, if not three sheets to the wind, attempted to dance along the ballroom floor.

As Muzak's first musical programmer, Selvin took surveys at places like Detroit's Ford Motor Company and the Arrow Shirt makers at Cluett, Peabody & Company in Troy, New York, concluding that the hotel orchestra (as it sounded back in the '30s and '40s) was the best background-music model. In 1943, the same year that Dr. Albert Hofmann experienced his first trip when accidentally absorbing a potent dose of the substance he had invented called LSD-25, Selvin took his findings to New York and presented them to the Acoustical Society of America with a paper entitled "Programming Music for Industry." In it, he advised that the best background music would be "strictly instrumental… and never over-arranged or tricky." From there, Muzak buttressed its product with scientific studies and bits of psychobabble to season the pitch.

By 1947, Muzak gave these studies additional scientific panache by divising "Stimulus-Progression"—a method of programming songs in fifteen-minute blocks of ascending tempo to give listeners a sense of "forward movement." Each composition got assigned a "stimulus value" according to rhythm, types of instruments, orchestra size, song sequence, and volume. Many of its tracks had the sweet strings and pianos usually associated with Easy-Listening, but by the end of each quarter-hour, the tunes tended to stress percussion and perky keyboards, particularly when the average worker's mid-morning and midday blood sugar tended to sag. Still, Muzak adhered to the expression "lilting melody" to describe its music in a 1948 ad that appeared in *Time* magazine, touting its psychological effects inside of Otis elevators. This ad alone gave the term "elevator music" a descriptive, literal meaning—nothing negative.

By the early '50s, the Easy-Listening allure of commercial recordings was unquenchable, particularly in America with arrangers like Percy Faith and Andre Kostelanetz who continued on from the radio days, as well as such subsequent stars as Les Baxter, Ferrante & Teicher, and Roger Williams. From the U.K., Mantovani (Italian-born but musically nurtured in England) also became a star in America with his 1951 recording of "Charmaine," a waltz from the 1926 silent movie *What Price Glory*. He earned such affectionate sobriquets as "the Niagara Falls of fiddles," thanks to a "cascading" violin technique that his arranger Ronald Binge devised. Mantovani soon followed "Charmaine" with a "gush of lush" version of the sixteenth-century folk tune "Greensleeves" and went on to apply what some had called his "honeyed, caressing tones" to movie themes, show tunes, and many popular songs. "I wanted an effect of an overlapping of sound, as though we were playing in a cathedral," he would say.

Through the decades, "Easy-Listening" continued to elude "easy" definitions. In some ways, it has been the neglected stepchild of musical categories. Unlike classical, jazz, blues, country, and rock (in its various forms), Easy-Listening was more of a populist label that centered on the needs of listeners instead of the whims of players. Some of its recording artists understood the concept and embraced it, but others were somewhat delusional about their output and avoided the "Easy-Listening" tag, though this was the kind of music that made them lots of money.

Even so, Easy-Listening became a sound that often emerged by serendipity. If they recorded it thinking of themselves more as day laborers than virtuosos, the arrangers and players (oddly enough) gave the music more breathing space, allowing listeners to add their own contexts without the recording artists' "high art" pressures. Easy-listeners were free to find beauty in the tracks that some—not all—of the studio performers did not realize they were creating. Decades later, a former Muzak programmer named Christopher Case reached a similar conclusion: "When musicians are left to themselves, not considering public taste, demographics, or the psychology of music, and just think about art for the sake of art, they will put together something that won't please everyone. Our music has a wider audience appeal than any other form of music. Most other forms are targeted to a tight demographic group.

Since we have so many listening at once, we are forced to amalgamate."

Many Easy-Listening giants avoided the celebrity limelight, content to describe their work with the self-effacing manner that some of Hollywood's notable film composers also used. Dimitri Tiomkin once claimed, "The [film score] composer, by providing pleasant melodic music, can direct attention from what the make-up artist could not hide." Perhaps defiant in their departure from "respectable" musicianship, some of the major Easy-Listening arrangers and conductors avoided dry music-theory lingo, opting instead to describe their craft with more populist metaphors and similes. In the '50s, Percy Faith stated his goal of "satisfying the millions of devotees of that pleasant American institution known as the quiet evening at home, whose idea of perfect relaxation is the easy chair, slippers, and good music." The ever-comical Jackie Gleason felt freer to break decorum when instructing his orchestra to approximate "the sound of pissing off a high bridge into a teacup."

Easy-Listening got more popular and more engaging by the late '50s and early '60s with the advent of rock-a-ballads and other youth-oriented pop music that depended more than ever on the hook. Tin Pan Alley fare could only go so far, and a new progeny of songs and recording artists gave instrumentalists new places to explore. The growth of echo effects also helped. Ray Conniff, one of Percy Faith's cohorts at Columbia Records, became so enamored with echo in the '50s that he credited it as his creative cornerstone. Heeding what he called "recurring patterns" in the background of many popular songs, he discovered what he called "a ghost tune behind the apparent one." Easy-Listening allowed the "ghost tune" to sound even ghostlier. In 1963, with Columbia's release of *Themes for Young Lovers*, Percy Faith and His Orchestra spearheaded the fusion of Easy-Listening with pre-Beatles teenage dream songs—a surprising and winning mixture that would evolve just a few years later into "Easy" psychedelia.

Easy-Listening maestros turned out album after album; some had hit singles as well. Then in the early 1960s, confusion oozed when *Billboard* magazine's editors noticed demographic shifts, specifically the growing rock-and-roll youth market, and sought new category strategies. Lots of music still surfaced that did not have rock-and-roll or rhythm-and-blues appeal, nor did it fit into "purist" versions of country, jazz, or classical, and yet it continued to attract many record buyers. To help account for these changes, *Billboard*, in July of 1961, started including an "Easy-Listening" subset of twenty titles from their Hot 100 records to reflect so-called "middle-of-the-road" tastes.

In the process, *Billboard* compensated for the dearth of instrumental singles by including celebrity singers in the mix. The first twenty "Easy-Listening" songs included Don Costa's instrumental "Never on Sunday" as well as the Chordettes'

recording of the same song. Arthur Lyman's vibraphonic instrumental "Yellow Bird" and Ray Ellis and His Orchestra's lush rendition of Nino Rota's "La Dolce Vita" showed up, but so did Pat Boone's uncharacteristically morbid "Moody River." On September 7, 1963, when *Billboard* called the list "Middle-Road Singles," Kai Winding's instrumental of "More" (the theme from *Mondo Cane*) got listed with Vic Dana's vocal cover, alongside songs like the Kingston Trio's "Desert Pete," and at #1, Bobby Vinton's "Blue Velvet." From November of 1962 through May of 1965, the chart category went from "Middle-Road Singles" to "Pop-Standard Singles."

On June 5th, 1965, around the time the Byrds' "Mr. Tambourine Man" hit #1 on *Billboard*'s Hot 100, the magazine introduced its separate Top 40 Easy-Listening chart, a move to fit the needs of radio programmers, record dealers, and jukebox proprietors exploring a netherworld attracting older and younger listeners. Along with hit instrumentals like Horst Jankowski's "A Walk in the Black Forest" and Bert Kaempfert's "Three O'Clock in the Morning," this first official Easy-Listening tally included some names from the British Invasion, who had offered songs melodious enough for adult appeal. They included "Before and After" by Chad & Jeremy, with its lush arrangements by Muzak contributor Frank Hunter, and "This Little Bird" by Marianne Faithfull, arranged by Mike Leander, who provided sweet backdrops for several other British pop entries, including the score for the 1967 film *Privilege* and those plaintive strings behind the Beatles' "She's Leaving Home."

This mid-'60s juncture is where the merger of psychedelia and Easy-Listening began. For many older musicians who had played on sessions from the big-band days into pop's jet age, the world was not coming to an end after all, but rather the old one got reborn in paisley prints and Day-Glo hues. But Easy-Listening psychedelia faced obstacles, as hallucinogenic dreams also involved nightmares, and what sounded so pretty on the surface hid sadder and darker themes—much like the ambiguous tone of popular music in general.

"A demon had invaded me, had taken possession of my body, mind, and soul," Dr. Hofmann recounted after his first LSD trip. "I jumped up and screamed, trying to free myself from him, but then sank down again and lay helpless on the sofa." Though he would call the drug his "problem child," Hofmann also saw new dimensions of human potential in the lysergic experience. Doctors and therapists hoped it would help alcoholics and schizophrenics, but LSD seemed more resourceful for the CIA and its various mind-control capers such as the notorious MK-ULTRA program. For them, LSD was a great "incapacitator" that disoriented users who ingested it without their knowing, leading to one infamous "misadventure" in 1953, when Frank Olson, a previously dosed CIA agent, leapt to his death from a New York City hotel room.

Though the government scientists conducting these experiments are credited with coining the term "trip," optimistic LSD advocates got queasy about the scandals and wanted to proselytize their viewpoint with a more sacramental word, leading Humphrey Osmond in 1957 to coin the term "psychedelic." The music born from this chemical revolution also embodied this conflict. Hardcore psychedelic rock tore the mind apart, while the softer or at least more melodic psychedelic pop, with songs usually running under four minutes, entertained the imagination with alien sounds yet adhered enough to traditional structure to discourage nervous breakdowns.

Bob Dylan foretold this paradox in 1965, two years before the "Summer of Love," when he introduced "Mr. Tambourine Man." The lyrics, partly inspired by Arthur Rimbaud, suggest an insomniac trying to get a grip after a bad night of wrestling with an altered state. It is the early morning, and "evening's empire" has fallen, so the sleepless wanderer seeks a gentle song to reclaim a sense of logic, proportion, and inspiration. That contrast between psychological mayhem and peace of mind is what makes the link between psychedelic music and Easy-Listening so strange and yet so inevitable.

Despite Dylan's claim that he had yet to try LSD at the time he wrote it, "Mr. Tambourine Man" took on a lysergic life of its own. Still, Dylan's voice had a gravelly groan that chafed against prevailing standards of good singing. His

Polydor

249 002

Beat
In
Sweet

JAMES-LAST-BAND

I Got You Babe
Baby Don't Go
Eve Of Destruction
Mr. Tambourine Man
Like A Rolling Stone
Yesterday u. v. a.

messages too were assaults against the "norm." "If I told you what our music is really about," he warned an interviewer in 1965, "we'd probably all get arrested." Others, however, with more melodic skills softened Dylan's composition. That same year, the Byrds released their more intricate, high-pitched, electrified version that stripped away several verses but kept the parts about the "magic swirling ship" and its narrator's desire to sail into calmer waters.

The Byrds also coasted into a brighter, comelier pop direction with the "jingle-jangle" of Roger McGuinn's 12-string Rickenbacker guitar, enticing fans to embrace its cosmic mood. Soaring from the power of this one recording, the Byrds articulated "folk rock," a pop fashion corresponding roughly with the British Invasion that, by 1965 and 1966, would join the Beatles in a psychedelic phase-shift.

Where electric guitars led, lush orchestras soon followed. Among the first to embellish psychedelic pop with such luster was David Rose. A famous conductor, arranger, composer from the big-band era, and popular for, among other creations, that sleazy tune "The Stripper," Rose also composed and released the 1944 Easy-Listening classic "Holiday for Strings": a fusillade of plucked violins approximating the sound of laughter and the frenzy of shoppers. This song alone proved that Easy-Listening was not just for relaxing by the fire or for meditating. It could also be audacious and at times deliciously mad—in a calibrated manner.

Also in 1965, David Rose released the album

The Velvet Beat, which applied the shopper's pizzicato effect of "Holiday for Strings" to "Mr. Tambourine Man," tiptoeing through each note as a sprightly contrast to Dylan's angst-filled original. Rose ended up making some listeners suspect that Dylan, consciously or unconsciously, knew that his anguish had an Easy-Listening endgame, as more of his recordings got metamorphosed by similar pop orchestras.

England's Mike Leander assembled an orchestra for the 1965 album simply called The Folk Hits, where "Mr. Tambourine Man" again tripped across a wave of reverberant strings. That same year, Germany's Easy-Listening maestro James Last and his "James Last Band" also guided the "magic swirling ship" along smoother waves by combining orchestral strings and acoustic guitar on an album called Beat in Sweet.

"Mr. Tambourine Man" surfaced again on the 1965 album The Bob Dylan Song Book Played by the Golden Gate Strings. Here, Easy-Listening flaunts its playful and eccentric side. Instead of narrating the dregs of a bad trip, the tune suggests the Clampetts of The Beverly Hillbillies recovering from a moonshine binge. A lighthearted buggy ride through backwoods Americana replaces the "swirling ship," with the ringing of banjos, horns (including a tuba), sundry percussion, and of course, massed strings as the centerpiece.

This transition from Dylan to Byrds to Easy-Listening instrumentals continued. While

Grace Slick and Jefferson Airplane equated the altered state to *Alice's Adventures in Wonderland* and *Through the Looking Glass*, where "logic and proportion have fallen sloppy dead," Easy-Listening reflected psychedelia from another side of the Looking Glass: an alternative but much less threatening headspace, reinterpreted by studio arrangers and players challenged to rearrange into notes what the pop and rock performers often improvised as outbursts.

The merging of psychedelia with Easy-Listening rattled the sacrosanct altar upon which rock-and-roll (like blues and jazz) tottered. According to purist gospel, the "real" music had to be a "raw," "liberating" experience unsullied by pop's profane commercialism. "Rock and roll was a victim of its own success," authors Martin A. Lee and Bruce Shlain proclaim in their book *Acid Dreams*, "and the new music, despite its frequent anti-authoritarian overtones, was easily coopted by the corporate establishment." Such an assessment prompts a mischievous thought: if being "co-opted" into middle-class norms is rock and pop's natural evolution, then Easy-Listening versions have all along been ahead of the curve.

Generational tastes were not always at war during the psychedelic years. Relatively wholesome groups, including those sloppily attired tunesmiths the Turtles, appreciated the musical roots that their vaudevillian parents had handed down to them. Like the Byrds, the Turtles retained shadows of the past in their repertoire: both bands included versions of Vera Lynn's World War II anthem "We'll Meet Again" on their early albums. The Turtles also recorded "It Was a Very Good Year," a moody look backward that the Kingston Trio had introduced years before Frank Sinatra's recording.

The Strawberry Alarm Clock was a curious act that could fluctuate from harder acid rock to ballads that suggested lysergic Lettermen. In 1967, they were adorned in love beads, sandals, and caftans, embodying psychedelic pop's look as well as its sound. They could tickle the teenyboppers on *American Bandstand* yet appear in Hollywood counterculture spoofs like Richard Rush's *Psych-Out* and later in Russ Meyer's X-rated *Beyond the Valley of the Dolls*. Shortly after its 1967 release, their "Incense and Peppermints" commanded enough of an impression for Muzak to record an instrumental version by Charles Grean and His Orchestra, re-contoured for offices, restaurants, stores, and of course, elevators from coast to coast—with an upbeat combination of harp, horns, flutes, tambourine, drums, and yes, even furtive appearances from a high-pitched electric guitar. Grean had the temerity to allow a flowing harp to start the track and then have the harp's plucked strings replace the vocal lead. The harp is the chiming force behind Grean's recording; it keeps the track sounding heaven-bound, even without a string orchestra.

On the same day that they recorded their elevator-music tribute to the Strawberry Alarm

David Rose / The Velvet Beat

Lush String Interpretations Of Today's Hits

Mr. Tambourine Man • You've Lost That Lovin' Feelin' • Are You Sincere • And I Love Her
King Of The Road • (I Can't Get No) Satisfaction • I Can't Stop Loving You • Mae
Downtown • The Great Pretender • All I Really Want To Do • What's New Pussycat?

E-4307

Clock, Grean and His Orchestra also recorded Muzak variations on two other psychedelic pop songs from around the fall of 1967: the Monkees' wistful "Daydream Believer" and the one single capturing the Four Seasons' short-lived "freaky" phase, "Watch the Flowers Grow." A year later, Martin Denny added a sitar to his "Incense and Peppermints" rendition on A *Taste of India*, also omitting strings but providing a relaxing "exotica" that beguiled listeners without intrusive voodoo drums or birdcalls.

As the 1967 Summer of Love's leaves turned brown, and a sorrowful autumn prevailed, an English band called the Small Faces sang about a peculiar place called "Itchycoo Park," where teen-agers indulged in risqué fun. The song bent heads with mind-blowing sound effects but also baffled airplay censors with its suggestive refrain about getting high and touching the sky. Soon after its release, the Beatles' engineer and producer George Martin released an album called *London By George!* It included an alternative "Itchycoo Park": purely instrumental, with all of the original's melodic titillation but with ethereal effects resonating from a parallel world fit for a prim-and-proper English auntie serving up tea with cakes and dainties.

British teatime is an important factor when considering the soft, chewy, melodic center inside of England's psychedelic pop. The rollicking Rolling Stones could holler about their lack of "Satisfaction," but this rebel yell too succumbed to Easy-Listening charms when David Rose (on the same album where he soothes the "Tambourine Man") rearranged Jagger and Richards' innards with a slow, string-filled cover. The tune is still unmistakable, but Rose's version suggests that its creators and audience are already somewhat satisfied.

The idea of teatime with the Stones got more enticing when the band occasionally shed their rhythm-and-blues masks to play closer to their bloodlines. On "Lady Jane," they were already mixing tradition with studio enhancements in a haunting and beautiful melody. Some Easy-Listening adaptors caught on. In 1969, Mike Melvoin (among those who discovered a new life with the synthesizer) electrifies the tune yet sticks to the baroque niceties on *The Plastic Cow Goes Mooooooog*. With guitarist Al Caiola arranging and conducting, "Lady Jane" becomes a wedding of the acoustic guitar and sitar on the 1971 album *Living Guitars Play Songs Made Famous by The Rolling Stones*. Years later, the Gino Marinello Orchestra would adorn "Lady Jane" with more mystery on an instrumental that bolsters the echoes and allows the acoustic guitars to sound more like the sitar's kin.

Fantasies of eating scones with the Stones got even quainter with the 1967 release of "She's a Rainbow," arguably the group's greatest departure from their safe, spoon-fed, bluesy image. Nicky Hopkins provides the flighty, pirouetting piano while John Paul Jones (busy with session work before joining Led Zeppelin) handles the string arrangements. Brian Jones plays a Mellotron, and a celesta adds more storybook flavor. Without the vocals, the song's ever-heightening melody seems even more buoyant on an album called *Groovin' Strings & Things*, with the piano notes sounding more like the exhalations of the breathy White Queen of Lewis Carroll's *Through the Looking Glass* who, as the Beatles would mimic, squeals, "Better... better...better..." before nearly passing out. For those more familiar with the Stones' "Satanic" poses, "She's a Rainbow" might connote that ballet school full of witches that Dario Argento would later dramatize in the 1977 film *Suspiria*, but the melody remains one of the psychedelic era's most inventive and gleefully "twee" pieces.

As the Beatles, the Byrds, Donovan, and even the Doors churned out song after song, Easy-Listening echoes from various orchestras and ensembles multiplied like white rabbits. Behind the disorienting light shows, hypnotic strobes, and head-rattling guitar solos, more musical contradictions unfolded as Easy-Listening doppelgängers appropriated some of the most appealing and salvageable material. Such other names as the 101 Strings, the Hollyridge Strings, Ronnie Aldrich and His Two Pianos, the Johnny Arthey Orchestra, Mariano and the Unbelievables, the Cyril Stapleton Choir and Orchestra, the Marble Arch Orchestra, and the Nirvana Sitar and String Group joined the Easy-Listening Love-In.

Contrary to what some might suspect, the Easy-Listening—or elevator music (which is essentially a positive term)—did not silence the cultural and social upheavals of the '60s but rather complemented the seismic shifts with its toned-down counterpoint. While the Beatles shouted or crooned their mind-twisting melodies, Donovan sang about an "e-lec-tri-cal banana," Bob Dylan blew paeans of protest through his nasal passages, and the Byrds made Dylan's sentiments sound more like the ballads of a spaceman, the elevator-music songbook expanded. This is precisely because many pop and rock performers were leaving melodic trails ripe for revision.

In an April 1966 essay for *High Fidelity*, composer Glenn Gould, coming from an academic perspective, proved somewhat more genial when considering Muzak's impact: "In my opinion, the most important of the missing links in the evolution of the listener-consumer-participant … is to be found in that most abused of electronic manifestations—background sound. This much-criticized and often misunderstood phenomenon is the most productive method through which contemporary music can confide its objectives to a listening, consuming, Muzak-absorbing society…"

The late Morton Gould (no relation to Glenn) led symphony orchestras that included The Chamber Music Society of Lincoln Center, composed music for such films as the 1957 widescreen spectacle *Windjammer*, and also put out orchestral arrangements of the Beatles' "Eleanor Rigby" and the Lovin' Spoonful's "Daydream" on his 1967 album *Morton Gould Makes the Scene*. In 1992, while President of ASCAP, he was in a strategic position to assess age-old prejudices: "The so-called serious musician turned up his nose or her nose at light music in any medium for many understandable reasons. It was a way of giving the serious musician more importance. If you could be in a private club, you could feel superior. There were lots of psychological, physiological, and in some cases pathological reasons for these feelings."

Appreciating *elevated* psychedelia, and Easy-Listening instrumentals in general, involves three paths that can sometimes overlap. The first and most obvious path is to simply enjoy these recordings either as unobtrusive background or to listen actively for the unusual mélange of musical styles, influences, and confluences.

The second path involves *layered listening*: instead of functioning as only a relaxing background, Easy-Listening can encourage those aware of the originals (with their social and historical contexts) to hear them through a psychological prism. The voice and music of Donovan and the Vic Lewis Orchestra's lilting version of "Sunshine Superman" form a dynamic interplay: deep-focused listening— an aural depth of field—that allows the original and the Easy-Listening apparition to alternately phase in and out of the mind.

The third path is for those who, through propaganda and the lazy temptation to follow groupthink, fancy they dislike this music but are at least curious enough to give it a chance. Theirs is a queasy quest as they enter an alien portal full of unexpected joys or delicious dangers. The adventure might be akin to visiting the "uncanny valley" that often awaits those who encounter some CGI or other AI creation: an *un*Easy place that seems foreign yet familiar at the same time. There await such marvels as the Hollyridge Strings' rendition of the Beatles' "Strawberry Fields Forever" that hovers like an astral apparition, Mike Curb and the Waterfall's homage to the Doors' "The Crystal Ship" that underscores Jim Morrison's romantic side, or Billy Vaughn's take on "Time of the Season" that is in some ways eerier than the Zombies' Top 40 classic.

In the early 1930s, Irving Berlin composed "Soft Lights and Sweet Music," a song that yearned to "hear a beautiful tune" while basking "in a light that is mellow." It was among the first ditties to prescribe an ideal musical "set and setting"—a concept that later went from the psychological theories behind Music by Muzak, to the psychedelic propaganda of Timothy Leary, and to the laid-back lifestyle suggestions of the Mystic Moods Orchestra. Even in those turbulent days when the strobe light's beam and the bad hallucinations stripped the senses, the Easy-Listening sailed in, like a magic ship, guiding weary travelers to a safer harbor and another alternate world. ✤

FIXING A HOLE WHERE THE WAVE CRASH IN

"TRIPPING IS A VERY SPECIAL TYPE OF ACTIVITY, MENTALLY AS WELL AS PHYSICALLY. IT CAN INCLUDE MOMENTS OF ASTONISHING INSIGHT AND SUPERMELLOW SERENITY... BUT ALWAYS LURKING AT THE EDGE OF THE PSYCHEDELIC AURA IS THE SPECTER OF SOMETHING DEADLY SERIOUS."

—MARTIN A. LEE AND BRUCE SHLAIN, *ACID DREAMS*

Years before George Harrison's first sitar strum or Donovan's mantra about "gazing with tranquility," the mating of psychedelic pop with the Easy-Listening instrumental emerged, like many vibrant forms, from the sea. The California shore, the sun and fun, the tanned surfers and radiant waves, would all seem ideal "set and setting" conditions for a peaceful LSD excursion. In its softer, more romantic incarnations, the surf instrumental provided an otherworldly, pre-raga seduction, as its electric guitar's eerie tremolos and hypnotic twangs reflected the slack-key reveries of its Hawaiian roots.

An intriguing example is "Pipeline," the 1963 hit by the Chantays, which evokes a sense of mystery and impending disaster. There is something Far Eastern in the guitar work, suggesting another time and place beyond the mindset of a typical sun-bleached beach bum. In this case, the actual "Pipeline" is an aquatic curve that threatens the unwary surfer. Those versed in surf lore recognize the allusion to one of the most treacherous parts of the ocean: the Banzai Pipeline, a fierce, swirling wave near Sunset Beach that, coupled with flesh-shredding coral, could drown and devour those hoping to "hang ten."

The underlying terror of "Pipeline" makes its relationship with Lawrence Welk all the more ironic. Welk, starting in 1955, took television viewers each week into another kind of alternate reality: polished smiles, perfectly tailored clothing, and songs fashioned with bubbly, happy persuasion. But as the unruly "teenage" market expanded, Welk didn't flinch; he instead envisioned a joyful challenge and had a surprise in store for his audience expecting their weekly waltz fix. On May 15th, 1963, the Chantays appeared on his show to join his champagne players for a generational marriage: a joint performance of "Pipeline." This was the same year that Welk recorded his own version, which retained the catchy tune but re-patterned it to conform to his hotel-orchestra tradition.

Then again, the Chantays' original had enough deceptively sweet charms. In 2015, when Chantays guitarist Brian Carman died, Dean Torrence of Jan & Dean shared with the *Orange County Register* his own affection for the song: "To me it had that kind of laid-back quality that some of the other surf songs didn't have. And it seemed to shift gears as it went along, which is kind of what the art of surfing would pretty well be."

As early as 1959, the Islanders foreshadowed the spooky yet "Easy" side of surf music with "The Enchanted Sea." The creeping guitars and wraithlike whistler suggested sirens leading seafarers to their doom. It also lured Easy-Listening artists. Martin Denny employed a small combo for a stereo-engorged version on his album of the same name. Alfred Newman and the Ken Darby Singers pushed it further out to distant shores on the Capitol album *Ports of Paradise*, with the sirens sounding ghostlier and a masculine choral response suggesting seamen in submission. Italy's Fausto Papetti attempted a nautical seduction with his woozy saxophone. Soon, Brooklyn's Santo & Johnny enlisted the orchestral skills of Mort Garson, an arranger/conductor who would show up on similar recordings that included a collection of Beach Boys tunes performed by the Hollyridge Strings.

That uncanny connection between surf music, Easy-Listening, and mind-altering acoustics (harbingers of kaleidoscopic sounds to come) also resonated across the pond, when surf fans in England, confined to the craggier Atlantic coast, shared their own Southern California fantasies. Venturing further into creamy-melody territory than the Ventures themselves, the Shadows, a backup group for pop idol Cliff Richard, emerged as instrumental stars with their 1962 hit single, "Wonderful Land." It is a dazzling olio of electric guitars and a string orchestra, connoting what Southern California might seem like to a Brit forced to stay content with the Beach at Blackpool.

The Shadows also had the savvy arranger, producer, and conductor Norrie Paramor. His name showed up as the co-composer or musical supervisor for several late-'50s and early-'60s British "youth" movies, often starring Cliff Richard and the Shadows, such as *Expresso Bongo* (1959), *The Young Ones* (1961), and *Summer Holiday* (1963).

"Wonderful Land" crested on the peak of the U.K. charts. Shadows guitarist Bruce Welch recalled, in Jon Kutner and Spencer Leigh's *1000 UK #1 Hits*, the group's enthusiasm about the orchestral addition: "Norrie Paramor was a great help to us, a father-figure if you like, an older man but a trained musician. Jerry Lordan had given us 'Wonderful Land,' and we recorded it knowing there was something missing. What we'd done wasn't enough. We had it in the can for nine months and while we were on tour, Norrie added French horns, strings, and a little vocal bit. Then it was a classic record, and we were so excited about it. It was the first time that a rock group had used an orchestra, and it was #1 for weeks." When "Wonderful Land" showed up on Atlantic Records in the U.S., Americans of varying ages were still reeling from the sunburst of Percy Faith's 1960 hit "Theme from *A Summer Place*." Though not a surf tune, Faith's recording popularized another kind of visceral effect: high-pitched strings processed through studio echoes for a pleasing effect analogous to sonic air conditioning. Its composer Max Steiner played the same theme with a Hollywood orchestra in the eponymous 1959 film, in which Sandra Dee and Troy Donohue portray lovelorn and alienated teens, seeking refuge from the stormy waves on the coast of Maine as well as from their invasive parents. Theirs is the longing for a "safe and warm" port in a sinister world that would recur in other "Easy"-friendly pop songs.

Jan & Dean, favored fellows of the California sands before the Beach Boys gained prominence, had already provided pretty harmonies similar

WONDERFUL LAND · MIDNIGHT

STARS FELL ON STOCKTON 36-24-36

mono

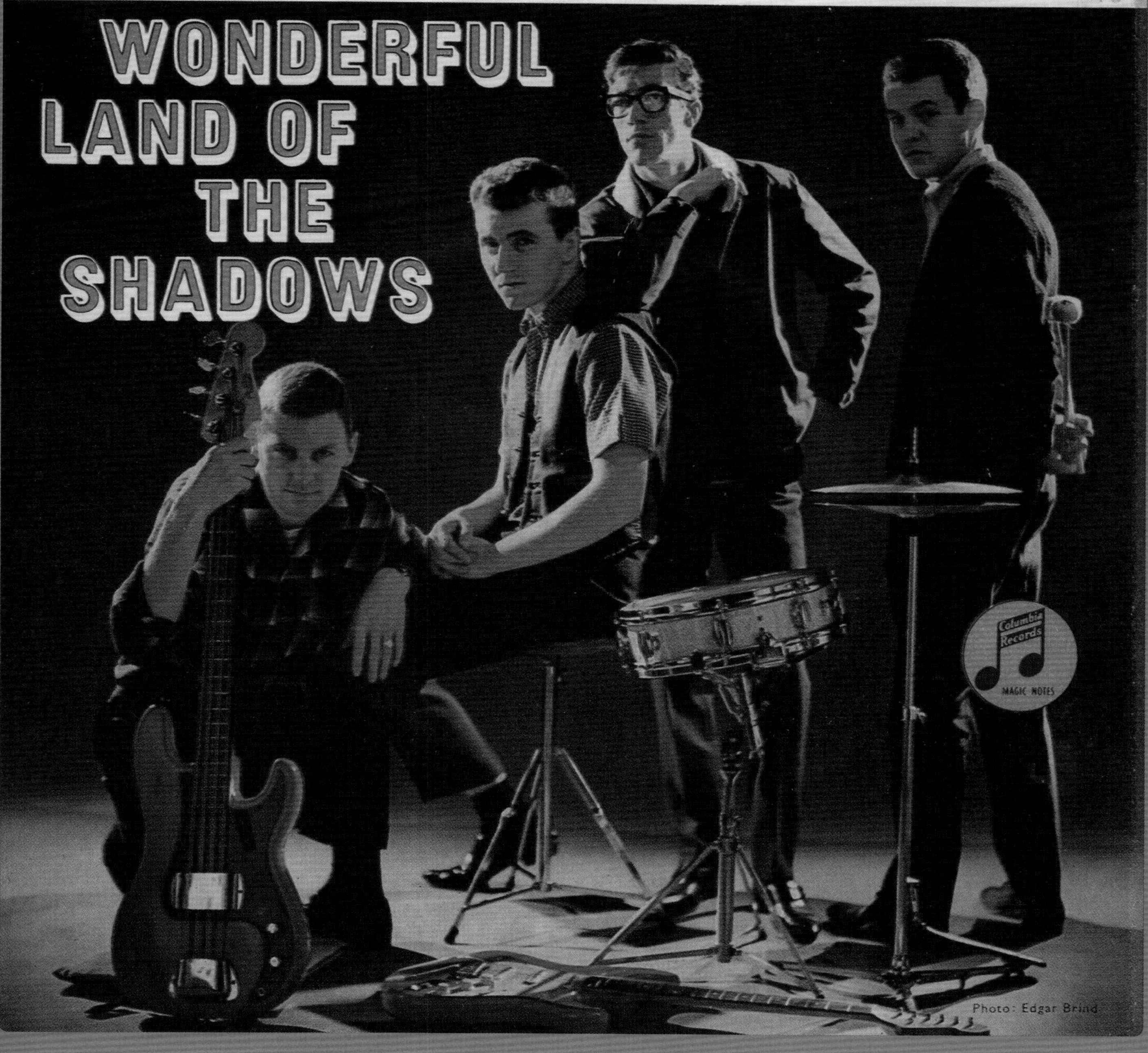

Photo: Edgar Brind

File Under: Hollyridge Strings · Top Forty · Instrumental · Beach Boys

ST 2156

CAPITOL FULL DIMENSIONAL STEREO

THE BEACH BOYS SONG BOOK

romantic instrumentals by

THE HOLLYRIDGE STRINGS

SURFIN' U.S.A. • DON'T WORRY, BABY • I GET AROUND
IN MY ROOM • LITTLE SAINT NICK • FUN, FUN, FUN
SHE KNOWS ME TOO WELL • WENDY • SHUT DOWN
THE WARMTH OF THE SUN • GIRLS ON THE BEACH

Arranged by STU PHILLIPS

Capitol
RECORDS

HIGH FIDELITY

to such clean-cut quartets as the Crew-Cuts and the Four Preps. But Jan Berry nurtured another ambition when he re-engineered some of his duo's hits into the extravagant 1965 release, *Bel-Aire Pops Orchestra: Jan & Dean's Pop Symphony No. 1.* Berry transforms "The Little Old Lady from Pasadena" into a spirited waltz, "Surf City" floats from pizzicato heaven to the ritual signals of a Japanese gong before the strings, horns, and drums place the production back onto the California fault line. The album's delicious version of Frank Loesser's "Heart and Soul" contains the expected electric bass guitar and drums, but violins are both plucked and stroked, along with burnished brass, woozy woodwinds, harpsichord, xylophone, chimes, and a low-key piano that arouses thoughts of Phil Spector's "Wall of Sound."

The Bel-Aire Pops Orchestra allowed even a bummer of a splatter-platter like "Dead Man's Curve," with its unnerving premonition of Berry's own crippling mishap in 1966 at the wheel of his Corvette to dodge thoughts of an oncoming, high-speed hearse. Instead, Berry (and his co-arranger George Tipton) opted for the sound of a parade, replete with a patriotic fife and drum, until some frantic violins hint that a hell-bent hot rod might be zooming in the distance.

Another practitioner of mind-altering, massed violins was Bernard Alfred "Jack" Nitzsche. Nitzsche showed his fondness for pop melodies when collaborating with Sonny Bono on "Needles

and Pins," which the Searchers made into some of the best "jingle-jangle" folk rock imaginable. When working with Phil Spector, he was among those who built the reverberating and thunderous "wall of sound" effect—or what Spector called "little symphonies for the kids." Nitzsche worked with several performing artists and musical forms, held an assortment of opinions about music and life, and had the reputation for being moody. He at least chilled with a fair share of "Easy"-pop, arranging such ear-cream-sodas as Bob Lind's "Elusive Butterfly" and subsequently laying a bed of strings over Tim Buckley's 1966 debut album.

In the summer of 1963, Nitzsche released "The Lonely Surfer," a sullen brew of pulsating guitar bass lines, a garish French horn, and mellifluous strings that went against the grain of what hardcore surf fans might have expected. The title and its musical execution stress the solitary soul amidst the daunting waters. "The Lonely Surfer" is, however, more in keeping with the garish Italian soundtracks in vogue during the early to mid-1960s, most notably the 1962 shockumentary *Mondo Cane.*

Nitzsche delved into more sardonic psychedelia by 1968, mimicking the popular conceptions of what Muzak sounds like in the 1970 cult film *Performance.* The track is entitled "Harry Flowers," named after the film's sadistic head gangster who represents a brutal side of London during the era of the Krays. "Harry Flowers" starts with a Mantovani-inspired blanket of fiddles but emits flashes of audio nausea when the rhythm and the sound warp to complement the corruption and troubled psychology of the characters.

By the mid-'60s, surf music's role as a halfway house between outdoor escapism and introspection surfaced in the movies. Bruce Brown's 1966 documentary *The Endless Summer* had a pensive theme song by the Sandals: a relaxing guitar that guided other tracks with such fitting titles as "Drifting," "Trailing," "Wild as the Sea," and "Lonely Road." The soundtrack, combined with the hypnotic serenity of Brown's voiceover narration, helped viewers to almost forget the torturous and sometimes lethal sport that the film celebrates.

Filmmakers Jim Freeman and Greg MacGillivray offered generous amounts of *elevated* tracks in their 1967 film *Free and Easy*. The narrator takes viewers on tours from California to Hawaii, flavoring the travelogue with soothing serenades that include George Martin's versions of "Good Day Sunshine" and "Here, There, and Everywhere." A high point is right at the start of the film, with shots of surfers braving the waves to the trippy sounds of "Strawberry Fields Forever" and "Penny Lane" by the Hollyridge Strings.

That same year, the Ventures dove into bolder lysergic waters by mixing soft-pop tunes with fuzz guitar on the album *Super Psychedelics*. Though without an orchestra, the Ventures manage to combine guitars, mixing folk with bits of flamenco,

soft percussion, and keyboards that take on different sonic personalities. "Reflections," for instance, includes a spooky interlude that suggests a wailing theremin. Their cover of "Strawberry Fields Forever" includes some semblance of a harmonium, sounding almost identical to the Mellotron on the Beatles' original, along with intermittent doses of distorted piano. "Endless Dream" combines wistful guitars with a sitar, suggesting that surf music's sonic warping had been approximating raga all along.

However, the most intriguing and disturbing blend of surf, psychedelia, and Easy-Listening comes from Brian Wilson. Behind his usual themes of sweet and lovely beach scenes, fast cars, and pretty girls, Wilson wallowed in private nightmares: visions of a saltwater maw gulping him up. He more or less hated the sea but thought that composing ditties about it could help to quell his phobia.

Wilson's warring thoughts harken back to 1964, when Timothy Leary, along with Richard Alpert and Ralph Metzner, refashioned the Tibetan Book of the Dead into a book called *The Psychedelic Experience*. It emphasizes something called "ego death" to invoke a state of mind when socially imposed selves burn away: "depersonalization" that supposedly frees the mind to "float downstream." John Lennon heeded this call when he wrote "Tomorrow Never Knows," but Wilson likely reacted with nausea. For him, "float downstream" could have been trigger words for darker thoughts than Leary (or Lennon) had imagined.

As the Beach Boys' poet laureate, Wilson also understood that he was creating a musical mirage, one that he could only admire from afar. Getting his head hit with a board the first and only time he tried to surf did not help. He compensated by conjuring a mental paradise that celebrated harmony over discord. Yet behind a song like "Fun, Fun, Fun," there was always a "Lonely Sea," and later something as puerile as "California Girls" contrasted with the more reflective and tortured psyche behind "I Just Wasn't Made for These Times."

The Beach Boys assumed a new incarnation shortly after they became world stars, thanks to arranger/producer Stu Phillips. Phillips took previous sonic gambits when having Paul Peterson from *The Donna Reed Show* intone a lushly arranged hit called "My Dad," while also helping Peterson's co-star Shelley Fabares etherize the Top 40 frequencies with "Johnny Angel." He had more surprises in store when taking over the Hollyridge Strings, Capitol Records' studio orchestra. Starting in 1964, he transposed Beatles songs into echo-laden treasures, pairing the orchestra with woodwinds, French horns, generous helpings of electric guitars, and drums on *The Hollyridge Strings Play the Beatles Song Book*. The success of this album launched a Hollyridge Strings series that would cover such other pop icons as Elvis Presley and the Four Seasons.

When it was time for a Hollyridge tribute to the Beach Boys, Phillips was already making a foray into surf culture by composing the score for the 1964 film *Ride the Wild Surf*, where gushing fans got to see Fabian and Tab Hunter pretend to navigate the waves while the illusion of a studio set's rear-screen projection kept their hair in place. The Beatles could maneuver from romantic to sassy to scary, but the Beach Boys' output consisted primarily of innocent adolescent yearnings, desires for love and security in an iffy world. In many ways, the Beach Boys offered Phillips more leeway in presenting the melodies as both sweet and torturous. Assembling members of the Los Angeles-based studio musicians known as "the Wrecking Crew," including the same rhythm sections that played on actual Beach Boys releases, Phillips expanded songs like "I Get Around" and "Surfin' U.S.A." from their initial teenybopper appeal into a vast, spectral soundstage.

Stu Phillips (in a telephone interview from 2002) was direct and technical when describing his Hollyridge technique:

"The high-end violin sound also depended on the amount of violins. The more the better! Most of the time, I didn't use violas. I found that cellos playing in the viola register had a better, less muddy, recording sound. There were about 14 violins and six celli. But I was also trying to get more of a rock sound. Once I replicated the rhythm sections of the rock beat, I would then throw the strings over instead of voices."

For those who judge the worth of a record based on the buying habits of those who rifled through record bins decades ago, *The Hollyridge Strings Play the Beach Boys Song Book* made a respectable showing (#82) on *Billboard*'s Top 100 albums of 1964.

When Brian Wilson and Mike Love collaborated on "The Warmth of the Sun," the lyrics reiterated the longing for a "safe and warm" summer place. But Phillips' Hollyridge arrangement made up for the missing words with emoting instruments, switching from bowed to plucked violins. Despite some subtle bossa-nova bounce to offset the song's sentimental edge, the overall mood retains the original's hints of fear.

The Beach Boys' 1963 release "In My Room" (which Wilson co-wrote with Gary Usher) was among the first of several '60s laments about young men seeking solitude and escape from encroaching social norms. The insular theme of "In My Room" also reflected Wilson's social withdrawal and his mounting dread of touring that eventually led to a nervous breakdown. The song also connotes another side to the surf music culture: simple guys becoming convoluted, forsaking their fetishes for the car, the girl, and even the big wave for solipsism and poetic contemplation. This was a prelude to the cerebral themes of the psychedelic years when, on *Sgt. Pepper*, the Beatles added Day-Glo wallpaper to Brian's "Room" as Paul McCartney sang about "Fixing a Hole."

When the Hollyridge Strings interpreted "In My Room," the ensemble made Wilson's message

more pensive. The Beach Boys' original—particularly as they performed it in 1964 on *The Red Skelton Hour*, looking like a nattily attired glee club but singing like heartbroken swains—sounds moodier when Phillips enlists pianist Lincoln Mayorga, a respected Los Angeles studio musician, to carry the tune. With a gentleman's dexterity, he begins with a mystifying glissando resembling "Aquarium" from *Carnival of the Animals*, but soon slides into a rhapsodic duet with violins (accompanied by a soft drum beat) that respects the original tune but more than compensates for the missing lyrics with a style that is both sweet and brooding.

Though he claims to have met neither Beatle nor Beach Boy, Phillips was creative with his orchestral-pop treatments of their work, proving that elevator versions could be simpatico with their foreground co-habitants. According to the booklet notes for the 2008 CD entitled *The Hollyridge Strings: The Beach Boys Song Book — Vol. 1 & 2*, Wilson appreciated the Hollyridge touch, with particular praise for Philips: "He did a beautiful job. I was very thrilled when I heard it… I loved it. It's beautiful … It's very interesting to hear this treatment, after we've been so used to the way we do these songs."

By 1967, when Capitol Records released *The Hollyridge Strings Play the Beach Boys Song Book — Vol. 2*, Phillips was busy with endeavors at another label. At this point, the Beach Boys' meditative side conformed to the changing times,

HAPPY TOGETHER · STRAWBERRY FIELDS FOREVER
A LITTLE BIT ME, A LITTLE BIT YOU · WESTERN UNION
THE VENTURES

KANDY KONCOCTION · PSYCHEDELIC VENTURE · 1999 A.D. · REFLECTIONS
VIBRATIONS · ENDLESS DREAM · PSYCHED-OUT · GUITAR PSYCHEDELICS

Included inside!
Exciting full color photo-story of the Ventures

SUPER PSYCHEDELICS

particularly with "Good Vibrations": a complicated structure noted for its tickling theremin. The arranging and conducting duties shifted to a joint venture by Mort Garson, a pop arranger/composer and future Moog enthusiast, and Perry Botkin, Jr., who conducted one of the very first Hollyridge Strings records back in 1961. Together, they re-engineered some of Wilson's acid-era output to create what sounds at times like the soundtrack to an animated fantasy.

The soundstage equivalent to CinemaScope was still there, with the outlandish echo stretching across the stereo spectrum, making the songs soothing, sprightly, yet sometimes oddly aggressive. The album opens with "Good Vibrations," including the acoustical bells and whistles reminiscent of the Stu Phillips sessions. The Hollyridge variation pays tribute to the song's intricacies, but the orchestra is surprisingly more conventional. The instruments glisten, especially the bold pizzicato, while what at least sounds like a theremin purrs softly in the background.

This is a contrast to Nashville's star pianist Floyd Cramer, who took a friskier approach to "Good Vibrations" on his RCA album *Class of '66*, pairing his trademark slip-note piano with an instrument that at least simulated a theremin. By 1969, when the musical worlds of pop, rock, classical, and Easy-Listening reached an extreme collision, Hugo Montenegro, always thirsting for new sounds and instruments, flavored the title

song for his album *Good Vibrations* with a vanilla vocal chorus singing the lines, along with guitars, violins, keyboards, horns, and a makeshift theremin provided by the professional whistler Muzzy Marcellino.

By 1966, when releasing *Pet Sounds*, Wilson absorbed other musical influences. He has claimed that his instrumental "Let's Go Away for Awhile," the flipside to the "Good Vibrations" single, is a tribute to Burt Bacharach, though it sounds more like an exotic ode to Martin Denny—with the bonus of a string orchestra. Here was Wilson conducting a composition that reminded the world of how desperately he needed what Jim Morrison later called "soft asylum."

In his book *1965: The Most Revolutionary Year in Music*, author Andrew Grant Jackson summarizes life's imitation of art, as an LSD-infused Wilson got the idea to write "California Girls": "In the midst of the trip, Brian suddenly yelled that he was afraid of his parents and fled to his room to hide his head under a pillow. He pulled himself together, though, by riffing off Bach on the piano, an exercise that evolved into the introduction to the Beach Boys' anthem…"

"California Girls" was a winner with record buyers, but the teenybopper gushes in its lyrics did little to project the Beach Boys' image as more than that of naïve West Coast kids. On the surface, it is simplistic and, considering Wilson's headier ambitions, retrograde. This posed a challenge to the Hollyridge orchestra. Instead of just repeating the tune, they chose Easy-Listening's alternative tactic: the playful and eccentric approach. Garson and Botkin perhaps knew of the song's lysergic origins when they decided to escort "California Girls" into an acid-flashback time machine that interpolates phrases from "California, Here I Come" and Bronislau Kaper's title song to the 1936 Clark Gable film *San Francisco*. Just as Brian Wilson often comforted himself by singing Stephen Foster's "Beautiful Dreamer," the Hollyridge Strings use this track to rearrange Wilson's mind, offering some historical continuity as an emotional buffer during uncertain times.

In David Leaf's 2004 documentary *Beautiful Dreamer: Brian Wilson and the Story of "Smile,"* Wilson is candid about his waves of depression and auditory phantasms: "In 1965, I started hearing voices, after I took LSD. I started hearing these voices saying, 'We're going to kill you! We're going to kill you!' And I would say, 'Don't kill me; please don't kill me!' And I would carry on a conversation with these auditory hallucinations, as they're called."

Amid the voices of death, the melodies lingered. And the instrumental Beach Boys variations got much closer to home when his father Murry, with whom Brian had a strained relationship, recorded his own version of a semi-elegiac Beach Boys tune. Back in the summer of 1963, Murry Wilson spoke to *Billboard* and threw some shade

at his sons: "Surfing music has to sound untrained with a certain rough flavor in order to appeal to teenagers. As in the case of true C&W, when the music gets too good, and too polished, it isn't considered the real thing." By 1967, however, Murry had no trouble augmenting his definition of "the real thing" on his album *The Many Moods of Murry Wilson*. He might have been a bad dad, but he apparently had a tender relapse when interpreting "The Warmth of the Sun" as a creamy, orchestral soft-serve. This track alone epitomizes Easy-Listening kindness, offering a musical dream world that can assuage even a father's wrath and allow the mind to "relax and float downstream" despite the approaching rip tides. ✳

45

WE SKIPPE
THE LIGHT
FANDANG
INTO A
FUNERAL

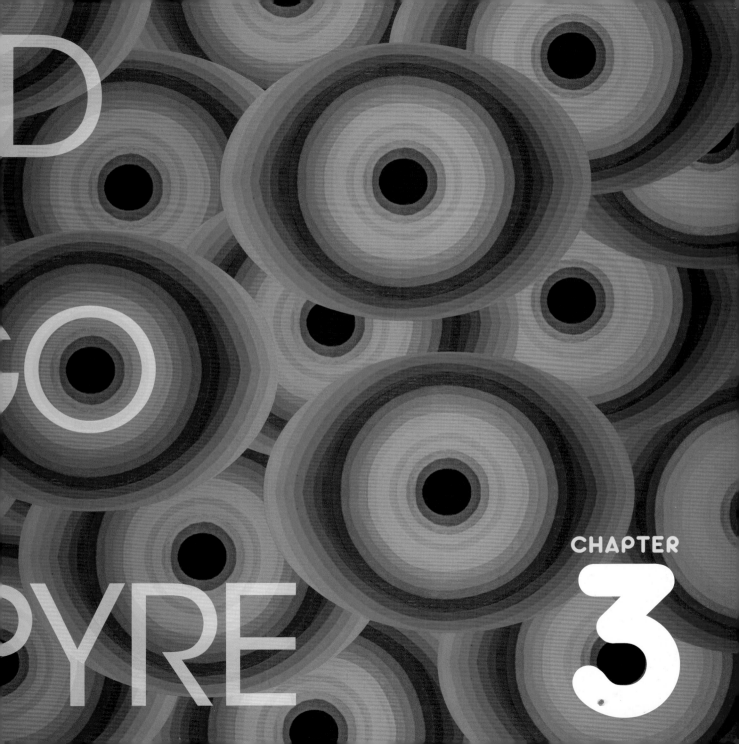

CHAPTER

3

"SOMETIMES I'LL BE IN AN ELEVATOR AND I'LL HEAR A CORNY INSTRUMENTAL VERSION OF 'LIGHT MY FIRE.' BUT IT'S NOT SELLING CIGARETTES OR DEODORANT, AND THAT'S WHERE WE DRAW THE LINE."

—THE DOORS' DRUMMER, JOHN DENSMORE

When surf guitars merged with string orchestras, the fun, sun, and dangers of scaling the waves also became moments for listeners to relax, meditate, and sometimes drift into scary but fascinating reveries, adding new identities to songs that might otherwise have been confined to youth-oriented AM radio. There was another trend that some rock and pop artists followed by the mid-'60s: just when the mood seemed so new and so subversive, many also expressed the desire to discover old musical forms and old songs that were hits before their mothers were born.

In contrast to "heavy" groups like Cream and their forebears the Spencer Davis Group, pop-oriented artists like the Beatles, with their sparkly yet often-spooky side of psychedelia, dovetailed with songs like the Small Faces' "Itchycoo Park" and the Lemon Pipers' "Green Tambourine," mixing in "classical" influences with British music hall, vaudeville, sea-shanty folk, and other precursors. It's as if some psychedelic frolickers snuck away from the noisy living-room love-in to explore the more enigmatic attic, where they uncovered such artifacts as musty sheet music and scratchy 78s an eccentric granny had left behind.

While Grace Slick and Jefferson Airplane envisioned an altered state where "the White Knight is talking backwards," other psychedelic performers shifted backwards to integrate old tunes that might otherwise have never reached a '60s recording session. The results were a tonal time fugue that sounded the way the cover of the *Sgt. Pepper* album looks: a jumble of generations, both living and dead, merging into a shared hallucination. Lennon and McCartney, Donovan Leitch, and John Phillips deserved a seat at the Great Composers' Commissary alongside Cole Porter and Noel Coward.

Some of the Memory Lane detours slid into direct nostalgia. The New Vaudeville Band's founder, songwriter, and producer Geoff Stephens wrote a song recorded in 1964 by England's Dave Berry called "The Crying Game" that tugged at teenage hearts. He co-wrote "There's a Kind of Hush" for the New Vaudeville Band before Herman's Hermits re-recorded it a year later and took the fame. Stephens also helped to discover and promote Donovan, who was already becoming Britain's psychedelic troubadour.

The Grammy Award-winning "Winchester Cathedral," and the New Vaudeville Band's follow-up single "Peek-A-Boo," harken back to a time when crooners like Rudy Vallee sang in front of hotel orchestras through megaphones. A bigger hit in America than in its native U.K., "Winchester Cathedral" stimulated instant elevator offshoots, with versions by the Alan Tew Orchestra, Ray Conniff and the Singers, Floyd Cramer, the Bob Crewe Generation, Xavier Cugat, Lenny Dee, the James Last Band, David McCallum, George Martin, Paul Mauriat, Peter Nero, Nelson Riddle, Billy Vaughn, and Lawrence Welk—all within a year after the initial Top 40 release in the fall of 1966.

The '60s-pop connection is more apparent when considering that "Peek-A-Boo" was co-written by John Carter (a pseudonym for John Shakespeare), who also co-wrote Peter & Gordon's psychedelic-era "Sunday for Tea" and an English answer to Scott McKenzie's "San Francisco (Be Sure to Wear Flowers in Your Hair)" called "Let's Go to San Francisco." All three Carter tunes could have easily been on song lists for those quaint little bands that, decades before, played discreetly behind potted plants at hotels.

Other examples of England's linking the "now sound" with the past include Peter & Gordon, who, like their counterparts Chad & Jeremy, enjoyed letting their pop style get swept up in orchestral mists, where melodic ghosts congregate. Mike Leander, an alumnus from the Trinity College of Music, offered string backings to the Rolling Stones' "As Tears Go By" and Marianne Faithfull's "This Little Bird." He had also composed the music for some of Peter & Gordon's best "retro" songs from those times, including "Lady Godiva," "Knight in Rusty Armor," and "The Jokers."

Another flirtation with old forms predated *Sgt. Pepper* by a month when, in May of 1967, Procol Harum's "A Whiter Shade of Pale" contrasted vocalist Gary Brooker's "blue-eyed soul" with a J.S. Bach-derived backdrop: an organ set against a thumping guitar that took rock into a paradoxi-

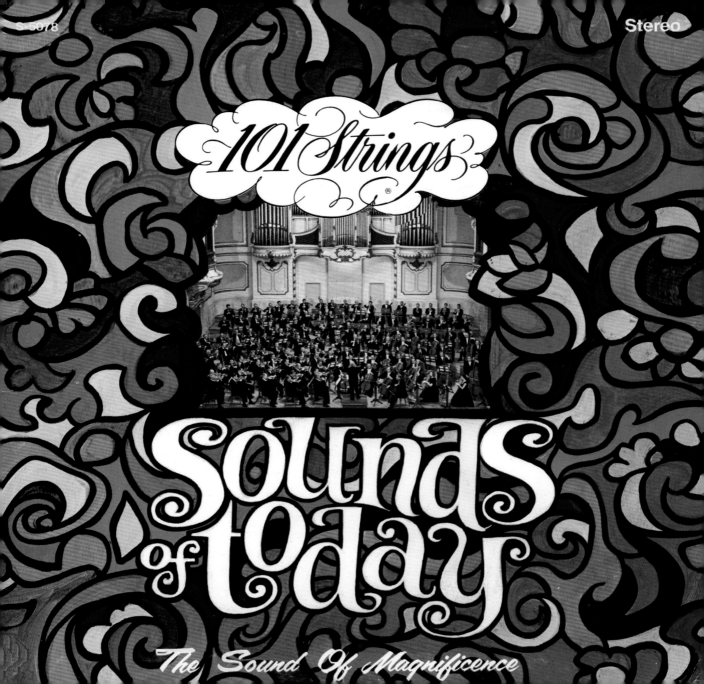

cally more conservative direction. Its psychedelic reverberations could have bounced as easily off the Church of England's walls as they did in chic London discotheques. The lyrics were disorienting. What could listeners make of those "vestal virgins," "feeling seasick," "doing cartwheels 'cross the floor," and that opening bit about skipping a "light fandango"?

Without the purple words, "A Whiter Shade of Pale" sounded closer to an electrified death knell, but it promised new beginnings for various Easy-Listening players. Ronnie Aldrich and His Two Pianos with the London Festival Orchestra, the Big Ben Hawaiian Band, Living Guitars, George Martin and His Orchestra, 101 Strings, the Anthony Ventura Orchestra, and others glommed onto its Bach template, letting the massed strings, pianos, organs, and guitars replace Brooker's vocalese.

Adding to the vogue for psychedelic soundtracks with traditional overtones were three brothers from Manchester, England, who had the advantage of a bandleader dad named Hugh Gibb. The three had showbiz goals early on as they perfected their harmonies by listening to Everly Brothers records. They played their callow rock-and-roll shows at various local theaters in the '50s and fit the bill as the generation's "angry young men," getting into fights and literally lighting fires around the town. The arson was likely one of the reasons why the Gibbs felt pressured to pack off to England's former penal colony, Australia.

By the early '60s, the Gibb brothers appeared on local Oz radio and television stations, singing Everlys-style folk and Lonnie Donegan-style skiffle. By then, they were already the Bee Gees. They signed a record contract while still teenagers, catching the interest of producer Robert Stigwood. They wrote songs and tried to make hit records. At last, in 1967, they darkened flower power with a bouquet of black roses on a time-warping lament about entrapped miners trying to make contact with those outside whom they will never see again.

Not long after the Beatles had hung funereal drapes over America's Top 40 with "Eleanor Rigby," the Bee Gees' "New York Mining Disaster 1941" made a sad song even sadder with somber guitar strums and woeful violins. It was full of doom, gloom, and voices from the tomb, but it catered to the era's desire for musical mind journeys that did not always involve balloons, daisies, and a dream date. It was also the summer of 1967, and radio ears were getting accustomed to songs reflecting both the comic and tragic sides of mind excursions, humming along to both.

Once "New York Mining Disaster 1941" became their first American success, the Bee Gees returned to England to record *Bee Gees' 1st*—an album that offered more whimsy mixed with melancholia, including psychedelic cover art by Klaus Voormann, who designed the Beatles' *Revolver*. With two extra members making it a quintet, the Bee Gees, still relatively young (the oldest Gibb being about twenty), seemed to shoulder the world's weight long before their time. Musically, they often thrived and wandered in their own Penny Lane with songs full of archaic fantasies. "Turn of the Century," with its harpsichord and oboe introduction, opens the album with the overt wish to go back in a "time machine." "Red Chair Fade Away" and "Cucumber Castle" continue with escapist wishes, and "I Close My Eyes" prefers social withdrawal, with warped acoustics similar to those on the Beatles' 1966 recording of "Rain."

Their most fascinating composition on the album—and perhaps the greatest of their entire repertoire—is the heart-wrenching "Holiday." The song, which appears to be about a misconnected romance, has a gorgeous, sobbing melody in a minor key and ambiguous lyrics. At one point, the narrator says, "Put the soft pillow on my head," which could imply that he simply needs to unwind and slow his racing thoughts or possibly that he requests to be put out of his misery and into a permanent sleep via euthanasia. "Holiday" offers an additional puzzle with its eerie wordless chorus that chimes in at the middle and the end to a dirge-like march. The solemn music collides with the cheery associations that the word "holiday" usually connotes, suggesting that the holiday could perhaps be the disheartened narrator's planned memorial.

Without the lyrics, the Bee Gees' melodies still convey much of their narrative meaning. Stigwood intuited this and assembled instrumental

arrangements by Bill Shepherd on the 1968 album *The Robert Stigwood Orchestra Plays Bee Gees' Hits*. "Barry, Maurice, and myself are completely thrilled by this L.P.," Robin Gibb wrote on the back cover, "a life-long ambition has been fulfilled to hear our music played by a full orchestra. They have done it splendidly, and I shall cherish it always, and I hope it will be the first of many such albums."

Robin Gibb's unbridled praise notwithstanding, the Stigwood Orchestra recreates the group's moods of contemplation and sorrow at least most of the time. The album includes a pleasing cover of the country-inflected 1967 hit "(The Lights Went Out in) Massachusetts," which shares thoughts of a transient returning to his New England roots and regretting his San Francisco sojourn. The orchestra offers a striking mixture of acoustic guitar and a celesta to fill in for the vocals, while the strings and horns follow the exact Gibb song formula.

The Stigwood Orchestra allows a sprightly, Disney-ish echo to sparkle throughout, a strategy that brightens (with mixed results) the Bee Gees' heavier thoughts. Even the doleful "New York Mining Disaster 1941," while keeping the mournful violins, leaps into a bolder, brassier chorus for a few upbeat and out-of-context seconds. Stigwood's version of "Holiday" is also not the album's best moment. It begins with swirling violins and a persuasive piper, but a brassy interval intrudes, along with energetic drums, putting the song through an entirely different identity that, at one point, digresses into cocktail jazz and instant camp.

That same year, arranger Bill Shepherd assembled (with varying success) his Bill Shepherd Singers to add what the back cover calls a "large lush choir" on the album, *Aurora (The Bill Shepherd Singers Sing Bee Gees Hits)*. At times, Shepherd makes futile attempts to "swing," but the tracks are generally fine interpretations that take the songs, as Shepherd proclaims, "straight down the middle of the road." Those remarks, far from implying anything dismissive, address a preference for some who might not usually listen to pop music but would also enjoy a Bee Gees tune in reconstituted form. This was a common practice at the time when songs like the Turtles' "Happy Together" (per the Percy Faith Chorus) or the Association's "Never My Love" (per the Johnny Mann Singers) won an additional audience.

Sometimes the reinterpretations could misfire, as when the Shepherd Singers briefly turn the beatific "Holiday" into snappy jazz, replete with a peppy background "do do do" expected from groups like the Swingle Singers. The wordless vocal treatment sounds more psychedelic when the chorus seems to enter a sci-fi dimension on "Red Chair Fade Away."

As the Bee Gees championed their pop music influences from another place and time, a handsome young man from Buenos Aires entered the era's expanding carnival of sounds. Mariano Moreno was a teenage star on Argentine radio and television, a keyboard prodigy who favored both the piano and harpsichord. Coming to America, he assimilated into such showbiz shrines as Vegas' Tropicana, L.A.'s Century Plaza, and San Francisco's Fairmont. In the meantime, Mariano assembled a string quartet of equally young and talented men to fit fashionably with the baroque-pop craze. Their first album on Capitol, released in 1968, was simply titled *Mariano and the Unbelievables*.

Mariano appears on the album cover, sitting proudly at his keyboard beside his co-players who are adorned in period costumes, ready to embellish hits of the day like "There's a Kind of Hush" and "Windy" with a combination of harpsichord, violin cascades and pizzicato dewdrops, as well as various types of background percussion—all sparkling across the stereo spectrum with what the back-cover copy describes as "melodic ease and big-sound moods that are irresistible."

One particular track deserves special mention: a cover of Spanky and Our Gang's "Sunday Will Never Be the Same." The 1967 hit adapted a traditional French carol known in English as "Angels We Have Heard on High." Mariano's version skips the original's beginning strains from J.S. Bach's church cantata "Gloria in Excelsis Deo" to concentrate on the main melody—in a slower, more pensive mode. The song was also perfect for other instrumentalists, including a raga melody from the Nirvana Sitar and String Group on their 1968 LP *Sitar and Strings* and a Muzak version from

STEREO

THE ROBERT STIGWOOD ORCHESTRA
Plays
BEE GEES' HITS

J. RAILTON

Arranged & Conducted by Bill Shepherd

Charles Grean and His Orchestra that retains the "Gloria" prelude.

On their follow-up album *The 25th Hour*, Mariano and the Unbelievables (now consisting of nine young men garbed again in period gear) use a similar combination of instruments on these pleasing covers of hits like "Love is Blue" and a refreshingly upbeat version of "A Whiter Shade of Pale." With composer Mort Garson as their arranger, Mariano and the Unbelievables do a much better job at handling "Holiday." They let the song go upbeat in parts while keeping the Bee Gees' subdued mood intact, with a hearty blend of harpsichord, drums, and most of all, the chamber strings that vary in tempo from a soft promenade to a marching beat and to a glossy pizzicato that remains eerie despite any surface cheer.

In 1967, the same year when Harpers Bizarre brought back Mack Gordon and Harry Warren's "Chattanooga Choo-Choo" and Cole Porter's "Anything Goes," the Stamford, Connecticut-based group the Fifth Estate dusted out Harold Arlen and E.Y. Harburg's "Ding Dong, the Witch is Dead" from *The Wizard of Oz*, adding plodding electric guitars to a tune that was already inscribed into childhood minds. They also added a bonus: two interludes of "La Bourrée," from Michael Praetorius' seventeenth-century *Dances from Terpsichore*—a royal revelry number that, in turn, evokes "The Sailor's Hornpipe," an old sea shanty that became one of Popeye the Sailor's cartoon themes.

San Francisco's The Sopwith Camel was less consistent with its nostalgic salutes, as it sometimes favored distorted guitars while swatting at the drums on tracks like the nightmarish "Frantic Desolation." Yet they came up with an uncanny fusion of psychedelic guitars and an original Easy-Listening-friendly melody on the semi-instrumental track "Maybe in a Dream." The Sopwith Camel's major public impact arrived in early 1967, when they channeled spirits from vaudeville on "Hello Hello" and "A Walk in the Park"—songs so sprightly that Claudine Longet soon recorded versions (with husband Andy Williams helping her on the latter). Tiny Tim also treated "Hello Hello" to his trademark falsetto.

Even harder British rockers like the Yardbirds were breaking loose from their blues fixations: the military cadences on "Shapes of Things" and the Gregorian mysticism on "Still I'm Sad" are two examples. The Johnny Mann Singers were effective when re-engineering 1965's hit "Heart Full of Soul" into an Easy-Listening vocal track (with guitars still present) on their 1968 album *Heart Full of Song*. Johnny Mann himself, who started singing at the age of five in the choir of St. Paul's School for Boys in Baltimore, insisted that "cleanliness, accuracy, and pitch" were essential for his Singers: "No matter what kind of material we did, we would not sound as if we were yelling or screaming." The 101 Strings also braved the harder stuff on their 1967 album *Sounds of Today* when adapting the

Spencer Davis Group's "I'm a Man," along with such softer material as "A Whiter Shade of Pale" and "San Francisco (Be Sure to Wear Flowers in Your Hair)."

And then there were the Doors…

As years transpire, these four troublemakers leave behind a richer, more complicated legacy far beyond the standard pabulum about their role as bluesy rock icons wallowing in the "modal jazz" mire. When not channeling John Coltrane or John Lee Hooker, the Doors offered so much more: shadowy invocations to such Romantic poets as William Blake, soft and sometimes sentimental ballads about lost love and paranoia, and at least one waltz. Many of their tracks were so new, odd, and difficult to classify that they often alienated rock audiences who had problems coping with the guitar and organ making carnival sounds or playing to Old World German oom-pah-pah on their version of "Alabama Song (Whiskey Bar)." Bertolt Brecht and Kurt Weill wrote "Alabama Song" in 1927 for the musical play *Little Mahagonny* as a parody on Western consumerism, but Morrison's love for whiskey gave the Doors' version a new meaning. The band appeared comfortable taking a breather from hard rock to indulge in what the Germans call "schlager" and what English-speaking snobs call "schmaltz."

When Elektra Records president Jac Holzman watched the band play live at the Whisky a Go Go, he was puzzled about their appeal until he heard them perform "Alabama Song." At that point, he signed the band to his label, impressed by how they demonstrated what he called "austerity, cleanliness, and simplicity." "Alabama Song" also reveals the blatant contradictions in their first album. Just as he discovered he could add the unexpected to "Light My Fire" with the Bach touches, Ray Manzarek helped to make the Brecht-Weill tune reflect the fantasy world where they cut the album: Sunset Sound, owned by Tutti Camarata, the same musical director who chaperoned such Annette Funicello tunes as "Pineapple Princess." There, Camarata made many Disney cartoon and voice-over recordings and had several instruments on the premises: an opportunity for the Doors to enrich their carnival sounds. Manzarek enhanced the oom-pah beer-garden style with a Marxaphone, an instrument resembling an autoharp that went well with Disney's cartoon scores and also turned out to be an extra flavor for the one song on *The Doors* that alerted listeners that there was more to the band than just stuff about back-door intercourse and Oedipal hang-ups.

On their second album *Strange Days* (released appropriately in the gloomy autumn of 1967), the carnival music got darker and more prominent. The Doors recorded a memorable track resulting from one of Morrison's many depressive moods, as he looked over Los Angeles from Laurel Canyon and thought up "People are Strange." The finished product defers to the style of European cabaret, and the tinny piano interlude suggests the part in a silent film when the villain enters. Give or take its paranoia, it was a wonderful tune fit for piano, orchestra, and, in the case of Tiny Tim who had falsetto fun when recording his version, a ukulele.

Strange Days did not go over as well with the "knowing" circles as the band and its producers had hoped. "The Beatles and the Stones are for blowing your mind," a critic from the *L.A. Free Press* contended. "The Doors are for afterward, when your mind is already gone. It's like screeching your fingernails on the blackboard." The Doors seemed to have Edgar Allan Poe as their muse, but several of their songs were fit for elevator-music makeovers, though mostly in a minor key.

The Doors sent out other elevator-music teases, performing a waltz on "Wintertime Love" for their 1968 album *Waiting for the Sun*, along with "Summer's Almost Gone," a lost and languid ballad that seems to echo from a lonely crooner's grave. Among the mainstream, adult-oriented vocalists, the Lettermen sang a slow and bewitching medley of "Touch Me" with that less likely horn-dog hit from 1968, "Hello, I Love You." The Enoch Light Singers did "Hello, I Love You" on their 1968 album *Whoever You Are, I Love You* with glitzy panache. Other than that, the Doors offered up many wonderful melodies that, once performed and recorded on Elektra, were dressed to the nines with nowhere else to go. That is, of course, with the exception of their greatest hit of all.

"Light My Fire" is a curious concoction that sounds "hip" and "sexy," yet suggests a more intricate, at times morbid, state of mind: a love song about death. Instead of shining an eternal flame, passion is as fleeting as the spark on a short fuse. By then, a phrase like "get much higher" lost its larger metaphorical meaning of reaching what a Broadway lyricist on "The Impossible Dream" called "the unreachable star" and instead got reduced to a petty drug reference. Ed Sullivan bought into this myth and forbade the Doors from ever returning to his Sunday night show when Morrison accidentally sang the phrase after Sullivan's sultans demanded they replace it with the limp and rhyme-free "get much better."

Despite so many pretty melodies in the band's repertoire, "Light My Fire" became the one Doors tune that garnered a surprising share of Easy-Listening clout. How so? It is loud, the erotic allusions make it more of a *back-seat* than a *front-seat* song, and the singer practically screams at the closing. Yet, something about its novel structure—precisely in the shorter single version—set it apart from the usual rock tune.

Had it played as the band initially planned it, "Light My Fire" might not have had such an instant appeal. It was supposed to start with the trite Latin-jazz beat similar to the opening of their first and failed single, "Break on Through." John Densmore, in a 1982 interview for *Modern Drummer*, claimed "we had this song where we just hit kind of a Latin groove and we would play it for fifteen minutes. That was 'Latin Bullshit #2,' and we had 'Latin Bullshit #1,' which was a different lick of some Latin feel, samba." These "LBS" references had nothing to do with the Spanish influences of Robby Krieger's distinctive flamenco guitar but rather with the repetitive bossa nova that many hipsters, as well as mainstream pop singers, ended up relying on as a conditioned reflex in order to sound "cool" while trying to fill the awkward silences.

Along with flamenco, Krieger also followed the lure of Eastern raga. Manzarek and John Densmore, though immersed in jazz, also took Transcendental Meditation classes and likely used those moments to conjure different, more inventive musical approaches. As Manzarek explained to NPR in 1998, "I put my Bach back to work, put my Bach hat on, and came up with a circle of fifths." That addictive keyboard turnaround at the beginning and end allowed the "Fire" to flicker in an indefinite musical category. The tune alone was novel, catchy, and "weird" enough to reflect new times when people started seeing and hearing life differently, but it also attracted showbiz hangers-on waiting at the "middle of the road" for fresh material with an easy singalong tune. But trouble flared when Buick wanted to use a version of "Light My Fire" in 1968 to promote a new car with the slogan, "Come on Buick, light my fire!" As Densmore told *Forbes* in a 2015 interview, "When

Buick came to us to use 'Light My Fire' in its commercial… we were all salivating. We were young and the money was big. Jim didn't really write that song—Robby did—but he still went nuts."

"Light My Fire" is also legendary for its two identities. When the band recorded it in August of 1966 with the rest of their first album, it ran close to seven minutes, due to Krieger's extended guitar jam with Manzarek's organ and Densmore's drums. The song's plunge into free-form jazz, partly inspired from an occasion when Manzarek heard Coltrane's improvised version of Rodgers and Hammerstein's "My Favorite Things," became so emblematic of the era's turned-on, tripped-out, lose-track-of-time aesthetics that the instrumental stretch reappeared decades later as background music for an academic-hipster party in the 1980 movie *Altered States*.

On the single version, however, the song has a different personality. In order to get popular airplay, which would eventually make it *Cashbox*'s #1 song of 1967, producer Paul Rothschild edited it down to less than three minutes. As studio edits go, it was among the most creative and arguably a major upgrade. Instead of the album's drawn-out pot fog, the shorter single was like a quick, high-octane jolt that retained enough song conventions for Easy-Listening spinoffs. Later on, even Krieger admitted to liking the edit, if only because it had greater volume power and was about a half-step faster than the album version.

59

The Doors, with this hit alone, embodied the creative identity confusion that would leave "Light My Fire" (in spite of the suburban bossa nova wallowing behind the verses) suspended over several musical categories: not quite rock, not quite jazz, absolutely not country-and-western, but with enough of that beguiling baroque to make it another psychedelic "classic." That is, until Jose Feliciano complicated matters when releasing a simpler, South-of-the-Border-flavored folk rendition. This soon became the version that lazier players adopted, even though it sounds funny and forced, especially when Feliciano yells out the song's title over and over again like a delirious street addict crying out for the impossible fix.

Despite the song's indirect homage to crooner tunes of the past due to Morrison's smooth baritone, "Light My Fire" is nowhere near as nostalgic as "Ding Dong, The Witch is Dead" or "Anything Goes." In its shortened version, "Light My Fire" remains a "standard" fit to sit beside the sheet music of "My Old Flame." Julie London, Astrud Gilberto, and the Enoch Light Singers took the Feliciano bait, but Mae West, edging toward eighty, was more of a trooper. She adheres to the Doors' edited arrangement on her 1972 LP *Great Balls of Fire*, mouthing the lyrics in a manner expected from the icon who would become the elderly erotic centerpiece in the 1978 cult movie *Sextette*.

Frank Sinatra, who resented rock and '60s pop music in general, had a special antipathy toward "Light My Fire" because he fancied that Morrison was stealing his vocal thunder. Ol' Blue Eyes, stewing in this narcissistic assumption, saw red one day when driving from Palm Springs back to Los Angeles, irate over hearing what he fancied Morrison's mocking imitation of him on practically every station. He might have mistaken his car radio for one of the snarky reporters he used to punch out, allegedly yanking the contraption out of the car and stomping on it.

From the time "Light My Fire" ignited radios in the summer of 1967, and the Doors lip-synched the recording on *American Bandstand*, many performers with musical agendas clamored to thrust their torches into Morrison's funeral pyre. Jazz aficionados, gobsmacked by the album version's jamming middle section, easily converted it into another improvisation exercise. Surf music enthusiasts hung up on *loud* could enjoy the Ventures' recording loaded with booming guitars.

Instrumentally, "Light My Fire" varied in quality depending on listener tastes. By the time Chet Atkins was ready to record it on a bed of Nashville Strings for the album *Solid Gold '68*, he robotically played it Feliciano-style, his guitar imitating that same repetitive yammer toward the end. Even Ronnie Aldrich, among the most inventive in the art of making a pop song more elevator-friendly, capitulates to jazzishness on his 1968 album *It's Happening Now*. Blending a grand string orchestra and an acoustic guitar, he proceeds to allow

THE BILL SHEPHERD SINGERS SING BEE GEES HITS

AURORA

his moody keys to slip through notes that a sober Morrison would have hit on the mark. Aldrich does allow the London Festival Orchestra to sweep along, but he seems more preoccupied with showing off the ping-pong effect characteristic of his Decca Phase-4 "Two Pianos" technique. In 1970, Edmundo Ros and His Orchestra drag it further into equatorial ennui, converting it to a cha-cha on the album *Heading South… of the Border*.

The Berlin-born fiddler Helmut Zacharias had a somewhat better interpretation, at least in parts. He was an instrumental *wunderkind* who tackled pop songs of many varieties. Hailed as "The Magic Violinist," he achieved U.S. fame in 1956 as a "light music" champion, with a recording of "When the Lilacs Bloom Again." As the '60s progressed, Zacharias fiddled about on such albums as *Happy Strings, Happy Hits* in 1967 and *Happy Strings of Zacharias* in 1968. In 1969, on *Zacharias Plays the Hits*, he slows the tempo and hits the notes in the Feliciano manner, but he does get closer to the Doors' original when supplementing his solo violin with some superb pizzicato. Nonetheless, he too treats it as just another oleaginous moonlight serenade and tries adding extra sizzle with come-hither female voices piping in the background.

Jack Pleis is more successful. Like many pop arrangers, Pleis started with jazz ambitions but moved on to more populist fare by the mid- to late '50s, assembling his orchestra for albums with such titles as *Music from Disneyland* and what *Billboard*

described in 1958 as "relaxed, pleasant mood music" on *Music for Two Sleepy People*. On a 1968 collection entitled *The Sounds of Our Time Play "Hey Jude,"* Jack Pleis and His Orchestra adapt the Doors' version to an acoustic guitar for the opening verses, as horns lead to a clarinet, and finally the faithful strings pick up the melody, before the ornate keyboard's finale. It is brassy but readily recognizable: pleasant to hear either on the home stereo, an Easy-Listening FM station, or through public ceiling speakers.

Mike Curb, while busy supplying soundtracks to movies like *Mondo Hollywood* and cutting albums with his own pop chorale The Mike Curb Congregation, took the time to assemble a studio band called The Waterfall for a decent instrumental tribute on the 1968 album *The Doors Songbook*. On "Light My Fire," they keep to the Doors' beat while sneaking in a few Feliciano strums at the very end, perhaps as an obligatory gesture, or just to be smart alecks.

Yes, *The Doors Songbook* includes some restless, brassy tinkering on its cover of "Break on Through," but "The Crystal Ship," with its soaring piano and plaintive vocal melody, gets full respect with strings, woodwinds, piano, and accents of a xylophone. Still, a song this darkly sentimental could have broadened its impact with interpretations from Ferrante & Teicher, Ronnie Aldrich & His Two Pianos, or Roger Williams. Curb's Waterfall combines a banjo with a bit of Dixieland on the main melody to "People are Strange," but on "Love Street," the quaint violins (reminiscent of the Rolling Stones' "As Tears Go By") make the melody slower while the added harpsichord makes it more reflective.

Some of the more exotically "Easy" attempts to capture "Light My Fire" were also compelling. In 1970, Ravi Shankar's nephew Ananda released a self-titled album of sitar-inflected pop tunes. Not wanting to quake in his uncle's more traditionalist shadow, Ananda had no problem with taking the Doors' melody and transposing it to the raga twang. At just over three minutes, Shankar's version is fit for background in an Indian restaurant, a World's Fair pavilion, or a psychedelic elevator ride.

Among the very best "Light My Fire" interpretations comes from the Norwegian composer-arranger Sven Libaek. Sven Erik Libaek had been famous from his boyhood as a pianist who performed on Oslo radio.

Eventually settling in Sydney, Australia, Libaek would go on to become an accomplished musician and ultimately a Muzak contributor. Libaek's "Fire," which aired on Easy-Listening FM stations as well as on Muzak, starts with low-key horns substituting for Manzarek's keyboard. The opening verse uses gentle brass, somewhat like Chuck Mangione's flugelhorn on "Feels So Good." Heroic strings soon materialize to secure each note of the chorus. The second verse continues with the same brass, along with an added saxophone, as the echoing background drums hasten the beat, and two sets of strings bounce back and forth. For the final verse, a flute takes on the main melody until the strings, the flute, and the burnished brass unite to play out the Bach-ish closing. This being the late '70s, Libaek was likely unbound to Feliciano's influence, as his version is closer to the Doors' tempo and structure than most other instrumentals. Refurbished and rekindled, "Light My Fire" proved to be more than just another "wild child." ◉

63

ST-F-1020

THE DOORS
SONGBOOK

SONGBOOK
THE DOORS

Forward
Records

MIKE CURB & THE WATERFALL

SHADOW OVER SGT. PEPPER

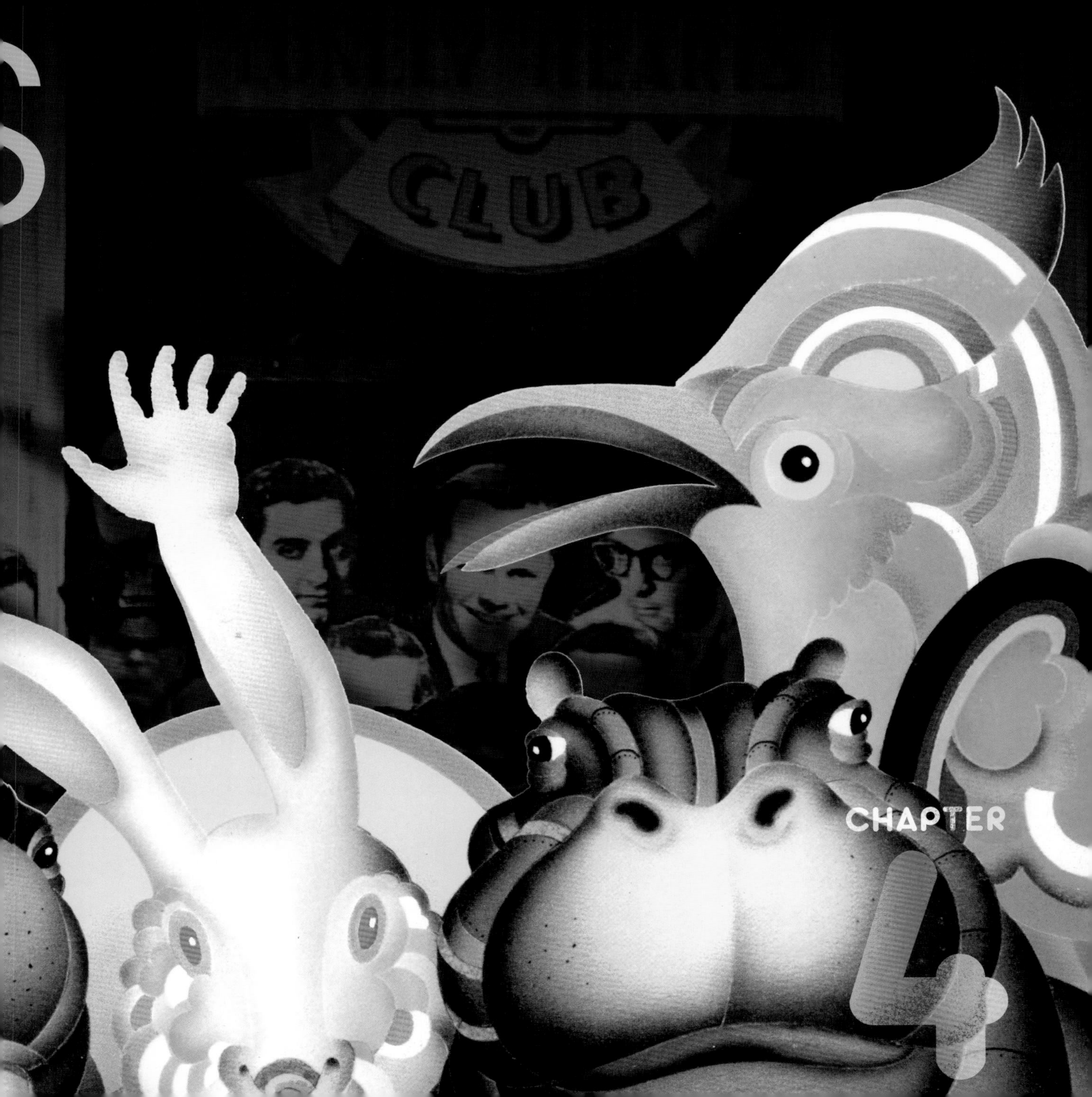

CHAPTER 4

"THEY RELISHED THE IDEA THAT THE FOUR MOST FAMOUS POP MUSICIANS IN THE WORLD SHOULD CREATE MOCK BANDSMEN AS THEIR ALTER EGOS, AND PRESENT THEIR MUSIC AS A NONSTOP STAGE SHOW, INTERSPERSED WITH THE 'OOHS' AND 'AHS' OF CHILDHOOD VISITS TO THE CIRCUS AND PANTOMIME."

—PHILIP NORMAN,
SHOUT! THE BEATLES IN THEIR GENERATION

Paul McCartney's legendary death in the fall of 1966, though officially a myth, continues to set a tone for the elegiac and spectral themes lurking through *Sgt. Pepper's Lonely Hearts Club Band*. The album's introspective, mostly melancholy mood had already permeated *Revolver* and some memorable singles recorded around the time of *Pepper*'s release. *Sgt. Pepper*, however, is the album that turned the sentimental, humorous, sad, and musically creative accomplishments of the twentieth century into a collage of styles from different periods, slipping through categorical cracks to surprise Beatles fans. They also turned the heads of previous detractors who were at last convinced that the Mop Tops were adding quality melodies to an endangered Euro-American Songbook.

From the marching brass-band nostalgia of its opening title to the apocalyptic and semi-classical closing on "A Day in the Life," *Sgt. Pepper* offers discrete stories told by voices from "the beyond." They are akin to those that would later wander about the Overlook Hotel in *The Shining*, which Stephen King likens to "the residues of the feelings of the people who have stayed there. Good things and bad things." *Sgt. Pepper*'s time-traveling band was tailored for the reality-warping psychedelic years, when past and present whirled in the same synesthesia that had people smelling colors and hearing butterflies scream.

Timothy Leary was apparently hallucinating when he claimed that *Sgt. Pepper* "gave a voice to the feeling that the old ways were over." To the contrary, the *Pepper* sessions allowed some of the old ways to creep back like fragmented memories—musical vestiges that complemented the psychedelic flourishes of distorted guitar, sitar, and such newfangled inventions as the keyboard tape manipulator dubbed the Mellotron.

"It was twenty years ago today," as the moldering chestnut of the future began, when the album arrived in the summer of 1967. The song refers to 1947, a year that yielded several milestones. In America, test pilot Chuck Yeager broke the sound barrier, while UFOs became a major news event that summer when aviator Kenneth Arnold spotted a fleet of nine alien lights in the skies near Mount Rainier. As the Dead Sea Scrolls surfaced in the Judaean Desert, America's OSS morphed into the same CIA that conducted nefarious experiments with LSD and mind control. In England that year, in time for Christmas and the winter solstice, occult showman Aleister Crowley, dubbed the "Great Beast," and one of the many faces glaring from *Sgt. Pepper*'s cover, passed on to whatever afterlife he had conjured.

1947 was also when Mantovani and His Concert Orchestra helped to energize the Easy-Listening craze with a 78 RPM single version of Charles Trenet's "La Mer" (or "Beyond the Sea")—waves of billowy violins that sounded mesmerizing even before he and his arranger Ronald Binge perfected a "cascading" effect, an overlapping of strings that turned Mantovani into "the Niagara Falls of Fiddles." It was also by the late '40s when Muzak, after several scientific trials, perfected its Stimulus-Progression method of programming music to match the daily mood curves for those occupying offices, factories and, of course, elevators.

A heady mishmash of events, 1947 offered comedy, music, mystery, and touches of horror that rebounded two decades later, as the *Sgt. Pepper* album combined the marketable "magick" of Crowley, the technological advances of studio pop, and mass media's ongoing obsession with the dead coming back to life. Such factors crowded into the Beatles' menagerie that included the hallucinatory "Lucy," the sexually complex "Lovely Rita," and the sorry fellow who "blew his mind out in a car."

Paul McCartney, as the Lonely Hearts Club Band's master of ceremonies, had the added advantage of his father Jim, a self-taught pianist who played in dance bands during the '20s and '30s. With aid from the family's upright piano and a collection of old 78s, he educated his son on the melodies and harmonies popular during the British music hall days. Jim and Paul dabbled into many yesterdays, but they still had to contend with rock-and-roll "purists" who fetishized the street-lingo of jazz, blues, and bluegrass in order to appear more "real" and less (as the British say) "posh."

At the same time, the emerging psychedelic era in England was subverting this "noble savage" conceit. Suddenly, English rockers, without flinching at the thought of seeming "twee," took a break from channeling Bo Diddley and explored their own folk and theater traditions. In an era celebrating the altered state, the country that produced Lewis Carroll and his *Wonderland* of oddities tripped down a sonic rabbit hole where "nothing is real," and some of the living who danced the Frug also waltzed with the dead.

McCartney might have inherited a knack for older music, but when considering the art of the string-laden lilt, he initially suffered what the British call "the screaming habdabs." In 1965, when George Martin suggested that strings accompany "Yesterday," McCartney initially scoffed at the prospect of a Mantovani sound. With baby steps, however, Martin talked him into using a more minimal and somber quartet. The *Pepper* sessions two years later revealed that McCartney expanded his musical palette when he sought more orchestral luster to accompany his downhearted "She's Leaving Home." Reacting to a *Daily Mail* article about a real-life young runaway, Paul wanted the tone to be melodramatic, semi-tabloid, and sentimentally lush, but George Martin was indisposed at the time. McCartney instead sought out Mike Leander, whose sweeping backgrounds had already demonstrated how pop and rock could tap into Easy-Listening's currency.

MERCURY STEREO SR 61132

INSTRUMENTAL BEATLES THEMES FROM

Sgt. PEPPERS LONELY HEARTS CLUB BAND

PETER KNIGHT & HIS ORCHESTRA

Mercury Record Corporation, 35 E. Wacker Drive, Chicago, Illinois 60601 • Printed in U.S.A.

The Hollyridge Strings
play: Magical Mystery Tour
and
Hello Goodbye · I Am The Walrus · All You Need Is Love

A Day In The Life · Your Mother Should Know

Baby You're A Rich Man · The Fool On The Hill

When I'm Sixty-Four · She's Leaving Home

Sgt. Pepper's Lonely Hearts Club Band

The Beatles Song Book Vol. 5

Like England's Leander, North America's Percy Faith realized how the studio orchestra could generate pop permutations by replacing vocals with added strings, pianos, and horns while boosting the melodies. On his 1963 Columbia album *Themes for Young Lovers*, Faith reached a watershed of sorts. He dispensed with guitars but used the near-addictive acoustics of high-pitched violins when recasting pre-Beatles hits like Skeeter Davis' "The End of the World," Little Peggy March's "I Will Follow Him," and the Cascades' "Rhythm of the Rain" (replete with pizzicato raindrops).

In 1964, the year the Beatles invaded American living rooms via *The Ed Sullivan Show*, Jimmie Haskell and His Orchestra released *Teen Love Themes* on Capitol, using techniques similar to Faith's but with the added kick of an electric bass guitar. The passing of a single year from Faith's album revealed some changes, which Haskell acknowledged when including echo-redolent versions of the Beatles' "Love Me Do," "A Hard Day's Night," and the Lennon-McCartney gift bestowed on Peter & Gordon, "A World Without Love." This was just before the Beatles flirted with psychedelia on *Rubber Soul* and three years prior to their cavorting under "marmalade skies." "She's Leaving Home" is not overtly psychedelic, but it still characterizes what much of *Sgt. Pepper* addresses: contemporary issues and troubles bedeviled by yesteryear's heartaches that never really go away.

Sgt. Pepper as well as cuts from *Revolver*, *Magical Mystery Tour*, and accompanying hit singles "Penny Lane," "Strawberry Fields Forever," "Hello Goodbye," "I Am the Walrus," "All You Need is Love," and even the warbling "Baby, You're a Rich Man" were laced with sonic codes that might have sounded reactionary to tougher rockers still craving a harder edge.

"Eleanor Rigby" goaded young folks to fast-forward into possible futures when they too might become old and lonely. In contrast, the otherwise kid-friendly "Yellow Submarine" got spiked with drug associations. Being that the Rolling Stones had already sung (in their native English as opposed to pseudo-blues) about the "little yellow pill" on "Mother's Little Helper," some interpreted the "submarine" as a metaphor for the barbiturate Nembutal. Whether minds were tranquilized or "psychedelicized," the Beatles were tripping backwards on "Your Mother Should Know," cajoling fans to "get up and dance to a song that was a hit before your mother was born"—preferably in a mind-bending ballroom that paired the traditional mirror ball from earlier hotel-band days with the "now generation's" stroboscopic lightshow.

Sgt. Pepper blended its rock and pop with bits of "classical," vaudeville, Salvation Army bands, East Indian raga, and circus calliopes. It was retrofitted to fashion, as swinging London's denizens and tourists flocked to a boutique called I Was Lord Kitchener's Valet. There, they could purchase

Edwardian military uniforms, seeming to rebel against convention while tacitly acknowledging the majesty of Britain's fallen Empire.

A prime example of the album's tribute to England's eccentric past is "Lucy in the Sky with Diamonds." Even the obvious acronym in its title sparked controversy when Lennon denied the connection and claimed he got the title from a picture that his three-year-old son Julian drew in nursery school. The "LSD" story—much more fascinating and suitable to posterity—took on its own life when the BBC banned the song's airing.

The Beatles had combined Lennon's multi-tracked voice with processed guitars, the Mellotron, Harrison's droning tambura, and McCartney's Lowrey organ as parts of a larger audio experiment that makes this the album's dreamiest track and what BBC critic Chris Jones would describe decades later as "nursery rhyme surrealism." Lennon was also keen to trace the song's origins to Lewis Carroll, that progenitor of acid dreams, who writes in the final chapter of *Through the Looking Glass* about Alice inside "A boat, beneath a sunny sky / Lingering onward dreamily..." For "Lucy in the Sky with Diamonds," Alice's boat ride also suggests the "magic swirling ship" in "Mr. Tambourine Man."

As late-twentieth-century teenagers got exposed to music that had "been going in and out of style" before their moms and dads were even zygotes, the *Sgt. Pepper* songs also seemed to be transmitted from the astral world, giving after-death

assessments of life's illusions and game plans: the bad tempers, broken families, childhood joys, adult failures, flighty romances, religious delusions, banal routines, shallow careers, petty annoyances, and chronic fears of aging in isolation.

A good bellwether for how the older intelligentsia received *Sgt. Pepper* is a review from *High Fidelity* in August of 1967. Gene Lees, a Canadian critic, lyricist, and author of several music biographies, sent mixed signals. He got negative when concentrating less on the music and more on the lyrics, dismissing most of them as "meandering, unstructured, free-association, do-it-yourself-Rorschakism [sic]." He was particularly stumped on "With a Little Help from My Friends": "What are the friends? Roaches? Who knows whether they mean drugs, or actual real-live friends? This lyric isn't profound; it's just indefinite."

The song's provocative words do evoke multiple interpretations: from popping pills to choking the chicken. Future Vice President Spiro Agnew, then Governor of Maryland, was among the censorious "establishment" who perceived the "friends" as narcotics, though he did admit it was "quite a catchy little tune." That "catchy little tune," with McCartney's skip-happy bass, was a lock for any "Easy" instrumental arranger with half an imagination and a good ear.

Lees put his generational biases aside when responding more favorably to other *Pepper* offerings, recognizing "Lucy in the Sky with Diamonds" as "almost certainly a deliberate evocation of the visual ef-

74

fect of an LSD high." He appreciated the Mellotron's "eerily beautiful accompaniment," recognizing it as "an electric keyboard instrument that here sounds like a reverberated harpsichord." He perceived the switch to a more rocking rhythm when Lennon repeats the title refrain as having "a flavor of mild hysteria" and recognized the song's "genuine beauty and startling shimmering interflowing images."

Some of the younger critics, on the other hand, did not react to *Sgt. Pepper* with open arms. Though *Cash Box* magazine deemed it America's best-selling album of the season, Richard Goldstein, writing for *The New York Times*, called it "busy, hip, and cluttered"—a dismissal that elicited lots of angry letters to the paper. The album was as sociologically confusing as it was musically creative. "Few of their old fans could have anticipated their present course or wished for it," Robert Christgau wrote in *Esquire*. "Yet the Beatles have continued to please more of the old-timers than anyone but they—and the old-timers themselves—could have hoped." He cited "Being for the Benefit of Mr. Kite" to augment his claim that the album is "a kind of long vaudeville show."

"Being for the Benefit of Mr. Kite" conjures sounds and images of carnival acrobats, flame throwers, and tightrope walkers. It also features an electrified waltz tempo: one of the album's most psychedelic moments, even though it is essentially mimicking a dance beat that European socialites enjoyed at least a century before.

Oddly, poor "Mr. Kite," readymade for elevator music interpretations, was also among the most ignored. Perhaps this was because "Henry the Horse" had heroin connotations that prompted the starched shirts at the BBC to add it to its forbidden list. "Fixing a Hole," also branded with drug rumors involving needles, got subsequent radio neglect that might explain why it too eluded the Easy-Listening radar. Decades later, when the post-new-age instrumental vogue demanded recordings with "tasteful" solo performances, guitarist Al Di Meola recorded an offbeat version on a Beatles tribute recorded at Abbey Road Studios.

Critic Naphtali Wagner hailed "the act you've known for all these years" for its "psycheclassical synthesis," but other, more populist, influences from previous generations allowed the Beatles (and such contemporaries as the Bee Gees) to balance on a tightrope between being melodic and ironic as they steered a threatening drug culture into an Easy-Listening comfort zone. Procol Harum's "Shade of Pale" had its Bach template ready for the taking, but the songs on *Sgt. Pepper* posed a greater challenge to instrumentalists. The tracks were unique, fresh, busy with multiple tone colors, tempo changes, cultural influences, and loaded with audio gimmicks for which conventional studio orchestras often required substitutes.

Among the arrangers to make the first moves was Peter Knight who, just months after the Beatles' release, came out on Mercury Records with *Instrumental Beatles Themes from Sgt. Pepper's Lonely Hearts Club Band*. Knight and the Orchestra recast *Sgt. Pepper* into what the back cover calls "mind-shattering instrumental happenings," including every track except "Fixing a Hole" and once again the forlorn "Mr. Kite."

The crowd's roar, the raucous guitar, and horn-drenched introduction are nearly as jarring as on the original, but a quainter "With a Little Help from My Friends" follows, with a sweet guitar, a harpsichord, a muted trumpet, discreet drums, and of course, glazing strings. Lennon and McCartney composed it for Ringo's limited vocal range, except for the ending, which forced him to totter over an octave cliff. Knight's rendition compensates for Ringo's absence by layering on different instruments to distinguish each verse, a nuanced approach that demonstrates why Easy-Listening should not be confused with lazy playing.

On "Lucy in the Sky with Diamonds," Knight makes the journey through "kaleidoscope eyes" seem more like a quaint parlor theme as he stresses the waltz beat of the verses, with horns and strings replacing the vocals while forging an unexpected friendship with the electric guitar. Knight combines the kinetic rock with constant shifts between a vaster orchestra and a smaller chamber ensemble. On the chorus, which switches from a waltz to more of a rock beat, Knight keeps the mood serene with a smaller chamber section.

Treated piano keys replace the Beatles' guitar opening on "Getting Better," another of the *Sgt. Pepper* tracks that got scant attention from other instrumentalists. Knight starts with thumping horns and percussion, but an interlude of baroque-style fiddles makes at least part of this another example of a soundtrack suitable for English teatime. This track alone bolsters the album's claim that "when you play this LP, you won't be listening to the Beatles' session minus the vocal tracks." Knight avoids what decades later would degenerate into the "karaoke" effect of merely miming the original backgrounds in order for soused party animals to slobber the words into portable microphones.

Knight's "She's Leaving Home" is not far removed from the ornate arrangement that Mike Leander did for the Beatles. On the original album, Lennon and McCartney alternate singing parts to contrast their narratives about the confused cries of parents over their missing daughter's motives. Knight compensates for the omitted words with harder tugs at the heartstrings. He preserves the original's opening harp but makes the mood more hyper-romantic by letting a harpsichord and French horn alternately substitute for the McCartney-Lennon duet, while a mournful trumpet occupies one line, violins follow another, and woodwinds also chime in. Knight converts the song's story into the instrumental equivalent of cautionary nursery rhymes against youthful indiscretions routinely drilled into children's minds.

Along with his album version, Knight also released a single of George Harrison's "Within You, Without You," using, like Harrison, a genuine sitar and tabla. Harrison recorded this raga lecture to the West with the aid of Britain's Asian Music Circle, but George Martin added violins and cellos from the London Symphony Orchestra. How authentically Indian it sounds is left for raga scholars, but learned and provincial listeners alike might detect stubborn traces of Western sing-song (and the laughter at the end on the original is one of those mysteries left for anyone to interpret with a grin). Knight's version is also the first of four arrangements on the album by Bob Leaper, who, among other duties, provided the orchestral shimmer on another Lennon and McCartney gift to Peter & Gordon, the 1966 hit "Woman."

Knight and Leaper take "When I'm Sixty-Four" further down the corridors where hotel-band shadows loom: the lightheaded clarinet, the muted trumpets, and the sweet violins await Al Bowlly or Rudy Vallee apparitions to materialize out of the ether and croon. The track also includes a Lawrence Welk champagne-style finale: an open invitation for other instrumentalists to turn this into another chirpy ballroom number tailored for a Guy Lombardo New Year's Eve gala. Lennon, perhaps paranoid about not letting his image as the testy "intellectual Beatle" slip away, dismissed "When I'm Sixty-Four" as "granny music" and was content to let McCartney take the credit.

Knight's "Lovely Rita" uses what had become a folk-rock staple: the tambourine. Here, it guides the melody's shift from piano to bolder brass. The piano is the star here, hammering away "plunk-plank-plank" flourishes similar to those of Liberace or Roger Williams. The cock crows as "Good Morning, Good Morning" opens with an electric guitar approaching Lennon's part until the string orchestra and brass join in. The album even simulates the title song's "Reprise," with constant crowd roars and the same rowdy guitar as in the beginning, but it does not last long.

"A Day in the Life," despite its dark tone, betrays bits of "granny music" as Lennon relives the humdrum existence of a middle-class Liverpudlian during Britain's postwar days. Knight substitutes the original's grand piano with a harpsichord, a lightly thumping bass guitar, the support of a string section, and a solitary trumpet to replace the vocal. He also makes the song's infamous freak-out moments conjuring "end times" from the Book of Revelation sound more like descending planes about to crash-land.

Playful bass lines, drums, piano, flutes, and lustrous strings substitute for McCartney's brief appearance on the "Woke up, fell out of bed" interlude, before the familiar notes of a grand orchestra return to Lennon's reflection. The trumpet again supplies the voice, and the track's fade-out is much less resonant than on the *Pepper* version. Knight even approximates the "run-out groove" that the

Beatles had slipped in at the very end, just when listeners thought that the second side would fade into oblivion.

A year later, Knight would conduct the London Festival Orchestra on *Days of Future Passed*, his collaboration with the Moody Blues. He had already helped to set an instrumental trend with his *Sgt. Pepper* tribute, but Knight soon faced numerous competitors.

"Penny Lane," one of the songs that got away from appearing on the album, inspired several tributes. Notable for its sly, sexual lyrics and other wordplay, it translates "instrumentally" into perky yet "granny"-friendly pop. The piccolo trumpet interlude on the Beatles' single was an afterthought, when McCartney marveled at the New Philharmonia's BBC television performance of Bach's *Brandenburg Concerto #2*, particularly David Mason's piccolo trumpet. Bach (who inspired the Doors, Procol Harum, and Spanky and Our Gang) became another impetus for Lennon and McCartney's retrospection on the mixed blessings of postwar life. Mason became a special guest of the recording session, rekindling the piccolo energy from his Philharmonia performance and pulling "Penny Lane," like a pied piper, further back in time.

The Beatles' recording had already made the instrumental adaptors' job easy. Paul Mauriat, on his 1967 release *Blooming Hits*, engorges the song with strong studio echoes on the higher- and lower-pitched strings, harpsichord, and horns.

That same year, on his album *The French Touch*, Franck Pourcel, France's other major "Easy" arranger, adds a similar orchestral luster of horns and strings. Attached to a drumming backdrop, Pourcel's interpretation is the ideal cinema score for depicting frenzied trendies crowding into a Carnaby Street boutique.

The ethereal love song "Here, There, and Everywhere," from *Revolver*, has been another favorite among pop arrangers. John Cameron, who had arranged several tracks for Donovan, allows his orchestra to respect the song's romantic meditation on the 1968 album *Warm and Gentle*. Mike Leander, on his 1969 album *Migration*, also gives it a grand orchestra treatment that played on BBC's Radio 2. Also in 1969, on his album *A Brand New Me*, Liberace massaged it with elegant keyboard strokes.

When the Beatles performed "All You Need is Love" live on television for world viewing, Mike Vickers conducted the orchestra. Vickers was by then the former flautist, guitarist, and saxophonist for Manfred Mann and would be among the first British musicians to use a Moog synthesizer. In 1970, he continued orchestrating pop songs as a founder of the Baker Street Philharmonic, whose album *Yesterday's Dreams* includes a version of "Here, There, and Everywhere" that starts with a mournful organ and acoustic guitar before the violins and an intermittent feminine chorus make it more cryptic.

George Martin was ahead of the game on his 1966 album *George Martin Instrumentally Salutes the*

INCLUDING
Hey Jude · Good Night
Ob-La-Di Ob-La-Da

The Panoramic Sound of

Lennon and McCartney

Cyril Stapleton, His Choir and Orchestra

(NEW IMPROVED FULL DIMENSIONAL STEREO)

The Beatles Songbook more great instrumental arrangements Vol. 4
The Hollyridge Strings

Penny Lane

Strawberry Fields Forever

Eleanor Rigby

Yellow Submarine

Eight Days A Week

Good Day Sunshine

Act Naturally

Drive My Car

Taxman

You've Got To Hide Your Love Away

I've Just Seen A Face

Beatle Girls, giving the song a brassier treatment that became part of the soundtrack to the 1967 surfer documentary *Free and Easy*. As the reputed "fifth Beatle," Martin perhaps felt qualified to enter more daunting territory, finding a melodic imp hiding inside of Lennon's mystically morbid "She Said, She Said."

"She Said, She Said" screamed into the world sometime in the summer of 1965, while Lennon and George Harrison stayed at a rented house in Hollywood's Benedict Canyon. Peter Fonda was among the guests, tripping with John and George on liquid acid from the Sandoz Laboratories. George was having some problems during his altered state when he imagined he might be dying. That is when Fonda attempted to comfort him by recalling how he survived his own near-death experience on an operating table at age ten after he mishandled a .22 caliber pistol and shot himself. John Lennon, no Pollyanna, nonetheless took umbrage when overhearing Fonda's mortality monologue. According to Fonda, in his autobiography *Don't Tell Dad*, Lennon shot back: "'Who put all that crap in your head?' he asked angrily. 'You're making me feel like I've never been born.'"

Martin's instrumental homage to "She Said, She Said" avoids much of the angst but retains a bit of the psychological edge in Lennon's dirge. He manages to engineer something hummable for those who cannot access or abide the original's dark lyrics. With bossa nova pulses, billowy strings, piano flourishes, and woodwinds that hint ever so slightly at Lennon's off-kilter attitude, Martin's track stays pleasant enough for casual listeners choosing not to detect anything sinister afoot. However, those aware of the song and its gloomy allure can still enjoy Martin's approach by exercising an aural depth of field that allows them to imagine an additional pall over the already shadowy creation.

In contrast, another *Revolver* track, which instrumentalists overlooked despite its baroque invitation, is McCartney's "For No One." Floyd Cramer both honors yet has some fun with this crestfallen account of a relationship gone sour on the RCA album *Class of '67*. The Beatles used a French horn and several other period instruments to fill *Revolver*'s melodic museum, but while reclining on a bed of soft strings, Cramer replaces McCartney's clavichord with his trademark slip-note piano. Then suddenly, Cramer switches the ballad from somber to manically chipper, an abrupt transition that somehow works, thanks in part to the moral support of fellow Nashville players.

Curious *Sgt. Pepper*-era arrangements came from another unexpected source. England's Cyril Stapleton had been a working violinist since the days of silent movies. He went on to play with other symphony orchestras and to accompany American vocalists like Dick James and Frank Sinatra. In 1969, he was still kicking and eager to acclimate to a mutable landscape with *The Panoramic Lennon and McCartney*, a collection from

Pye Records. Stapleton also uses voices singing the words—a technique that others like Ray Conniff, Percy Faith, and Johnny Mann used to accomplish the seemingly contradictory feat of reciting the lyrics without detracting from the music. Ordinary star vocalists insist on occupying the foreground, but Stapleton's singers allow the words to function as additional instruments. At the same time, those familiar with the Beatles' songs can choose to focus on the messages while hearing them from a new and sometimes more haunting angle.

Stapleton, his orchestra, and choir go into friendly territory with soft ballads like "When I'm Sixty-Four," but the collection also includes a version of "With a Little Help from My Friends" that makes an unexpected detour from the Beatles' simple and childlike approach. In 1968, confusion reigned again when Joe Cocker turned it into a pseudo-gospel shriek rite, with an equally baleful chorus and lots of ear-grinding electric guitar. His version threatened to overwhelm the original even more when he famously stumbled about and flailed his arms while performing it at Woodstock. Like an intrepid explorer, however, Colonel Stapleton forged on with his singing safari into the wilds of Cocker country, duplicating the lyrics with the controlled inflections of a Church of England choir and giving the "blue-eyed soul" a refreshing vanilla makeover.

On his 1969 album *Cinemagic Sounds*, Richard Hayman applied some musical contortions to "Lucy in the Sky with Diamonds," which he squeezed into the collection because "Lucy" was part of the *Yellow Submarine* soundtrack. Hayman's presence on the pop instrumental scene goes back to his creepy 1959 *Voodoo* album, but he also knew how to soothe. A harmonica stylist by trade, he was also an associate conductor for the Boston Pops Orchestra and an arranger for several Muzak sessions. On "Lucy," however, Hayman ignores the poignant, unsettling key shifts on *Sgt. Pepper,* opting instead for an incessant beat that should have been listed as "The Fool in the Sky with Diamonds." Hayman fused "Lucy" with the dance-party rhythms that Sergio Mendes & Brasil '66 imposed onto a Top 40 version of "The Fool on the Hill" that occupied AM radio throughout the summer of 1968. Andre Kostelanetz also recorded a version of "The Fool" on his 1969 album *Traces* with the Mendes arrangement, but his gleaming orchestra yields more pleasurable results. To be fair, Hayman does preserve one creative twinge from the Mendes version: the dizzying carousel crescendo.

Meanwhile, Hungarian guitarist Gabor Szabo took a breezier elevator ride on his 1967 album *Wind, Sky, and Diamonds*, backed by the California Dreamers, a ghostly choral amalgam of Ray Conniff's traditional "bah-bah-bah"s with then-trendy word chimers like Roger Nichols & The Small Circle of Friends. The Dreamers consisted of several in-demand background vocal performers: Ron Hicklin, Al Capps, Loren Farber, Ian

Freebairn-Smith, Sally Stevens, Sue Allen, Jackie Ward (a former Ray Conniff Singer who had dubbed herself "Robin Ward" on her effervescent 1963 hit "Wonderful Summer"), as well as brothers John and Tom Bahler, who also founded the sunshine-pop group the Love Generation.

Szabo's opening guitar on "Lucy in the Sky with Diamonds," paired with a sitar, keyboards, drums, and the occasional tambourine, forms a dreamscape, especially as the singers make the words sound more like guitar extensions. On "A Day in the Life," the California Dreamers sing the lyrics along to the ever-present harpsichord and imitations of Ringo's drum trappings, but Szabo skips the strident noise of the apocalypse and goes right into McCartney's interim dream to (only momentarily) show off his improvisational guitar.

An obscure fragment in American television history occurred sometime in 1968, when the professional curmudgeon Henry Morgan appeared on *The Merv Griffin Show*, reading the words to "Hello Goodbye" from the sheet music, inciting audience chuckles as he misled them into overlooking the catchy and elevating tune behind the Gertrude Stein-ish lyric repetition. "Hello Goodbye" was light, humorous, and the kind of nursery-rhyme melody that invited numerous interpretations. The Marble Arch Orchestra stresses the humor with eccentric touches on the 1968 album *Tomorrow's Standards*—a busy and ever-shifting arrangement that includes strings, horns, harpsichord, chimes,

tambourine, and drums. (On the same LP, the Orchestra has fun with the banjo when covering the 1968 novelty single "Thank U Very Much" by the Scaffold, a British pop group that included Paul McCartney's brother Michael.) Others with more of an affinity for horns could choose *The Baroque Brass*, which combines trumpets, flugelhorns, euphoniums, and the sackbut trombone. A little later in the '70s, Enoch Light and His Orchestra give "Hello Goodbye" a more imperial, symphonic nod on *Beatles Classics*.

Of the many mood maestros on songs like "Hello Goodbye," the one studio orchestra that stood out among all of the others was, of course, the Hollyridge Strings. They were the Ectoplasmic Beatles. Starting under the baton of Stu Phillips, the Hollyridge variations provided what one of the album's notes called "tuneful, gorgeously listenable versions" of Beatles songs. These were modest words because their recordings, like most Easy-Listening, connoted more than simply music for relaxation. Unlike other musical categories with more obvious contexts, Easy-Listening is more amorphous, suiting the listener, who can have various emotional reactions and perceive complicated meanings behind what might be a deceptively simplistic façade.

Phillips became an expert at reconstituting the Beatles through a resounding and lovingly processed world that was beautiful for domestic backgrounds yet mysterious for those probing deeper into Planet Hollyridge. "The strings had that great echo because of tape delay," Phillips recalls in a coyly technical manner, "which offered almost a repetition of a note. This was especially effective with the pizzicato. Those string players' fingers almost bled from plucking so hard. But their bravery helped to produce that distinctive sound."

By the time the Hollyridge sessions graduated into the *Sgt. Pepper* phase, Phillips was at Columbia Records' Epic label, recording Monkees songs as the Golden Gate Strings. Perry Botkin Jr. and Mort Garson took over. In the process, these two seasoned arrangers and composers continued with Phillips' techniques, retaining the spooky reverberation that made the Hollyridge sessions so distinct. They also added their own innovations to offer some of the most intriguing and intrepid Beatles renditions. Botkin was already part of Hollyridge Strings history when (under the moniker Bunny Botkin) he conducted some of their early '60s Capitol entries, including the 1961 single "Lucy's Theme" from the Troy Donahue film *Parrish*.

Garson, on the other hand, established his pop-history niche in 1963, when he, along with lyricist Bob Hilliard, composed "Our Day Will Come." He was also the arranger for an in-house orchestra at Liberty Records marketed as the Sunset Strings, with albums of echo-laden Italian movie themes as well as a Roy Orbison tribute. About a month before *Sgt. Pepper*, Garson was already tripping on the Big Moog and other electronic toys for an album of his own material, *The Zodiac: Cosmic Sounds*.

When the Hollyridge Strings released *The Beatles Songbook, Vol. 4* in 1967, Botkin and Garson included "Strawberry Fields Forever." Like "Penny Lane," it was supposed to be part of *Sgt. Pepper*'s "glass onion" gaze at the present through the past. "Strawberry Fields Forever" was truly psychedelic terrain, where the rhythm switches into differing dimensions, and the electronic effects are their own drug. Recreating Lennon's hallucinatory meadows as a glistening instrumental, Botkin and Garson retained all of the Beatles' melody and rhythm but added more conventional instruments that nonetheless made this the star track of the LP and arguably the most fascinating of Hollyridge revisions.

Through the Hollyridge echoplex, "Strawberry Fields" acclimates to the Beatles' eccentric altering of keys and recording speeds, at times sounding more outré than the Fab Four. Botkin and Garson draw it into another kind of time warp by layering the slow, enveloping strings with a torpid saxophone that morphs into a wistful clarinet. The result is a seductive and peculiar tone reminiscent of the "come hither" sound that the Jackie Gleason Orchestra used for its creamy "vanilla music." This also made the Hollyridge "Fields" an ideal track to introduce the 1967 surfing film *Free and Easy*.

The following year, *The Hollyridge Strings Play Magical Mystery Tour* (or *The Beatles Song Book Vol. 5*) took on several *Sgt. Pepper*-era tracks. The Hollyridge approach to "A Day in the Life" is a highlight. It starts out with the acoustic guitar's pensive strumming and the creeping piano, but the strings, like orchestral body-snatchers, envelop some of Lennon's baleful attitude to make the mood more ambiguous. There are no references to war movies, crashed cars, or dead bodies to grab the attention: just music to evoke something profound and bizarre that listeners can interpret any which way. When it gets to the bridge, with McCartney's story about waking up, falling out of bed, having a smoke, and going into a dream, the sprightly melody offers a farthing of relief from the existential woes, recalling those perky production-music library tunes with such titles as "Workaday World" and "Holiday Playtime."

While working on the Hollyridge sessions, Mort Garson arranged tracks for Mariano and the Unbelievables' second album, *The 25th Hour*. It honors "Hello Goodbye" with the harpsichord, violins, and a rocking drum beat that sparkles enough to fascinate varying ages, despite the era's much-ballyhooed "generation gap."

Other Hollyridge tracks on the collection, such as "Magical Mystery Tour" and "Your Mother Should Know," employ a playful and wistful shoppers' pizzicato. Even the Beatles' originals of both songs were likely to confuse hardcore rockers as much as they pleased older listeners who discovered that Pepperland might have alluded to drugs, but it also offered the auditory equivalent of cream-filled crumpets.

Among the *Sgt. Pepper*-era pieces, "I Am the Walrus" proposes the biggest Spike Jones dare. It is quirky, at times dissonant, and threatens to laugh back at any earnest attempts to take it seriously. "The first line was written on one acid trip one weekend," Lennon revealed to David Sheff in a 1980 interview that appeared in *Playboy*. "The second line was written on the next acid trip the next weekend, and it was filled in after I met Yoko." It is also another of Lennon's pranks: a parody of Dylan-style verbosity that took hold in the mid- to late '60s. These were times when an American folk artist like Bob Lind could enthuse about "the canyons of your mind" and "the bright, elusive butterfly of love," while Jonathan King, a Brit at least as flamboyant as Lennon, could clutter his 1965 psychedelic ballad "Everyone's Gone to the Moon" with elaborate metaphors. King predated the Beatles' "yellow matter custard" by two years with his "mouths full of chocolate-covered cream." His "Moon" was enough of a delectably strange concoction to inspire America's Percy Faith and England's Ivor Raymonde to cover it with orchestral gauze.

Botkin and Garson's "Walrus" variation also crosses generational tastes. Beneath the original's obtuse lyrics and frenetic textures, the "Walrus" (at least in parts) bears enough of a traditional melody for various interpreters to either ignore or mimic the daffy blips. Even stiff-lipped, bowler-hatted bankers of the time could flit down Fleet Street and

85

Columbia
Stereo
C 30097

THE PERCY FAITH STRINGS
THE BEATLES ALBUM

Let It Be / Michelle
Here, There And Everywhere
Norwegian Wood
The Ballad Of John And Yoko
Something

Eleanor Rigby
Because
Lucy In The Sky With Diamonds
Yesterday
The Fool On The Hill

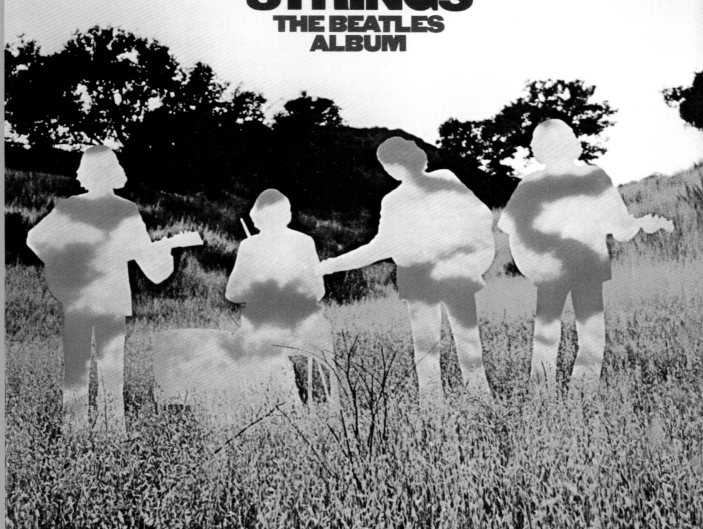

pretend for at least a few seconds that they were, as the Brits say, "mad as a March Hare." The Hollyridge "Walrus" treatment captures much of this madness while remaining conventionally listenable to attract those who might not care for the Beatles' release. The best part occurs when the strings spray a shower of pizzicato tears at the moment when Lennon is supposed to sing "I'm crying."

As the master of crying violins, Percy Faith covered songs like "Lucy in the Sky with Diamonds" with string-saturated finesse on his 1970 release, *The Beatles Album*. Faith had been among the foremost advocates of large and glossy orchestras liberating themselves from the "classics" and adapting to pop. To enhance this sonic chiffon, he accompanies the Beatles' songs with "The Percy Faith Strings," a special ensemble he had formed twelve years beforehand, consisting of thirty-two violins, eight violas, and eight cellos. Producer Irving Townsend's back-cover notes help to summarize the effect:

"…forty-eight of the finest string players in the world spread out from the podium like four exquisite ribs in a delicate fan of sound—a Beatle ballad as familiar as a friend woven into countermelodies so precisely right that they too sound familiar. Then, the startling individuality of a flugelhorn, an alto sax, a trombone, or a flute appears warm and confidential, and then disappears again into the flowing strings."

In a November 1970 review in *High Fidelity* of *The Beatles Album*, critic Morgan Ames betrayed a snippy aversion for recordings of this sort but was more reverent this time. He recognized how "Faith took this album seriously. He searched out those Lennon-McCartney songs which 'play for strings,' and then set the tunes orchestrally with infinite grace." Ames seemed on the verge of becoming an Easy-Listening convert when concluding, "This album is recommended as first aid for your ruined nerves and despairing spirits."

As the '70s unleashed lots of melancholy Top 40 ballads, records by piano-dependent singer-song-writers, hyper arena rock, and eventually Kiss and disco, Easy-Listening records adapted to the mutable times and tunes. The minds behind the 101 Strings released dedications to the Carpenters and Carole King, but they also listened for chirrups of psychedelic nostalgia. When Elton John revived "Lucy in the Sky with Diamonds" in 1975 (with John Lennon accompanying him on backing vocals and guitar), they also shined their ever-loving light on the "tangerine trees" with a white-bread chorale for the 1976 album ceremoniously titled *101 Strings Orchestra Play & Sing the Songs Made Famous by Elton John, Featuring The Alshire Singers*.

The maestros behind these Easy-Listening recordings from the *Sgt. Pepper* days, whether they realized it or not, bore an ethical burden. They had to lighten the load cast upon the Beatles that resulted partly from the group's own misadventures: the tussles they caused with authorities and censors, the umbrage they had elicited when mocking middle-class mores, and Lennon's cracks about Christ and Christianity that played right into their hecklers' hands.

Additional mysteries hover over *Sgt. Pepper*. The jaundiced tone that pervades even the most accessible melodies reflects the less-than-easy time the Fab Four had when experiencing Dr. Albert Hofmann's "problem child" for the first time. The book *Acid Dreams* tells of Lennon and his then-wife Cynthia joining George Harrison for dinner at a friend's home. Without warning, the so-called "friend" slipped acid (in the form of sugar cubes) into their after-dinner coffee. "John was crying and banging his head against the wall," Cynthia recalled. "I tried to make myself sick, and couldn't. I tried to go to sleep and couldn't. It was like a nightmare that wouldn't stop..." Lennon's recollection was just as glum: "We didn't know what was going on. We were just insane. We were out of our heads."

Using their *Sgt. Pepper* guise to channel the past, the Beatles evolved from lovable Mop Tops to musical mediums as they summoned childhood memories full of light and shadow. When the trip got too scary, they retreated into their hall of illusions to find refuge in another room where there is "nothing to get hung about." The Beatles' originals continue to delight, but fans can also enjoy the Easy-Listening alter egos—elevator music piped into Pepperland, where the living, the dead, and the purportedly dead linger together. ♦

Easy-Listening Acid Trip

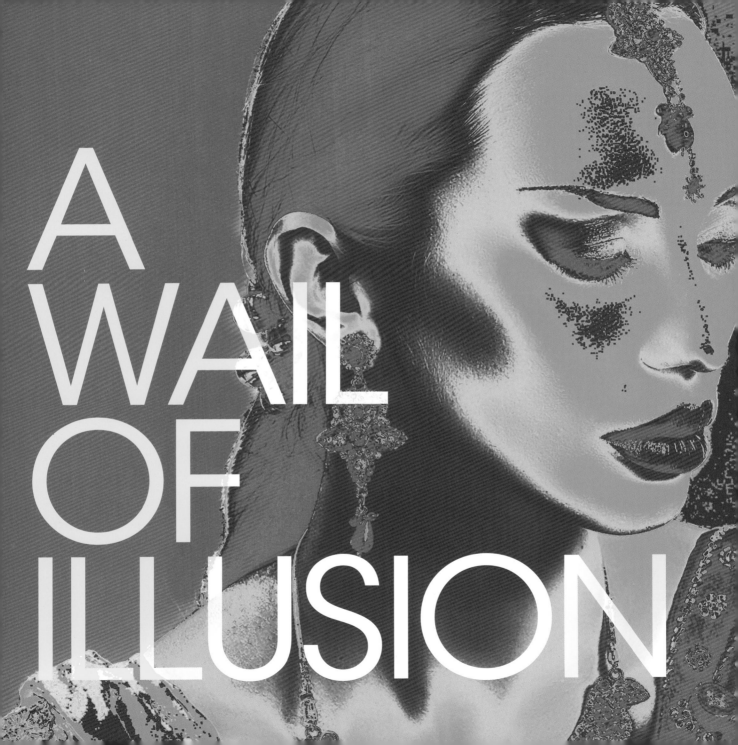

CHAPTER

5

"THE RAGA FAD IS IN FACT CLOSELY LINKED WITH THE PSYCHEDELIC SADNESS—SO MUCH SO THAT THE SELF-MADE CHEMICAL MADMAN TIMOTHY LEARY IS A FREQUENT SOURCE OF LINER-NOTE QUOTES THESE DAYS."

—GENE LEES, FROM *HIGH FIDELITY*, JULY 1967

Sci-fi visionary J.G. Ballard once gave a dismissive but honest assessment of the sitar's troubled relationship with the average North American and European listener. In Ballard's story "Venus Smiles" (from his *Vermilion Sands* collection), the narrator speaks of the "whining quarter-notes of this infernal instrument, so grating on the Western ear." Ballard depicts a dystopia, where "sonic sculptures" emit sounds that strike much of its population as unsettling. At one point, the narrator reacts viscerally to the intrusion: "The statue was now giving out an intermittent high-pitched whine, a sitar-like caterwauling that seemed to pull apart the sutures of my skull." By the time Ballard's book appeared in Great Britain in the early '70s, the "high-pitched whine" had already entered pop and some Easy-Listening recordings—to the point when many found it an odd yet amiable addition to the ever-mutating "modern" sound.

In 1965, George Harrison was among the first to introduce the sitar on the opening drones of the *Help!* soundtrack, where its needling presence alerts viewers to the movie's madcap vignettes. That same year, Harrison used it to make the setting on "Norwegian Wood (This Bird Has Flown)" sound more alienating, as Lennon sings about being invited to a stranger's home, hoping for intimacy and then being abandoned, or "had." Here, the sitar is a narrative weapon that warns listeners not to get too comfortable in unfamiliar

places. Despite Harrison's lofty intentions and genuine interest in the instrument and its culture, the average listener likely found the sitar akin to the theremin: an electronic "weirdo" widget that wails without being touched. Those preferring to spell "art" with a capital "A" might want to limit the theremin to classical recitals or avant-garde "performances." However, it is equally noble when tailored for popular entertainment, especially to dramatize unusual circumstances: movie scenes where a space monster invades a town, or in pop songs that drift into strange places.

The sitar too could induce anxiety without assaulting its audience with loud, nihilistic noise. In 1966, the Rolling Stones lured raga into a crypt on the hypnotically morbid "Paint It Black." The sitar simulates the wail of collective mourners, while Jagger rants about wanting to blot out the sun as funeral cars take his lover away. The optics of this performance on *The Ed Sullivan Show*, with Brian Jones arrayed in priestly white and sitting cross-legged with the sitar on his lap, indicated that the group, already an eye- and ear-sore for typical middle-class consumers, was traversing more uncharted (for some, unsightly) territory.

This cultural cross-pollination affected musicians from East India as well, but with different results. Ravi Shankar received the *Billboard* "Artist of the Year Award" in 1967 but felt a backlash in his home country for being associated with the drug culture of the West. Though he publicly denounced drugs, Shankar got absorbed into the hippie movement by osmosis, earning a standing ovation at the Monterey International Pop Festival and eventually Woodstock.

While the sitar and the percussive tabla got exposure through introspective ballads from the Beatles and Donovan, other recording artists flirted with the sound to add mystique to mainstream songs. One was Chim Kotari. In 1966, under the supervision of ace arranger Arthur Greenslade, Kotari released *Sound of Sitar* on the Deram label. The closest it gets to an actual psychedelic-era tune is a cover of "Eleanor Rigby," but Kotari mixes raga with strings and other more conventional instruments on selections like "Winchester Cathedral," "Strangers in the Night," and "Guantanamera."

Big Jim Sullivan (born James George Tomkins) was in high demand as a U.K. studio guitarist, chumming with fellow session musician Jimmy Page (in his pre-Zeppelin days). Sullivan's contributions go back to 1963 with Frank Ifield ("I Remember You") and in 1965 with Gerry and the Pacemakers ("Ferry Across the Mersey"). Sullivan also played on the Small Faces' 1967 hit "Itchycoo Park" and the 1969 Serge Gainsbourg-Jane Birkin duet "Je T'Aime … Moi Non Plus." His session colleagues nicknamed him the "Electric Monster" because he was, along with other sound pioneers like Vinnie Bell, among the innovators of "fuzzbox" distortion and the wah-wah pedal—techniques that helped to jolt psychedelia's neurons.

Sullivan made a conceptual leap in the mid-'60s when the Bengalese-born Vilayat Khan, who joined Shankar as one of India's prominent sitar players, inspired him to also pursue the raga path. Integrating these imported sounds into pop standards of the day, Sullivan filled his first album, the 1967 *Sitar Beat*, with homages to some of Britain's better-known psychedelic entries: the Beatles' "She's Leaving Home" and "Within You, Without You," Donovan's "Sunshine Superman" and "Fat Angel," and a perfunctory salute to Procol Harum's "A Whiter Shade of Pale."

A year later, Sullivan got more experimental with *Lord Sitar*. Most of the songs were famous, but his electric sitar got more aggressive, and the arrangements got quirkier. This time, he added American entries—from *Fiddler on the Roof*'s "If I Were a Rich Man" to the Monkees' "Daydream Believer." His tribute to British comrades continued with salutes to "I Am the Walrus," "Eleanor Rigby," and George Harrison's "Blue Jay Way."

By April of 1968, Martin Denny, perhaps tired of his continual sonic excursions into the South Pacific, reset his sights on *A Taste of India*. With sitar, tabla, tambour, assorted flutes, and his trusty keyboards, Denny imbued a faraway allure to such recognizable tunes as Francis Lai's title theme to the movie *Live for Life* and John Sebastian's "Amy's Theme" from *You're a Big Boy Now*. The star track, however, is Denny's venture into the Strawberry Alarm Clock's "Incense and Peppermints."

94

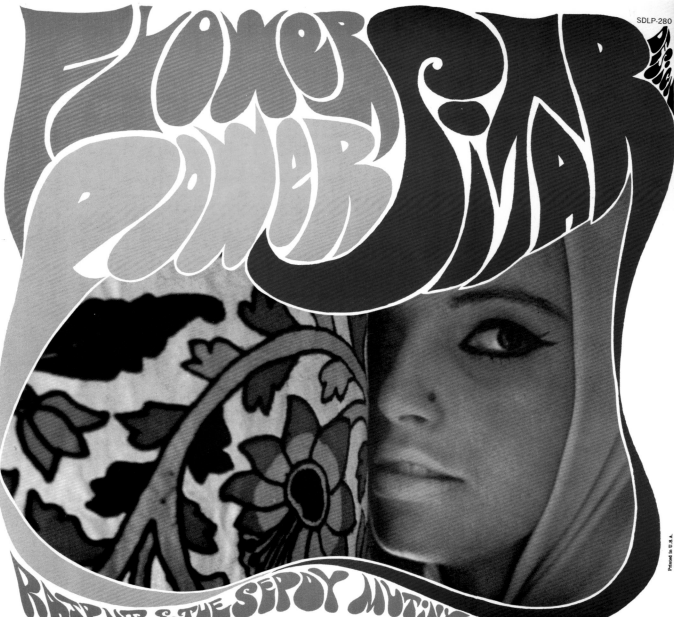

STEREO

SDLP-280

Printed in U.S.A.

FLOWER POWER SITAR

RAJPUT & THE SEPOY MUTINY

Raga pop had already shown signs of getting curiouser and curiouser when the American electronics wizard Vinnie Bell combined the sitar with the traditional guitar. Born Vincent Gambella, he was from Brooklyn's Bensonhurst but became an eminent New York (and sometimes Los Angeles) session guitarist—heard on records that played around the world. He was also a protégé of Tony Mottola (another session guitarist who appeared on Enoch Light's Project 3 Total Sound label and had worked on many Muzak recordings). Bell played guitar on Kai Winding's 1963 version of "More" (the theme from *Mondo Cane*), with Jean-Jacques Perrey, the other half of the Perrey & Kingsley duo, playing the song's star instrument, the Ondioline. He also helped the evolution of folk rock with his edgy electric guitar on Simon & Garfunkel's 1965 hit single "The Sounds of Silence."

Bell fits into the technical definition of a "luthier," an inventor of stringed instruments and string manipulations. Among them is his "water guitar"—a sound that dripped blood in the background on the Vampires' 1964 novelty instrumental "The Creep" and wept along to Beethoven's *Moonlight Sonata* on "Past, Present, and Future" by the Shangri-Las in 1966. A year later, just in time for the flower-power era, Bell led the Shangri-Las from their usual romantic melodramas into a psychedelic dreamscape on "The Sweet Sounds of Summer," including a bridge where the water

guitar and the voices make a brief but delirious departure from the tune. (1967 was also the year that some other radio-ready pop songs indulged in similar trip-time interludes, such as the discordant violins that interrupt the flow of both the Rolling Stones' "She's a Rainbow" and Nancy Sinatra's "Lightning's Girl.")

Also in 1967, Bell reached another watershed when he teamed up with a firm from Neptune, New Jersey, called the Danelectro Corporation. He had previously worked with Danelectro to create an electric 12-string guitar (with the body of the traditional teardrop Greek bouzouki) dubbed the "Bellzouki." He went on to assist them in designing the Coral Electric Sitar. It looked like a conventional electric guitar with a six-string neck, but to its side were thirteen additional strings that players did not strum but rather channeled as "sympathetic string vibrations" to provide the essential *whirr*.

A 1967 Universal Newsreel has announcer Ed Herlihy introducing the man and his invention, as Bell plays an electric raga tribute to "That Happy Feeling," an instrumental that Bert Kaempfert had released in 1962. The melody and rhythm are sufficiently identical to Kaempfert's recording, but Bell's quasi-Eastern textures are a winning match as the string orchestra and chorus swell in the background. The track appears on Bell's 1967 album *Pop Goes the Electric Sitar*, featuring mainstream love songs like "The Shadow of Your Smile," but slips in some psychedelic twang on "Eleanor Rigby." Bell would also lend his electric sitar to the 1967 album *The Lotus Palace* by the Alan Lorber Orchestra and its covers of "Lucy in the Sky with Diamonds" and "Within You, Without You."

The 101 Strings also entered the psychedelic fray in 1967 with *Sounds of Today.* The lush interpretations of "San Francisco (Be Sure to Wear Flowers in Your Hair)" and "California Dreamin'" are fine, but the Strings' arranger Monty Kelly takes big chances when composing three tracks for a sitar showcase. Two of them, "Strings for Ravi" and "Blues for the Guru," flounder more in a jam-session funk, connoting the kind of generic "freak out" music that Hollywood used for discotheque scenes in such LSD-themed films as Roger Corman's *The Trip.* Kelly was more successful with "Karma Sitar," which carries on with what J.G. Ballard's story calls "caterwauling," but has a beguiling melody: a better hybrid of the Eastern twang and the Western string-sweeps.

That same year, Gabor Szabo, on *Wind, Sky, and Diamonds,* harnessed the wonky proportions of Jefferson Airplane's "White Rabbit" with sitar accompaniment. This time, his California Dreamers chime a wordless chorus. Grace Slick's defiant anthem, favoring hipper pills over mother's little helpers, was not the most inviting to elevator-ready adaptations, but Szabo draws on the song's bits of Ravel's *Bolero* and other influences, while the sitar opening seduces listeners to fall deeper into the rabbit hole's escalating rhythm.

A year later, Design Records (a Pickwick Records subsidiary) released *Flower Power Sitar,* by Rajput & the Sepoy Mutiny, where a sitar leads the background of percussion, piano, and acoustic guitar on mostly original compositions with such pertinent titles as "Lullaby for Flower Children," "Flowers, Flowers Everywhere," and "Ragadelic." Raga scholars might declare the sitar out of tune, and media personalities have used the album's version of "Up, Up and Away" to characterize anything or anyone from India or South Asia in general. But those who reject it solely on what are often subjective or transitory musical dictums miss the point. This is still Easy-Listening, a musical terrain that has been ignored or belittled for so long that reappraising it often calls for aesthetic refocusing or perceptual cleansing. The album is a product of the late '60s, when the sitar was still a means of sending cryptic signals. Though it has an edge that is off-base, and for some off-key, *Flower Power Sitar* is still relatively relaxing background music that keeps its poise, even if it wobbles.

In contrast to Rajput & the Sepoy Mutiny, the Clebanoff Strings cater more directly to established musical tastes. Herman Clebanoff, a Chicago-born violinist, displayed his passion for the instrument when starting his Clebanoff Strings in 1945. His first LP, *Moods in Music,* appeared in 1959, using other instruments like the musette and echo effects for mostly light classics and waltzes. The Clebanoff Strings went on to record movie themes and ro-

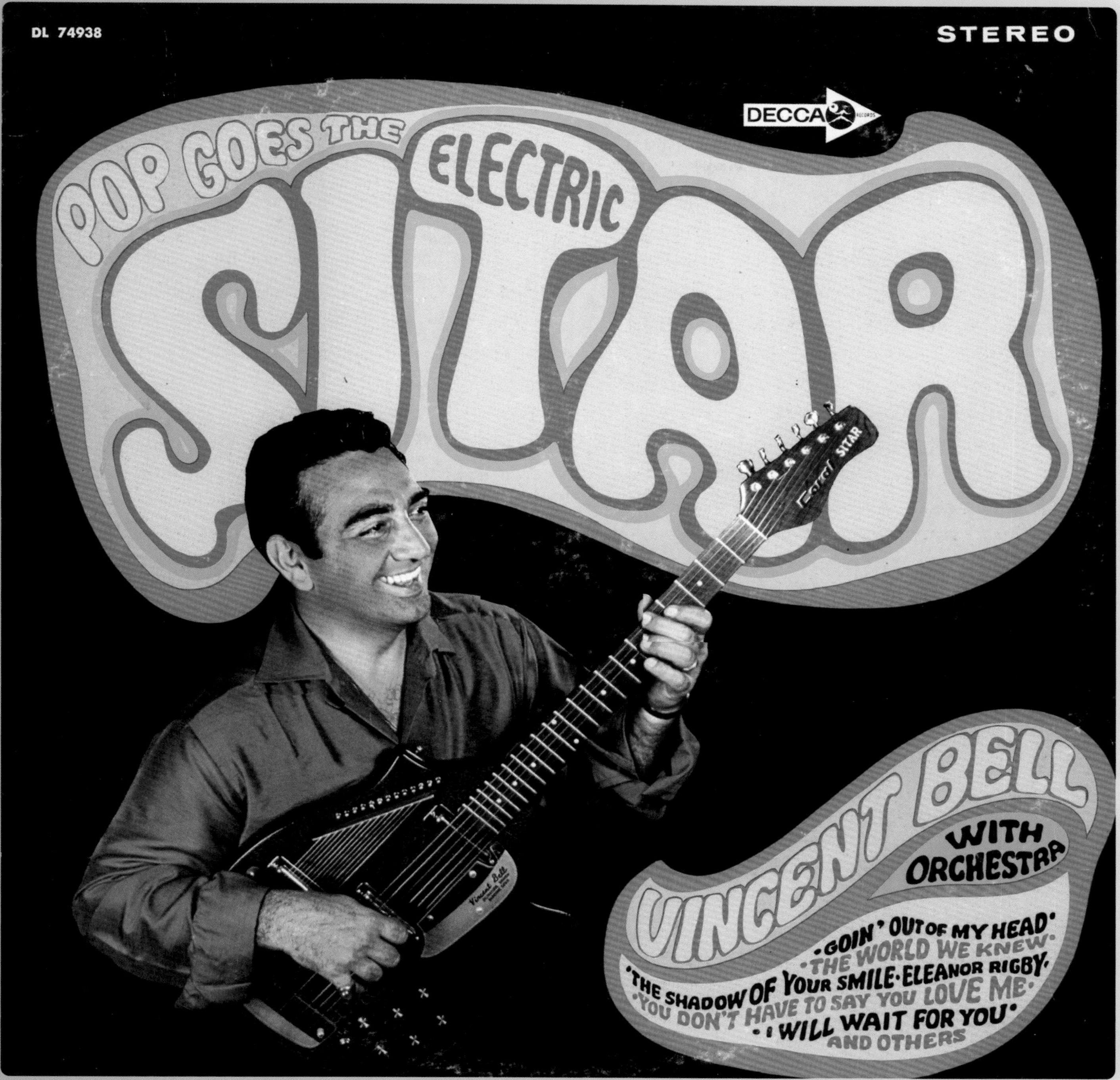
DL 74938
STEREO
DECCA RECORDS
POP GOES THE ELECTRIC SITAR
VINCENT BELL
WITH ORCHESTRA
•GOIN' OUT OF MY HEAD•
•THE WORLD WE KNEW•
•THE SHADOW OF YOUR SMILE•ELEANOR RIGBY•
•YOU DON'T HAVE TO SAY YOU LOVE ME•
•I WILL WAIT FOR YOU•
AND OTHERS

mantic standards and graduated to modern pop by the mid-'60s. The 1968 Decca album *Once Upon a Summertime* includes tracks like the title song that sound relatively more conservative, but the final track is a full-string orchestra version of "Within You, Without You." It blends a straight-on-the-notes Western melody with a layer of Eastern disguise, leaving out the sitar and tabla altogether yet keeping some sense of George Harrison's exotic resonance and shifting rhythms.

The *Living* Series, led by producer Ethel Gabriel for the RCA-Camden label, generated albums that highlighted strings, guitars, keyboards, marimbas, brass, and voices. The Living Guitars provide the same sitar effects (with Al Caiola's arrangements) on "A Whiter Shade of Pale" as well as a rendition of "Ruby Tuesday" on the 1968 album *San Franciscan Nights*. That same effect rebounds for "Lady Jane" on the 1971 album *Living Guitars Play Songs Made Famous by The Rolling Stones*, again with Al Caiola arranging and conducting.

The Nirvana Sitar and String Group offered creative variations on *Sitar and Strings* (alternately titled *Nirvana Sitar*). Released in 1968 on Mr. G Records, a subsidiary of Audio Fidelity, the string ensemble and percussion guide the sitar as it weeps gently over "A Whiter Shade of Pale," "Sunday Will Never Be the Same" (with the baroque introduction somewhat similar to that of "Light My Fire"), and a variation on the Vanilla Fudge version of "You Keep Me Hanging On." A highlight is

the intricate take on the Association's psychedelic choirboy hit "Never My Love," garnishing the full orchestra with xylophones and acoustic guitars. Amid the covers, the Nirvana String Group also indulges in a few self-composed out-of-body intervals, with such titles as "Mind Waves."

An outlier was a studio concoction called the Soulful Strings. Arranger/conductor Richard Evans aspired to what he hoped would be a "hipper" sound by using violas instead of violins. This was the exact opposite of the Hollyridge Strings approach that emphasized the violin's high-pitched sparkle. As a result, the Soulful Strings sound less than stellar, but the debut album *Paint It Black* at least makes the effort to interpret the Byrds' "Eight Miles High," another folk-rock hit that, while appropriately disorienting in parts, has enough of a tuneful appeal for other Easy-Listening arrangers to adapt had they taken the time. Here, the somber and more minimalist approach is murky, but the track remains close enough to the Byrds' structure, including the freak-out guitar sections that Roger McGuinn credited to John Coltrane's sinuous saxophone on "India," which, in turn, was likely Coltrane imitating raga. Some of the album's other tracks are also faithful enough to basic singsong melodies, prompting *High Fidelity*'s John S. Wilson to note how "… the feeling it gives off, the sounds it makes, are so essentially contemporary pop that it's more than just a jazz record."

Bell got more acclaim when he made his water guitar more prominent on such tracks as Ferrante & Teicher's outlandish yet soothing version of Bob Dylan's "Lay Lady Lay." The instrument achieved most fame on Ferrante & Teicher's 1969 "Theme to *Midnight Cowboy*" and Bell's own "*Airport* Love Theme" the following year. Shrewd enough to protect his patents, Bell claims "Les Paul went to his grave, still begging me to tell him how my 'water sound' pedal worked!" Decades later, Bell provided the haunting pedalboard tremolo on the main theme to David Lynch's *Twin Peaks*. As the '60s got more ornate and showed signs of apocalyptic excess with the musical *Hair*, Easy-Listening also showed glimmers of inspired madness. Vinnie Bell released his 1969 album *Good Morning Starshine*, showing off his sitar and other electronic baubles (with an occasional chorus) on the title song, along with "Aquarius," "Love Theme from *Romeo & Juliet*," and a timely salute to the Beatles' "Hey Jude." In 1970, Paul Mauriat surprised listeners with more eccentricity on his album *Let The Sunshine In / Midnight Cowboy / And Other Goodies*. On "Let the Sunshine In," he reveals *Hair*'s comic side: a frenetic sitar and plodding electric guitars contrast with the horns and his trademark violin flutters. And in 1972, Franck Pourcel kept the raga alive for a new context: a sitar-saturated version of Francis Lai's "Theme from *Love Story*" and a stark departure from the customary orchestra and piano of Henry Mancini's 1971 hit.

By 1969, another novelty instrument sidled, at times, into Easy-Listening territory. The Moog, when initially introduced by such recording artists as Mike Vickers, sounded the way a contraption called a "synthesizer" was expected to sound: a robotic voice. Several Moog albums by established arrangers arrived on store racks, one of them by Marty Gold entitled *Moog Plays the Beatles*. Most of the tracks have that flippant novelty appeal, but Gold does a nice job amalgamating his Moog with sitar on his version of "Norwegian Wood." Some of Muzak's regular session players such as Tony Mottola, Richard Hayman, and Dick Hyman looked to both Command and Project 3 Total Sound Records to engage in similar sonic horseplay with titles like *Moog: The Electric Eclectics of Dick Hyman*.

The Jackie Gleason Orchestra, which took over Capitol's "Mood Music" realm by the mid-'50s when Paul Weston switched to Columbia Records, contributed to the delicate craft of soft sutras with the 1969 album, *The Now Sound… for Today's Lovers*. The string arrangements are as rich as ever, along with an assortment of instruments from the private collection of Emil Richards that include the African and Thai marimbas, Dharma bells, and Gamelan gongs. The star instrument is, of course, the sitar, and a traditional wooden one at that, played by another L.A. "Wrecking Crew" associate, Mike Deasy.

Deasy had already performed on several psychedelic-pop sessions that included the acoustic guitar on Scott McKenzie's "San Francisco (Be Sure to Wear Some Flowers in Your Hair)." He also put out a 1967 solo album, with vocal backings by Curt Boettcher, entitled *Friar Tuck and His Psychedelic Guitar*. The same year he recorded for Gleason, he was traumatized when producer Terry Melcher inveigled him to join in on some sessions with the then-budding singer-songwriter Charles Manson. Deasy got increasingly paranoid and ended up departing from the Spahn Ranch in an acid-driven funk—all of this transpiring roughly two months before the Tate-LaBianca murders.

Amid the tempestuous days of the waning '60s, Deasy worked well with Gleason—an imposing media personality who earned his reputation as Middle America's roué and whose tippler exploits gave the expression "lush moods" an extra twist. Though this was among Gleason's more intriguing sound excursions, the closest the album gets to actual '60s pop is a cover of the Beatles' "Yesterday." The high point, however, is a raga variation on a much older song called "Two Different Worlds"—a track that reinforces psychedelia's recurring theme of traveling backwards and merging otherwise contrasting cultures. Deasy and the Gleason Orchestra embellish Al Frisch's lovelorn mid-'50s standard with surrealistic raga ruminations.

All in all, J.G. Ballard's assessment of the sitar, while mired in cultural differences, is forthright, and from a Western perspective, accurate. Lofty scholars of "authentic" raga and "world music"

can enjoy a Shankar concert for whatever cultural accuracy they seek, but when pop stars from North America and Europe appropriated it in the mid- to late '60s, the sitar functioned best as an alien appliance offering spells of exotic seduction, eerie foreignness, and emotional disquiet. At any time, these Easy-Listening raga forays are ready to reboot and resound through ceiling speakers overlooking international food courts of the future. ★

File under: Jackie Gleason/Easy Listening

SW 2935

STEREO
PLAYABLE ON
STEREO & MONO
PHONOGRAPHS

Jackie Gleason
The Now Sound...For Today's Lovers

Capitol
RECORDS

The Gleason Strings
with Sitar & other
exotic instruments

Goin' Out of My Head
Yesterday
It Must Be Him
Live for Life
Lonely Is the Name
Can't Take My Eyes Off You
Moon River
Two Different Worlds
I Won't Cry Anymore
I Can't Believe I'm Losing You

CHAPTER

6

FR

SAN
ANCISCO
AND THE
FLOWERS
ARE BLUE

"McKENZIE MIGHT HAVE RESEMBLED A HIPPIE STRAIGHT OUT OF CENTRAL CASTING, THE LYRICS MIGHT HAVE VERGED ON ADVERTISING COPY, BUT IT HAS A SOARING MELODY AND GREAT PRODUCTION—WITH A LIGHT, SHIMMERING ATMOSPHERE."

—JON SAVAGE, *THE GUARDIAN*

Love-In aspirants by the thousands arrived to bask under San Francisco's silvery sunlight as word of the encroaching 1967 Summer of Love reached across America, leading to one of the country's largest migrations. The prelude was the "Human Be-In" at Golden Gate Park in January. With it came the politics, the antics, the drugs, and of course, the music—all adorned with colorful revelers to replace the previous flocks of darker-clad "beats" who once swarmed the North Beach district in the late '50s and early '60s. Students from the area's City College, Berkeley, and San Francisco State University were among the disaffected seeking refuge from what they had then perceived as the evils of middle-class values. The *Oracle*, the local underground newspaper, touted it as "A Gathering of the Tribes." It was also a reaction to California outlawing the manufacture, sale, and possession of LSD. Authorities imposed the ban on October 6, 1966—a date that the "Be-In" organizers interpreted as the Book of Revelation's sign of the Great Beast: 666.

The "Be-In" played a crucial role in weaving the psychedelic culture's fabric. There, Timothy Leary espoused his infamous "Turn on, tune in, drop out" slogan, as he openly encouraged the audience to quit both high school and college. Poets Allen Ginsberg, Michael McClure, and City Lights Books co-founder Lawrence Ferlinghetti were also on hand, along with such local bands as Blue Cheer, the Grateful Dead, and Jefferson Airplane.

The Diggers (local activists and humanitarians) offered free turkeys, and Augustus Owsley Stanley was generous with his "White Lightning" acid.

From there, more and more "heads" crowded into the Haight-Ashbury area (that some nick-named "Hashbury") as activists for several causes goaded followers to "Question Authority." Many of San Francisco's establishment figures were less enthused. Civic-minded citizens, including a few of the original hippies, grew nervous about the drain on the city's infrastructure and the prospect of harder and more dangerous drugs seeping into the neighborhoods. The *San Francisco Chronicle* published the headline "Hippies Warn City—100,000 Will Invade Haight-Ashbury This Summer."

Another mass event slated to occur just south of San Francisco stirred more jitters. Monterey had hosted folk and jazz festivals, but the prospect of one dedicated to what its planners euphemistically referred to as "pop" signaled trouble. The Monterey International Pop Festival would unite two California factions that had been separate (and at times hostile). The San Francisco and Los Angeles scenes would merge to promote a new California for a new age, even though the focus would be on San Francisco.

John Phillips, lead singer and composer for the Mamas & the Papas, joined his wife Michelle and producer Lou Adler to organize the June festival. Though the Mamas & the Papas were among the more whitebread entertainers of the era, Phillips

seemed less interested in actual "pop" and more intent on foisting the so-called "progressive" acts, such as Janis Joplin with Big Brother & the Holding Company, Eric Burdon & the Animals, the Jimi Hendrix Experience, as well as Ravi Shankar's long raga improvisations.

Concerned about projecting a "cool" image, Phillips and company decided not to include the Monkees, who were still one of the most liked and successful pop groups. The Doors were also conspicuously absent, even though "Light My Fire" illuminated radio stations everywhere. They almost banned the Association because Phillips felt they had too much of a straitlaced look and sound. The Association did end up opening the revelries with a well-groomed performance, but their psychedelic choirboy appeal ultimately waned as the so-called "heavy groups" gained more traction with rock promoters.

To allay misgivings from San Francisco officials, Phillips assumed the task of luring people to the City by the Bay with an alluring song. It worked before when Gus Kahn, Walter Jurmann, and Bronislaw Kaper collaborated to write "San Francisco," which Jeanette MacDonald belted out in the 1936 movie of the same name. Decades later, composer George Cory and lyricist Douglass Cross (both from Brooklyn) wrote "I Left My Heart in San Francisco." In December of 1961, Tony Bennett performed it live at the Venetian Room of the city's Fairmont Hotel. Bennett soon made a record that won a Grammy in 1962, a year after *Billboard* made its fledgling attempts to list both instrumentals and vocals in the same "Easy-Listening" sub-category, where it reached #7. Through the years, many instrumental versions confirmed the song's historical mark, but by 1984, to the chagrin of some residents, "I Left My Heart in San Francisco" ended up competing with Jeanette MacDonald's rousing movie theme as the city's alternate anthem.

Phillips, who grooved far away from the Bay Area in his ritzy Bel Air mansion, aspired to give the town "where cable cars climb halfway to the stars" another melodic identity. Like a Madison Avenue ad man with an instinct for a good hook, Phillips thought up a captivating refrain that would be pleasant and non-threatening enough to make the coming concert seem more like a Renaissance faire. "San Francisco (Be Sure to Wear Flowers in Your Hair)" soon became a Top 40 confection that stuck to the brain like a moist, psychedelic lollipop. Phillips claimed that it took a mere twenty minutes to compose, yet it would exude a place in history longer than its composer had likely anticipated: the type of song that might have embellished living-room sing-alongs at the piano in a long-ago and faraway time.

The Scott McKenzie single got released in April of 1967, reached *Billboard*'s Top 10 the following month, and shortly thereafter became a "standard" born from an era that celebrated anar-

chy and transience: brimming with dulcet acoustic guitar chords, an inspiring tempo build-up, and an all-too-fitting Pied Piper flute. In addition, it avoided jam-happy Grateful Dead values with a tidy run time of about three minutes. Originally, Phillips had intended to use it as part of a PSA that he hoped would quell many local residents and politicians, whose fears got validated when, for three days, the Festival attracted at least 25,000 spectators, many of whom would travel from Monterey to remain in the city.

Considering Phillips' musical past, "San Francisco (Be Sure to Wear Flowers in Your Hair)" is no surprise. The Mamas & the Papas, though closely allied with the self-described "freaks" due to their hippie attire, drug scandals, and reputation for sometimes appearing drunk or tripping during performances, recorded lots of songs on the traditional and wholesome side of Tin Pan Alley. They even released a couple of Rodgers and Hart favorites: "My Heart Stood Still" in 1966 and "Glad to Be Unhappy" in 1967.

Phillips had already laced several of the group's sentimental melodies with old-fashioned honky-tonk pianos, orchestral backgrounds, tight harmonies, and Cass belting out her parts with blues-free precision. He also tried to stay as close as possible to his folk origins while acknowledging the wealth of pop influences, primarily the Beatles. An example of the Mamas & the Papas' penchant for time travel is the clever way they reshaped the early Beatles' "I Call Your Name" into a vaude-ville-era novelty. Songs like "Words of Love," "California Dreamin'," and "Monday Monday" also conformed to mainstream standards with their studio-enhanced echoes, string backings, and tunes that everyday people could hum to themselves without even realizing.

"San Francisco (Be Sure to Wear Flowers in Your Hair)" earned the added distinction of being despised by some of Monterey's "progressive" head-liners. Janis Joplin and the Grateful Dead suppos-edly sniffed at such melodic competence. Even so, when the Mamas & the Papas closed the Monterey show, they brought on Scott McKenzie to sing the song. On this tune at least, McKenzie, like Don-ovan, embodied the ideal romantic troubadour. The wistful air in his voice suggests he was already nostalgic for a flower-power era that was just about to end (or that essentially never really happened). His recording also opened D.A. Pennebaker's 1968 documentary *Monterey Pop*. Nowadays, it is an intrinsic part of Summer of Love retrospectives.

Nevertheless, in the Monterey aftermath, the proliferation of flower children, the traffic jams, the drug problems, and the worries of local busi-nesses worsened. Scott McKenzie merely showed the likable side of what others saw as the equiv-alent of a locust invasion. Mayor John F. Shelley and the city's Board of Supervisors declared a "war on the Haight." Even Charles Manson, who lived on Cole Street, felt creepy vibes from the area, and by the end of the year, took himself and some of his "family" down to Southern California.

Soon, the Summer of Love veered into an autumn of discontent. On the fair and foul day of October 6, 1967, a phalanx of disillusioned flower children staged—to the bemusement of *Time* maga-zine—a "Death of Hippie" happening. They carried and buried a coffin filled with love beads, flowers, incense, candles, and other bric-a-brac that would clutter a typical Haight Street boutique.

The *Atlantic Monthly* offered its own eulogy a month before in an article entitled "The Flowering of the Hippies." Its author Mark Harris noticed the paradoxes: "Hippies thought they saw on Haight Street that everyone's eyes were filled with loving joy and giving, but the eyes of the hippies were often in fact sorrowful and frightened, for they had plunged themselves into an experiment they were uncertain they could carry through."

American soldiers fighting in Southeast Asia—usually not privy to the protests—tended to per-ceive Scott McKenzie's recording with unadulterat-ed joy. Keven McAlester, writing for *The American Experience* on PBS.org, took a breather from an otherwise skeptical assessment of the song to cite a passage from the book *Voices from Vietnam*:

"I once read an interview with a Vietnam vet-eran who said that, to American soldiers stationed there at the time, the song was a 'tearjerker,' be-cause San Francisco was a common destination for soldiers en route home. In short: in the midst of a

110

LA LA LA (HE GIVES ME LOVE)

RAYMOND LEFEVRE
and His Orchestra

DELILAH

THE LAST WALTZ

**THE WORLD WE KNEW
(OVER AND OVER)**

**SAN FRANCISCO (Be Sure To Wear
Some Flowers In Your Hair)**

THE DAYS OF PEARLY SPENCER

ANGELICA

and others

STEREO

4 CORNERS OF THE WORLD

A KAPP RECORD

FCS-4250

grave situation, it gave him hope. And by my insignificant personal standards or any more substantial ones, that qualifies 'San Francisco' not as one of the worst songs ever written, but one of the very best."

Meanwhile, American youth and their open-minded elders, at least outside of San Francisco, fell in love with the melody and got entranced by the flute. Easy-Listening versions soon followed. On the 1967 album *Sounds of Today*, The 101 Strings promised "the most astounding 'trip' ever to be taped." Here, "San Francisco (Be Sure to Wear Flowers in Your Hair)" starts out with a harpsichord, followed by low- and high-register strings, an electric bass, the contagious flute, and the steady pace of a tambourine. There is a lot going on in this one track alone, as it combines the original's Elysian appeal with a larger symphonic style, peaking when the massed strings replace the lead vocal part.

That same year Jack Pleis conducted and arranged for his orchestra on *Music of the Flower Children*, embellishing the "San Francisco" soft touch with flourishing strings, horns, and pop-inspired drums. The album became part of the "Sounds of Our Times" series and also included instrumental makeovers of the Association's "Windy" and Harpers Bizarre's "Come to the Sunshine." Pleis, to reinforce the period mood, composed two of the album's tracks, the most notable entitled "Fable of the Flowers."

The Phillips-McKenzie flower anthem resurfaced with a Pacific Island treatment by The Big Ben Hawaiian Band on the 1968 album *Hawaiian Styled*. Here, sweet slack-key guitars blend with strings, an electric bass, and a chiming "jingle-jangle" backdrop, all tailored for stereo. Also in 1968, the Living Guitars paid respects to "San Francisco" and its "gentle people" on *San Franciscan Nights*: an acoustic guitar and chimes carouse with an electric sitar, drums, and organ. The album attempts to lend the same otherworldly sparkle when covering "San Franciscan Nights," Eric Burdon & the Animals' grittier city tribute.

England apparently loved the song even more. McKenzie's single reached #1 on the U.K. charts. Britain's star chanteuse Petula Clark, a barometer of "middle-of-the-road" decorum, felt comfortable enough to adapt her own version that same year. In truth, "San Francisco (Be Sure to Wear Flowers in Your Hair)" became the chime heard round the world. Italy's Fausto Papetti combined his saxophone with electric guitar strums, a subtle electric bass, and a harmonica to give this American theme a Continental flair. The tune also penetrated the Iron Curtain, as young people in Czechoslovakia, trying to free themselves from the yoke of the U.S.S.R., invoked it to help inspire their short-lived Prague Spring revolt in 1968—before the Soviets drove in with tanks to crush the rebellion.

By August of 1967, the U.K. continued inhaling its Bay Area contact high, as England's Flower Pot Men offered a Beach Boys-style tribute called

"Let's Go to San Francisco." It was harmonious and offered more of that hungered-for lighter pop, with the lead vocal by Tony Burrows, who would go on to sing on White Plains' "My Baby Loves Lovin'" and Edison Lighthouse's "Love Grows (Where My Rosemary Goes)." Its co-composer, under the alias John Carter, was songwriter and producer John Shakespeare, whose KPM library compositions like "Bell Hop" would play behind comedies in both England and America. In Ken Loach's 1967 film *Poor Cow*, "Let's Go to San Francisco" materializes as source music beaming from a transistor radio on the shore of a West Sussex beach, where children romp about in game arcades and elderly beachcombers project sour faces while attempting to enjoy vanilla ice cream.

"Let's Go to San Francisco" merited a sweet cover by John Cameron (who also provided arrangements on the *Poor Cow* soundtrack). On his 1968 album *Warm and Gentle*, Cameron uses the tender caresses of high-pitched strings and a flute to substitute for the lead vocal, while a harpsichord, horns, and drums lend additional support. That same year, Cameron arranged an upbeat version of "San Francisco (Be Sure to Wear Flowers in Your Hair)" for the John Schroeder Orchestra on an album called *The Dolly Catcher*, with some quirky horns, a somewhat manic organ, and a gentle wash of strings sounding more like a chamber quartet.

France's ace arranger Caravelli recorded a sweet, lush, and echoing version of "Let's Go to

San Francisco" called "Il Faut Croire aux Étoiles" on his 1968 album, *Si J'avais Des Millions (If I Were a Rich Man)*. He is among the four major French Easy-Listening maestros that include Raymond Lefevre, Franck Pourcel, and Paul Mauriat. In an unofficial pact, or perhaps a friendly competition, they became France's Four Musketeers of (to use the Gallic expression) *musique de fond*. They also gave "San Francisco (Be Sure to Wear Flowers in Your Hair)" their distinct interpretations while preserving the original's dreamy spirit.

Born Claude Vasori to an Italian father and a French mother, Caravelli developed his own orchestra by the '50s, recording popular tunes along with a few nods to classical works. Vasori adopted his fancier stage name in 1956, inspired by France's new twin-engine Aerospatiale Caravelle jet, with the "i" added as a nod to his Italian heritage. From there, he became known in America as Caravelli and His Magnificent Strings, releasing several albums, primarily on Columbia Records.

"San Francisco (Be Sure to Wear Flowers in Your Hair)" appears on the 1968 album *La, La, La A'la Caravelli*. Though he tends to adhere more to the trebly side of the spectrum with a minimum of bass, he stays faithful to the original's rhythm and tone yet does not hesitate to get creative with the arrangement. He starts with the strumming of an acoustic guitar, baritone strings leading to soprano strings, and the ringing of chimes as the main melody begins. At the song's (Golden Gate) bridge when the original has McKenzie singing, "All across the nation, such a strange vibration," Caravelli adds sweet horns before returning to the main verse with a harmonica and a wordless chorus. His version comes closest to the tempo of McKenzie's recording, reflecting the mellow viewpoint of a Haight-Ashbury reveler.

In May of 1968, Paris witnessed its own political turmoil from uprisings of students and workers. Still, the elevator music recordings multiplied, sharing a pool of French studio musicians that also contributed to movie and television soundtracks. On his 1968 album *La, La, La (He Gives Me Love)*, Raymond Lefevre gives "San Francisco" another high-frequency pitch of strings and vibrant horns. Starting with acoustic guitar strums, electric bass, and maracas for a soft backbeat, he soon lets the high-pitched strings control the tune. A harpsichord also joins in before an anxious horn leads to the "strange vibration" bridge. From there, the strings, horns, harpsichord, acoustic guitar, drums, and chimes maintain a complicated state of energized tranquility. Lefevre essentially provides a soundtrack that could have been perfect for a controversial documentary about the Haight-Ashbury jamboree.

Lefevre would appear on U.S. charts in February of 1968 with "Soul Coaxing"—an instrumental version of the French pop song "Ame Caline." The song had achieved fame a year before, when Michel Polnareff sang it in a style that ascended into a yodeling falsetto. Polnareff also helped to promote psychedelic pop in Europe. By April of 1968, America's Peggy March converted the French melody to English lyrics, releasing for RCA a vocal single of "Soul Coaxing" called "If You Loved Me." Earlier in the '60s, March had recorded "I Will Follow Him," which Petula Clark also sang in French under the title "Chariot"—a melody composed by Del Roma (an alias for Paul Mauriat) and J.W. Stole (an alias for Franck Pourcel).

Franck Pourcel was a violinist who also enjoyed merging traditional orchestras with novel studio gimmicks, especially intense echo reverb to make the previously unconventional union of massed strings and electric guitars sound more powerful. His early history resembles the boilerplate bios shared by other French musicians of his ilk. He too came from a musical family and studied at the Paris Conservatoire. By the end of World War II, he too went through a jazz-fancying period and admired the work of violinist Stéphane Grappelli. However, the power of pop animated his recording career in 1959, when he and his "French Fiddles" helped to meld Easy-Listening and rock-and-roll with an instrumental cover of the Platters' "Only You."

On his 1968 Imperial LP *Love is Blue*, Pourcel portrays the land of "gentle people" with a soft samba while keeping Scott McKenzie's silky and romantic tempo. Light percussion leads to woodwinds, flutes, and a bustle of strings that soon welcome an organ and again a tambourine. Horns, drums, and the increasingly energetic string section fill McKenzie's "people in motion" bridge, before the flute returns with sprinklings of a celesta and a heavenly autoharp on the final section. Pourcel's delicate touch moves through the Haight from the viewpoint of a curious yet somewhat cautious pedestrian ambling along a street adorned with headshops and volatile "heads."

As if by cruel synchronicity, the sad *adieu* to the Summer of Love occurred just as Paul Mauriat's instrumental piece called "Love is Blue" started its patient climb up the *Billboard* charts. At the end of 1967, *Billboard* had the song at the lowly #109 in its "Bubbling Under" category. Two months later, America's listeners got swept up in the command of its ricocheting strings, hypnotic harpsichord, appealing melody, and pop-infused cadence. Soon, it purred in *Billboard*'s #1 catbird seat, making Paul Mauriat one of few Gallic recording artists to earn such American plaudits.

As a melancholy complement to McKenzie's anthem about a communal love headed for loss, "Love is Blue" is worth a tale of its own as it shows how the listening public can sometimes be more intuitive and savvy than the songwriters or performers. Mauriat likely would not have heard about the song had its composer André Popp and its lyricist Pierre Cour not entered it in the 1967 Eurovision song contest held in Luxembourg. Popp and Cour, imagining themselves as creatures of loftier heights, did so reluctantly, and legend has it that they had deposited the sheet music into a waste bin before

wisely retrieving it. At Eurovision, the chanteuse Vicky Leandros performed "L'Amour est Bleu" to the world for the first time, but it lost out to the Sandie Shaw hit "Puppet on a String."

Mauriat had done arrangements for such seasoned performers as Charles Aznavour and Maurice Chevalier, a résumé that might have led him to think his standards were above the newer and seemingly simpler pop. "To be honest," he told *Billboard* magazine in January of 1996, "I wasn't very fond of the song. The song was published by Philips, so I covered it. It was quite an instant hit. In the U.S., a Minneapolis DJ called Alan Mitchell started to play the song and asked the audience to react. He was flooded with phone calls. It quickly took off in the whole country."

As early as January of 1968, *Billboard*'s Pop roster had "Love is Blue" at #1 for five weeks, and its Easy-Listening chart had it at #1 for eleven weeks. Mauriat's accompanying album *Blooming Hits* also occupied a five-week #1 spot among *Billboard*'s Top Pop Albums. Just before Valentine's Day in February of 1968, "Love is Blue" entered *Cashbox*'s #1 slot, with the Lemon Pipers' "Green Tambourine" at #2. Despite *Blooming Hits*' provocative cover featuring a naked woman gussied up in psychedelic paint, Mauriat had a talent for making even the Day-Glo turn blue. The album's music was ornate, but just as with "Love is Blue," sadness draped most of the tracks—a trait partly due to the originals. Great standards, after all, are not always about happy times.

Jim Morrison was astute as he sang about the "strange days" that were upon us: a time when a stately tune like "Love is Blue" could play on the same youth-oriented radio format with the Doors' sullenly antiwar "The Unknown Soldier" and Nancy Sinatra and Lee Hazlewood's Freudian duet "Some Velvet Morning." Alan Smith, writing for the *New Musical Express* in April of 1968, stayed upbeat, describing Mauriat as "a rocking Mantovani": "I'm enchanted about his style. So often the Mauriat sound is a nifty combination of the soaring lilt of French strings, and a big, pumping beat sound dear to the heart of every real pop fan."

Not to be outdone by his peers, Mauriat includes a vibrant version of "San Francisco (Be Sure to Wear Flowers in Your Hair)" on his 1968 album *Mauriat Magic*, with the strings, keyboards, horns, and rocking pizzazz that animate both "Love is Blue" and his follow-up single "Love in Every Room." Though primarily a keyboardist, Mauriat also favors echoing horns, acoustic guitars, gentle drums, the always-satisfying chimes, and most of all, the soprano violins that keep his interpretation in a melodic zone tottering between sunshine and the inevitable twilight. On the song's bridge, the rhythm oddly slackens, as if briefly startled by visions of the actual Golden Gate Bridge's chilling heights. At this point, the electric guitar chords sound more like percussive strokes, contrasting with a flowing harpsichord, and the calculating tambourine. All along, the prominent reverb

helps to make Mauriat's mélange of instruments more animated and deliciously odd. As a movie soundtrack, Mauriat's "San Francisco" could accompany the type of perky travelogue that once guided tourists on bus rides through Haight-Ashbury's wilderness: elevator music transmitted at high voltage.

As love turned blue, and the Haight-Ashbury light show dimmed, the Summer of Love became a jet-age folktale consigned for future historians to sort out. Even for those not alive to witness the rise and fall of "a whole generation with a new explanation," "San Francisco (Be Sure to Wear Flowers in Your Hair)" lingers on like all great melodies, inspiring an Easy-Listening afterglow that emits like so many electrographic waves. As other instrumental orchestras cast shadow versions of McKenzie's tune, the song's mixture of joy and pathos intensified precisely because the studio players were challenged to convey those same emotional conflicts without lyrics. Listeners heard melodic splendor, but they could also detect as much despair as their own personalities and past histories allowed.

Though counterculture purists at the time resented "San Francisco (Be Sure to Wear Flowers in Your Hair)" for its unabashed commercial potential and elevator-ready beauty, their scorn fades with each passing year as listeners grow less inclined to separate the so-called "reality" from the so-called "media-generated illusion"—if such distinctions were ever relevant in the first place. ❧

117

LOVE AND "THE INTERNAL MUZAK DENIAL IV

CHAPTER

7

"A MELODY OR A TUNE OR A WHISTLE IN YOUR HEAD STICKS WITH YOU MORE THAN ANYTHING I'VE EVER COME ACROSS. SO, I WANT TO PUT A NURSERY RHYME IN YOUR HEAD..."

—ARTHUR LEE

By November of 1967, *Billboard*'s confounding "Easy-Listening Top 40" reflected pop music's choppy waters. In the November 4 issue, the chart had Vikki Carr's "It Must Be Him" at #1, with Roger Williams' instrumental "More Than a Miracle" at #2. Harpers Bizarre's "Anything Goes" at #14 preceded Bobbie Gentry's "Ode to Billie Joe," both of which also secured comfortable places in the regular pop niche. Claudine Longet's "Small Talk" came in at a respectable #17 right ahead of Henry Mancini's spine-tingling instrumental theme to the thriller *Wait Until Dark*. At the very bottom of the list was Spanky & Our Gang's "Lazy Day." Notwithstanding the fact that the buying habits of consumers decades ago are marginally relevant, these conflicting titles appearing under the "Easy-Listening" rubric show how nebulous the category had gotten when pop and rock groups, adult-oriented singers, and elevator-music instrumentalists got corralled into the same cubicle.

As 1967 bled into 1968, other musical trends challenged the so-called "generation gap." All along, Herb Alpert and the Tijuana Brass, who also churned out the kind of music white suburbia enjoyed, got a fashion pass because their records were, after all, predominantly horns, with a chic Latin feeling, and a nod to jazz. 1968 was also a year for several hit instrumentals. Mason Williams' "Classical Gas" got intergenerational clout when he performed it on *The Smothers Brothers' Comedy*

Hour. The same applied to Hugo Montenegro's version of Ennio Morricone's Spaghetti Western theme for *The Good, the Bad, and the Ugly*—the funny noises, exotic percussion, and peculiar rhythm made it palatable to novelty-starved elders and rock fans alike. Yet by early 1968, Paul Mauriat's electrifying elevator music on "Love is Blue" commanded both the Easy-Listening and Pop charts, along with Raymond Lefevre's "Soul Coaxing (Ame Caline)."

While Easy-Listening sounds were sharing space on Pop charts with the Beatles and the Doors, the flower-power mood continued to wilt. All along, the dreamy instrumental tunes were ahead of the melancholy curve. Mauriat's recording of "Love is Blue" was a sad song wrapped in orchestral shimmer. When Brian Blackburn added English lyrics, it got even bleaker: "Blue, blue, my world is blue / Blue is my world; now I'm without you… Black, black, the nights I've known / Longing for you, so lost and alone." "Love" was no longer just a slogan for world peace, a noun depicting romantic agony, or a hippie euphemism for unencumbered sex; the word started connoting a reminder of love's absence in an increasingly alienating environment.

Despite the fact that "Love is Blue" became *Billboard*'s #2 song of 1968, Mauriat unknowingly fulfilled a dual purpose for pop music aficionados. He lulled many young people into liking his sound but also gave snootier critics an empirical villain.

This was the brazen sound of elevator music, broadcast daily on AM and FM stations across the country. It had already unnerved hipsters when it lurked in the background, but Mauriat brought the massed strings out into the Top 40 open to much acclaim but, in turn, rekindled sour attitudes some felt toward the music by Muzak piped in to so many restaurants and other public places. While Mauriat's rocking piano might have been a bit too distracting for a Muzak program, the general public was nonetheless correct in calling it "elevator music"—the term to which Muzak itself alluded in a 1948 Otis Elevator Company ad to boast of how its "lilting melody" comforted queasy elevator passengers.

Those who continue to use "elevator music" as a catch-all expression for this kind of sound are wrong only when thinking that the music is bad. Long ago, John Philip Sousa called *all* recorded music "canned music." As years passed, dismissive critics kicked the canned music down the road, making Easy-Listening assume the onus that many bluenoses had all along imposed onto popular music in general, especially once the live performance was no longer a sacred space, and the studio artifice got more advanced and enticing. Adjectives like "lush," "bright," "airy," "cheery," "summery," "romantic," and "sweet" got tangled up in the nastier term "soulless." To detractors, many with Cultural Marxist filters, this was the music of "capitalism" and (for the less polite) "whiteness."

PHILIPS

PHS 600-248 **STEREO**

PLAYABLE ON MODERN MONAURAL EQUIPMENT

PHILIPS

Blooming Hits
PAUL MAURIAT
and his orchestra

PENNY LANE

THIS IS MY SONG

(THERE'S A) KIND OF HUSH

Featuring
LOVE IS BLUE
(L'AMOUR EST BLEU)

MAMA

SOMETHIN' STUPID

PUPPET ON A STRING

INCH ALLAH

L'AMOUR EST BLEU (LOVE IS BLUE)

SEULS AU MONDE (ALONE IN THE WORLD)

ADIEU A LA NUIT (ADIEU TO THE NIGHT)

Mercury Record Corporation, 35 E. Wacker Drive, Chicago, Illinois 60601 • Printed in U.S.A.

Among the victims of this bias was a West Coast band inevitably called "Love." Love was a Los Angeles phenomenon, particularly along the Sunset Strip at places like the Whisky A Go Go—even before the Doors became the club's notorious showboats. The first band to get a contract on Elektra Records, Love placated fans on their first two albums: *Love* in 1966 and *Da Capo*, which followed in the early part of 1967. Both LPs played it safe with an often grim, bluesy, and "heavy" style. Plying the vocals and guitars with scream-and-slam abandon, their cries of angst and protest on the apocalyptic "7 and 7 Is," from the summer of 1966, near their finale with the bang of an exploding bomb.

Then in November of 1967, as *Billboard* turned the "Easy-Listening" category into a sonic blob engulfing many others, Love released *Forever Changes*, an album that was, for many, a traumatic break from the blues-folk-rock fusion that made the group's previous work so "Go Go"-compliant. Bruce Botnick claims that, while an engineer and co-producer at Elektra Records, he promoted the album's lush arrangements at a time when radio stations were nowhere near as narrow-casted as they became years later. Back then, Al Martino's "Love is Blue" could follow Herb Alpert's "This Guy's in Love with You," which could then lead to Richard Harris' "MacArthur Park" or Paul Mauriat's instrumental "Love in Every Room," or even the Troggs, when those unruly Brits also broke form with a string orchestra on the ballad "Love is All Around."

Forever Changes used a variety of elevator-music shock tactics, thanks to the Los Angeles Philharmonic as background and to violinist David Angel, who molded the string arrangements. Arthur Lee's sprightly voice also matched the more honeyed tunes. Love's ease into "Easy" was not so unusual. What is now classified as "sunshine pop" illuminated a fan base from the mid- to late '60s. Chad & Jeremy chimed in to the British Invasion with lush string orchestras arranged by names like John Barry and Frank Hunter. They were, after all, right near Marianne Faithfull on *Billboard*'s first forty-song Easy-Listening chart in June of 1965.

In early 1967, a New York-based group called the Left Banke released the creamy-on-the-melody "Walk Away Renee," followed by the diaphanous ditty "Pretty Ballerina." They also had a debut album of more baroque-pop sounds: strings, horns, harpsichords, romantic guitars, and tenderhearted vocals that scaled the higher notes. Around the same time, the Blades of Grass, another East Coast band, also basked in opulent strings and perky but gentle horns. Their strings were arranged by Irv Spice, whose Irv Spice Strings & Orchestra released an album on the Audio Fidelity label around the same time entitled *Starry-Eyed and Breathless*, including "starry-eyed" treatments of the Beatles' "And I Love Her" and "A Hard Day's Night."

Like Love, the Blades of Grass were not afraid to let the vocals ascend to the near-breathless heights of Lewis Carroll's White Queen. On

"Happy," their first single, Irv Spice spreads out the sonic chiffon to perfection while the Blades sing like cherubim. A regional tiff, however, clipped the record's wings when the Sunshine Company released their own version of the song from the West Coast. (Another twist had the Sunshine Company's version of "Up, Up and Away" overshadowed by the Fifth Dimension's recording.) The Blades' version of "Walk Away Renee" is arguably the best, or at least as good as the Left Banke's. Had the Beatles not already recorded "Help" and instead gifted it out as they had other Lennon-McCartney gems, the Blades' more textured treatment might have survived as the definitive version.

Other pop acts like the Mamas & the Papas, the Association, and Spanky & Our Gang had used similar techniques with nary a raised eyebrow. Yet, 1968 wrought the bloody Vietnam Tet Offensive, political assassinations, the Paris uprisings, and the summer riots at the Chicago Democratic Convention. Airwaves blasted such inevitable bummers as Arthur Brown's apocalyptic "Fire" and the Rolling Stones' "Street Fighting Man" (set to dissonant Paris police sirens). Even Bobby Goldsboro's tearjerker about a tree towering over the memory of a dead wife on the crossover #1 hit "Honey" contributed to the gloom. However, the same year continued to offer happy and giddy tunes as Tiny Tim's falsetto tiptoed from one ditty to another. John Fred & His Playboy Band's "Judy in Disguise (With Glasses)" goofed on "Lucy in

the Sky with Diamonds," which in turn triggered the Marble Arch Orchestra to do an instrumental parody of John Fred's parody on the 1968 album *Tomorrow's Standards*. On "Time for Livin'" The Association chimed about getting "a ticket to life" under the Southern California sun and inspired Percy Faith, His Orchestra and Chorus to echo the song's cheer on the 1968 album *Angel of the Morning (Hit Themes for Young Lovers)*.

Love's *Forever Changes* combined the pretty with the scary. "The Red Telephone," for instance, sounds melodically puckish, but paranoia and pessimism seethe beneath. The title alone suggests (for mid-'60s television viewers) the emergency line connecting Commissioner Gordon to Batman, but also the nuclear buttons at LBJ's fingertips. The song's pleasantries of strings, echoes, muted horns, and a sing-along melody evoke visions of surrealistic pillows wafting through the air, contrasting with lyrics about "sitting on a hillside, watching all the people die." Another highlight from the album offers sprinkles of whimsy, string pizzicato, and sweetness with a macabre under-taste on "The Good Humor Man He Sees Everything Like This."

Presaging the nightmares that grew darker both inside and outside of the counterculture, *Forever Changes* did so in a softer way that was more subversive than the spoon-fed pabulum of grating guitar solos and nihilistic calls for "revolution." However, Love faced an additional challenge. Though three of its five members were white, in-

125

cluding co-composer Bryan MacLean, Arthur Lee and his lead guitarist John Echols were not, which likely explains why many hipster nags, plagued with white guilt, shackled Love to the oppressive codes of "cool." Lee, Echols, and the rest of Love would have none of that nonsense as they broke free on *Forever Changes* with a breezier style that, like much Easy-Listening, sounded sweeter even as life got sadder.

Many Love fans in the U.S. regarded *Forever Changes* as an outright betrayal of what passed as "raw truth." The album's lackluster sales were partly due to Elektra's promotion machine focusing on the label's newer acquisition, The Doors. It also got a mixed reception from some of the critical illuminati who, by the late '60s, had mutated into aesthetic and political militants. They played a mean and hard game, tarring and feathering any music that sounded too commercial or flashed a toothpaste gleam.

Love also had previous ties to the "knowing" scene on the Strip, which made their dulcet violins, lilting pianos, bubbly guitars, happy horns, and angelic harps seem all the more disorienting: an excuse for guerrilla critics to intensify their Easy-Listening phobias. Love somehow messed with the mojo; it had hamstrung the hex that the programmers of emerging underground radio stations tried to cast on impressionable minds.

Just as "The Red Telephone" was Lee's paranoia in cute wrappings, Easy-Listening was the ideal armor for a man who disliked the messy hassles of touring and who craved nontoxic retreats from the strident crowds. Fenced inside of a private compound in Laurel Canyon, Lee regarded change as not only "forever" but also frightening. Brian Wilson might have confined his fears to the ocean, sun, imaginary voices, and a domineering dad, but Lee seemed to be afraid of the air and, literally, for his life.

Lee claimed that as he composed and performed the *Forever Changes* sessions, he sincerely thought this record would be what he called his "last words to the world." These quirks might explain his attraction to elevator music's psychological balm and the deeper focus it offers for those willing to read into its unassuming surfaces.

Forever Changes seems more significant for the now-historical critical reaction it elicited. Who was responsible? Were the members of Love tripping too often? Did the band "sell out"? Those unreceptive to Love's radical plunge into sonic lightness pulled no punches. In April 1968, Beatrice Wayne, writing in Hearst's new-and-splashy *Eye* magazine, tempered her contempt with confusion: "Like Muzak in the elevator, this album is elevated Muzak." She had problems processing Love's motives, so she rationalized. To her, this elevator trip must have been a cosmic joke: "Rather than contemplating for us, [Lee] speaks most eloquently when he's putting us down. Well, that's Love." Sandy Pearlman, in the March-April 1968 issue of *Crawdaddy!*, pondered the terrifying prospect that Love had, in some kind of Faustian pact, "come face to face with the spirit of Muzak," yet he still found *Forever Changes* "incredibly beautiful …in its own very, very odd way." Nevertheless, Mr. Pearlman had to find a comfortable "set and setting" in his own mind. While recognizing that *Forever Changes* "sounds really conventionally beautiful," Pearlman stated that there had to be a more sophisticated stratagem behind all of this. A kind of cognitive dissonance set in, as Pearlman went on to claim that the album "doesn't have the Muzak ring. But aren't all of this stuff's most significant referents Muzak?" If he liked it, and it sounded like elevator music, then how could he like it?

In the throes of self-doubt, he concocted a theory he called "The Internal-Muzak Denial Move." This is how he explained it:

"Specifically, they've modularized the Muzak components available, in overwhelming quantity, in the cultural pool. But this makes for the subordination of these components (given their traditional role). The usual Muzak pop homogeneity has been short-circuited… They have denuded Muzak of the soporific. Allowing even the words to be heard and enjoyed. And establishing a pretty gorgeous context that doesn't prevent cognition."

In short, Pearlman attempted to allow the more uptight listeners to keep clutching at their pearls by interpreting *Forever Changes* as "denuded Muzak." They could use irony as a psychic crutch while staying safe in their anti-establishment bunkers. Lee, likewise, could continue to play undisturbed inside of his elevator-music bubble, letting Pearlman and other like-minded journalists believe what they wanted to believe.

With *Forever Changes*, the counterculture's anti-Muzak shibboleth was official. Before then, those who adored the Rolling Stones at their rawest likely had no problem supplementing their tastes with something sad and tender like "As Tears Go By" or the even lusher "She's a Rainbow." However, the negative reactions to Love's album encouraged groupthink, signaling to much of the record-buying youth a more concrete idea of what "elevator music" sounds like and how or why they were supposed to despise it.

Three decades later, once *Forever Changes* achieved worldwide acclaim, Lee was free to sing its praises. Perhaps the "lounge" trend of the mid-to late '90s, which reclaimed some of Easy-Listening's cast-offs, helped this along. At last, American listeners started taking *Forever Changes* seriously, delighting in the elevator music that dope-and-granola-bloated "heads" from long ago rejected. By the twenty-first century, John Echols declared *Forever Changes* his favorite Love album because it moved in a different direction, challenging categories and expectations. In an interview with *Vinyl Rewind*, he also disabused assumptions about the album's cover: "People think it looks like Africa, but no, it's actually a heart."

In 2006, a *Slate* critic's appraisal might have given some readers pause: "With big, string-filled orchestrations and quirky song structures, *Forever Changes* reeks of ambition. Often, it sounds like a mess—an overreach by a drugged-up and not-quite-mature talent (Lee was 22 at the time)—but *Forever Changes* has proved irresistible to the kind of critic that likes to champion lost masterpieces and gives bonus points to black performers who have the good taste to play 'white' music."

Forever Changes has a more coherent context when considering other musical trends that coincided with its release. Back in 1967, as the mellower hippies sought harmony and peace, and the Bay Area-based Mystic Moods Orchestra attempted to allay the same generation with "Easy" melodies blended into sound effects of oceans, trains, and even car races, the engineers at Muzak had their own ambitions regarding music's power to forge a better world. Dr. James Keenan, a social scientist from Stanford University, presented to Muzak's Scientific Board of Advisers a paper entitled "The Eco-Logic of Muzak." In it, Keenan displayed his industrial psychology background with academic, post-Marshall McLuhan jargon to articulate the company's sonic goals. For him, Music by Muzak was "synomorphic with the modern world and interrelated with all matters of time and place: Muzak helps human communities because it is a nonverbal symbolism for the common stuff of everyday living in the global village."

Lee and Love apparently also sought some kind of musical language that was "synomorphic" with a utopia far away from the pandemonium. In 2003, years after long struggles with personal demons and two years before his death from leukemia, Lee had joined an ensemble, with added strings and horns, to perform live selections from *Forever Changes*, sounding as fresh as the original recording. By then, the ideal "set and setting" that psychedelia's Dr. Leary and Muzak's Dr. Keenan envisioned never came to pass. But the sounds of elevator music continued to surface, despite the hectoring of those who thought it was a soundtrack to the end of the world. ✿

129

A SEA OF GREEN TAMBOUR

Kama Sutra
(BMI)
Time: 2:21
M-1023

RANWOOD

R-801
Prod

RANWOOD

INES

RANWOOD, LOS ANGELES, CALIFORNIA • A DIVISION OF RANWOOD INTERNATIONAL, INC.

Kama Sutra
(BMI)
Time: 2:21
M-1023

R-801

Produced by
Randy Wood
Lawrence Welk
George Cates

GREEN TAMBOURINE
(P. Leka - S. Ping)
LAWRENCE WELK
and his orchestra
Arranged and Conducted by
Richard Maltby

"'LET'S HEAR THAT ONE MORE TIME,' SOMEONE MUST'VE SAID, AND SOON ENOUGH 'GREEN TAMBOURINE' SOUNDED GOOD ENOUGH TO THE BOYS IN THE BAND..."

—IAN VAN TUYL AND OWEN GROVER, *POPSTROLOGY*

In December of 1967, America and much of the world heard what many consider the first bona-fide bubblegum hit: the Lemon Pipers' "Green Tambourine." For about three months, Top 40 radio audiences encountered studio magic at full prowess: an almost-uncanny combination of raga sounds from the electric sitar, the glimmering strings, the strategic tape echoes on the word "tambourine," and last but never least, the jingle-jangle of the song's title instrument.

With no direct reference to drugs, "Green Tambourine" still created a psychedelic atmosphere. Accounting for the numbers, the record offered an international contact high: #1 in America, #3 in New Zealand, and the Top 10 in the U.K. and Australia. Fans liked its glistening style, sweet vocals, catchy melody, and ancillary reference to Bob Dylan's (via the Byrds') "Mr. Tambourine Man."

Billed as "the first hit for the fledgling Buddah record label," "Green Tambourine" also summarized the sound and spirit of the times. Its composers Paul Leka and Shelley Pinz were two fledgling songwriters connected with New York's Brill Building, where composers like Barry Mann, Burt Bacharach, and Carole King flourished. In fact, it was in front of the Brill Building, at Broadway and 49th Street, where Pinz claims she was inspired. Standing at the corner, she noticed an elderly busker offering a song to passersby for a bit of change. Pinz felt an instant story: a living metaphor for the vibrant yet volatile times when panhandling signified rebellion.

In a glaring contrast to Leka and Pinz, the Lemon Pipers were a "heavy" rock group from Oxford, Ohio. Lead guitarist Bill Bartlett wrote "Turn Around and Take a Look," the group's debut release that few noticed, but Buddah Records' president Neil Bogart liked it enough to make bigger plans for the band (who saw themselves as players of harder stuff) to embody the refreshing sound of psychedelic soda pop.

On the same month that "Green Tambourine" premiered, the Lemon Pipers were scheduled to open for Jefferson Airplane at the Cincinnati Gardens. Regardless of how they saw themselves, the "heavy" band quickly metamorphosed into "Easy"-psychedelic-pop ambassadors. Lead singer Dale "Ivan" Browne had an innate talent that facilitated the change: a light tenor matching the sparkly sound effects that tickled so many ears as he sang about a desperate street player acting like a happy outcast.

Shortly after signing with the New York-based Buddah Records, the Lemon Pipers entered the Cleveland Recording Studios, chaperoned by Paul Leka. Leka had formulaic ideas, including block chords and music charts, that he instructed the band to follow. He performed more of his wizardry when returning to New York with the master tape. There, he brought in Chinese bells and toyed more with the song's star instrument: an electric sitar that haunts each melody line.

Leka also brought in studio musicians for an assortment of violins, a viola, and a cello: the same Irv Spice Strings and Orchestra that provided gleaming backgrounds for the Blades of Grass that same year. Irv Spice would crop up in several other places, such as a strings arranger for another East Coast psychedelic pop group, similar in the spirit to the Blades of Grass, called Sounds of Modification and their 1968 self-titled LP on Jubilee Records.

After hearing the final New York mix, the Lemon Pipers could barely recognize themselves at the other side of Leka's echo chamber. As keyboardist Robert Nave recalls, "No one was talking about how we would recreate the record on stage." Indeed, "Green Tambourine" evolved into a studio creature: sound sensations merging human and machine that were impossible to duplicate on an ordinary, three-dimensional platform. It was, to use '60s jargon, a "happening"—but unique to a time and place when sound engineers and their devices became as vital as the musicians.

As "Green Tambourine" gave the Buddah label its first million-selling single, the Radio Industry Association of America (RIAA) certified it as a Gold Record by February of 1968. Both *Billboard* and *Cashbox* listed it as #1 in their Hot 100. The song soon caught on in Europe, compelling lead singer Browne to translate his trebly tenor into French and Italian. The Lemon Pipers' "Green" joined Paul Mauriat's "Blue" on the psychedelic-pop color spectrum. Co-composer Pinz was also part of the Peppermint Rainbow, a Baltimore group that released a version at roughly the same time but got more famous the following year with "Will You Be Staying After Sunday?" (#32 on *Billboard*'s Hot 100 and #22 on its Easy-Listening chart) and a less-remembered but equally colorful track called "Pink Lemonade."

With only three verses, reinforced by constant vowel repetitions that rhyme with, or come close to, the word "gleam," "Green Tambourine" also includes a wordless chorus that replaces lyrics with an electric-raga instrumental detour. What is most fascinating is the song's structure. Like "San Francisco (Be Sure to Wear Flowers in Your Hair)," its jangling jingle appeal inspires performers covering it to adhere to its basic tune and avoid needless improvising.

"Green Tambourine" is among those rare tunes that makes a great impression on the popular culture for a short period of time and is almost forgotten shortly afterward. Recording artists as varied as the off-base operatic Mrs. Miller to the heavier rock of the Status Quo forged their versions when the moment was right. Leka and Pinz found an ideal nursery rhyme to put into the heads of a ready audience, combining hit-maker hooks, mystifying accoutrements, and a strong enough melody to also inspire several elevator music elucidations.

Roughly a month after the Lemon Pipers' release, Muzak recorded an instrumental interpretation by Earl Sheldon and His Orchestra. It starts with the expected tambourine accompanied by an electric bass before an electric lead guitar picks up on the opening verse. Sheldon and his Orchestra depend more on happy Herb Alpert-era horns joining the shaking tambourine and the hiccupping guitar. An organ also surfaces as the tune moves forward, but the readily detectible main melody never slips away.

Sheldon's version could have used the Lemon Pipers' string coating, but Muzak likely programmed the track for areas where guitars, horns, and percussion were better at neutralizing urban noises. Back in the day when Music by Muzak was ubiquitous, many hippies and other young consumers who dropped their silver to purchase a copy of the Lemon Pipers' single were likely exposed to this elevator version as they traipsed in and out of mainstream retail nooks.

The most notable version was from the "Champagne Music" master himself. Lawrence Welk and His Orchestra released their "Green Tambourine" single on Welk's Ranwood Records label, with a carbonated sound that bubbled up *Billboard*'s Easy-Listening category to #27. Welk includes an echoing female chorus as his players apply the same harpsichord and other effervescent sounds that attracted television viewers to his weekly show.

In the midst of the psychedelic era, Welk continued with variations on the style he had devised in 1938, when his Honolulu Fruit Gum Orchestra performed at the William Penn Hotel in Pittsburgh, Pennsylvania. Amid the throng of patrons pledging champagne toasts between waltzes and slurry conversations, Welk became entranced by the dizzying splendor, particularly from the multiple mirrors reflecting the chandelier. For him, this light show simulated bubbles: a sensation inspiring him to showcase his music as visual and tactile as well as aural.

Welk met the demands of itinerant players not acquainted with the sheet music but still needing to stay in key by writing out what he described as "short, light, delicate musical figures," arrangements which, when paired with the harpsichord, created his lasting-trademark "fizz" effect.

The June 1, 1968 issue of *Billboard* specified that, along with Welk's "Green Tambourine," there were also recorded versions by Les Brown on Decca, Trombones Unlimited on Liberty, Mariano and the Unbelievables on Capitol, a children's version by the Do-Re-Mi Chorus on Kapp, the Lennon Sisters on Mercury, and Enoch Light on Project 3. The Enoch Light Singers made "Green Tambourine" their first single on Project 3 Records, the flipside of their take on Tommy Boyce and Bobby Hart's "I Wonder What She's Doing Tonight." Terry Baxter and His Orchestra covered it on *The Best of '68* while a keyboardist and composer going by the name of Sir Julian included it on his 1968 album from Unart Records, bearing the pervasive title *Love is Blue*.

File under: Instrumental

ST 2875

STEREO

Capitol
RECORDS

PLAYABLE ON STEREO
& MONO PHONOGRAPHS

Mariano
and the Unbelievables

The 25th Hour

Green Tambourine
Hello Goodbye
The Look of Love
Best of Both Worlds
Love Is Blue
Sunny · Holiday
A Whiter Shade of Pale
Live for Life
The Man Upstairs
25th Hour

Mariano and the Unbelievables once again stand out. With arranger Mort Garson's talent for studio reverberation, Mariano and Co. begin with a bouncing tambourine beat and drums, but the listening gets sweeter as a Bell triangle rings along to Mariano's sizzling harpsichord. The string quartet enters with that fluttering effect that the Lemon Pipers' single uses before the first verse and after that trademark echo following the line "Listen while I play…" All along, the continual scraping of a ratchet fortifies the pulse, up to the final verse, when the harpsichord and strings engage in a flirtatious duet.

The U.K. also paid tribute. Sounds Orchestral, on the 1968 album *Words*, has Johnny Pearson leading with the same piano gymnastics that distinguished the group's 1965 instrumental hit "Cast Your Fate to the Wind." The following year, RCA Camden's "Living" series brought out Living Percussion's *The Beat Goes On*, showcasing bongos, xylophone, and the new kid in the studio neighborhood: the Moog synthesizer. Dick Hyman (a New York City pianist who played on many a Muzak session) arranged this version of "Green Tambourine," with an electric sitar and a vibraphone as vocal substitutes before closing with a synthesized harp.

The Lemon Pipers followed "Green Tambourine" with other Leka-Pinz songs: such cosmic confections about castles and candy as "Blueberry Blue" and "Jelly Jungle (of Orange Marmalade)."

The latter introduced tasty and trippy descriptions: "a rainbow ladder to the sky," clouds "as fluffy as a parachute sail," a "yellow ball of butter," violins that "grow like peaches in the sun all day," and the more resonant "tangerine dreams." Then, by April of 1968, the "Green Tambourine" contended with composer Jimmy Webb's "sweet, green icing flowing down" on a love song with enough edible metaphors and similes to match the menus of both the Lemon Pipers and the "marmalade skies" of the Beatles.

Webb, whose "Up, Up and Away" had obliquely referred to altered states, went into freak-out mode with "MacArthur Park," a masterpiece full of lyrical twitches and musical switches. He had intended it for the Association, but when they balked at its unusual length and bizarre words, actor Richard Harris (still in the afterglow of his role as King Arthur in *Camelot*) was anxious to become a pop singer and chose "MacArthur Park" out of Webb's sheet-music pile. Webb and Harris bonded not on Orange Sunshine or magic mushrooms but with lots of Guinness, champagne, and liqueur. "When Richard did the vocals at a London studio," Webb recalled to the *Guardian* in 2013, "he had a pitcher of Pimm's by the microphone. We knew the session was over when the Pimm's was gone."

Though conceived in booze, Harris' recording of "MacArthur Park" yielded a Top 40 novelty rife with hallucinatory references that catered to younger and older fans. It also encouraged listeners to bend their minds, making them fathom the elaborate conceits involving a melting park, a dripping cake, a menacing rain, a vanishing recipe, and "a stripèd pair of pants." Another appeal was its length of seven-plus minutes, a feature that Webb later confessed to the *Guardian* was of grave concern:

"At first, we felt like the guys who'd created the A-bomb: we were a bit afraid of what we'd done. I didn't know I could write something like that. We had doubts about releasing it as a single, but when radio stations began playing it from the album in its entirety, I was asked to do a shorter version as a single. I refused, so eventually they put out the full seven minutes 20 seconds. George Martin once told me the Beatles let 'Hey Jude' run to over seven minutes because of 'MacArthur Park.'"

Through the years, Webb has tried to ease the concerns of the literal-minded who still fail to comprehend the song's larger meaning and focus too much on the cake. The melting cake was Webb's metaphor for a romance gone south, and the real MacArthur Park in Los Angeles' Westlake area is where Webb claims to have witnessed an old flame get hitched to someone else at an open-air wedding. Decades later, the park acquired a terrible reputation for drug deals, prostitution, and gang-related shoot-outs.

Just as "Green Tambourine" gifted Top 40 radio with striking sounds, "MacArthur Park" of-fered what Webb described as a "musical collage." Harris, with his hoarse and chronically unmelodic voice, valiantly shifts in moods, melodies, and time signatures—all boosted by Webb's harpsichord doses. These peculiar properties combine the best of the era's orchestral and psychedelic pop. No wonder the record soared to #10 in *Billboard*'s Easy-Listening category and to #2 on its more encompassing Pop chart.

Several "creamy-on-the-melody" artists accepted the "MacArthur Park" challenge. Even though the record broke a fundamental rule by running over three to four minutes, instrumentalists often abbreviated the song by concentrating on its most endearing parts. Francis Lai's 1971 album *More Love Themes* includes a tribute (running about four-and-one-half minutes) that starts with crisp and rapid harpsichord strikes and proceeds with studio-enhanced strings, a grand piano, subtle voices, and an organ—a mixture that previously distinguished his title theme to the 1967 film *A Man and A Woman*.

Conducted by Nick Perito with Arthur Ferrante's arrangement, Ferrante & Teicher, on their 1968 album *A Bouquet of Hits*, complement "MacArthur Park" with a grand orchestra, violins, and flutes as their twin pianos float into glissando bliss—all in just over four minutes. On his 1969 album *A Brand New Me*, Liberace melts it into two other Top 40 entries of the time—"Cherry Hill Park" and "Echo Park"—on a medley entitled

"Parks and Recreation." Other Easy-Listening versions (at varying lengths) arrived from Ronnie Aldrich, Frank Chacksfield, Floyd Cramer, Martin Denny, James Last, Raymond Lefevre, Doc Severinsen & Strings, and Hugo Winterhalter.

"MacArthur Park" became a tune so adored by so many that it joined others like "Theme from *A Summer Place*," "Love is Blue," and "Green Tambourine" as melodies so familiar that they were also subject to parody. Such mockery continued into 1982, in a scene from *Airplane II: The Sequel*, when wincing passengers cover their ears while rushing in and out of an elevator blaring "MacArthur Park" by 101 Strings at deafening decibels.

Meanwhile, the Lemon Pipers, despite the fame that "Green Tambourine" accrued, still languished through their identity crisis. A Gold Record and constant airings around the world, either through the original single or instrumentally piped in through a background music service, were not enough for the Lemon Pipers to pipe down and savor the spoils. They still aspired to be cogs in the "progressive rock" machine and were reluctant to record their subsequent Leka-Pinz hit: the violins- and harp-laden "Rice is Nice." They instead wrote off such efforts as "funny-money music" and yearned to return to performing psychedelic blues at venues like Bill Graham's Fillmore West with acts like Spirit and Traffic.

When guests at a New York awards show asked them to perform "Rice is Nice," the band's belligerent attitude went into overdrive as they decided to play it as a deliberately cacophonous mess. The horrified Buddah executives had to contend with the band's demands that future contract language specify when and where they would have to perform the song. Their snit worsened when they eventually refused to play "Green Tambourine" at live concerts. By 2011, however, with time to get years of sneering out of his system, Ivan Browne mellowed a bit. "I'll admit that 'Green Tambourine' was good, and Leka created a great orchestration for it," he told *Cincinnati* magazine. "But the other stuff they made us record messed with my mind for years." ❦

141

DONOVA BRAIN AND THE CEILING REFRAIN

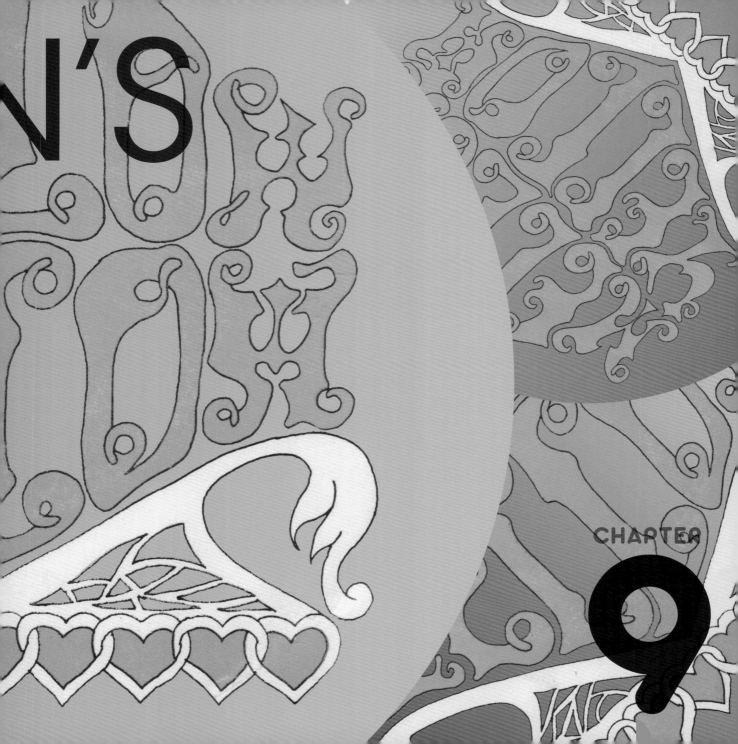

CHAPTER

9

"I'D LOVE TO GO INTO SOME OF THESE PSYCHEDELIC TEMPLES AND SING SOFTNESS AND CHANGE THE VIBRATIONS, 'CAUSE THEY'RE VERY SORT OF METALLIC AND GRITTY AND HARD, AND THEY NEED TO BE A BIT PURER."

—DONOVAN, *ROLLING STONE*, NOVEMBER 9, 1967

There are at least two cringeworthy scenes in D.A. Pennebaker's *Don't Look Back*, a 1967 *cinéma-vérité* glimpse into Bob Dylan's 1965 British tour. In one, a jittery Dylan listens in his hotel room as Donovan plays a song called "To Sing for You" and reacts with a giddy but patronizing air. He then takes the guitar, honoring Donovan's request to hear Dylan play "It's All Over Now, Baby Blue." Donovan, about five years younger than Dylan and still developing his unique style when this was filmed, looks on politely as a defensive Dylan appears to refer to him as the "Baby Blue" when twanging about a "vagabond who's rapping at your door."

Worse, later in the documentary, Dylan interrupts his stage performance of "Talkin' World War III Blues" with a bitchy remark: "I looked in the closet, and there was Donovan." The audience laughed and clapped, but the moment captured a sharp contrast between the two '60s songster-poets. Dylan seemed hard, petty, shaggy, and toxic in his black shades. Donovan, in contrast, was the shy gentleman, unwilling to lambaste journalists and reporters the way Dylan does throughout the movie.

Dylan, whose nasal whine flouted good-singing standards, wrote several fine songs that many thought sounded better when others performed them. Donovan Leitch, to the contrary, sang with the melodic and often haunting style of a traditional minstrel. Part of that talent is due to the skills he'd inherited from his Scottish ancestry and his wide-ranging knowledge of British folk traditions. He projected a mystique with often gaudy outfits and the audacity to brandish a bundle of peacock feathers on his famous infrared cover photo for *A Gift from a Flower to a Garden*. Donovan lived sincerely inside of his mystical dream and did not have to resort to the kind of parody that a sunflower-toting Henry Gibson displayed during his hippie-poet routines on *Rowan & Martin's Laugh-In*.

"I wanted to go into the beatnik bit of San Francisco," Donovan told John Carpenter in that first *Rolling Stone* issue from November 9, 1967. He sought to help clean up the bad vibrations with kindness, when others prowling in the Haight-Ashbury district's darker days exhibited amphetamine psychoses. Even when he tried being sassy with pseudo-jazzy numbers like "Mellow Yellow" or "Sunshine Superman," Donovan still came across as the stargazing visionary who effortlessly elided "Trans-Love Airways" into "Jefferson Airplane" on his song "Fat Angel." He also appeared to take the "flower power" ideals more seriously than certain Airplane members who crowed about collecting guns.

In *The Autobiography of Donovan: The Hurdy Gurdy Man*, Donovan claims that early on he "resembled what author Colin Wilson had described as the 'romantic outsider.'" He also addresses the different drummer he must have heard in contrast to his more hardened peers: "Critics of my gentle approach to music were still missing the point. In contrast to the wild exuberance of rock-and-roll, I was soothing with my songs. Peaceful music was needed then. Even more so now."

With a poetic manner that often came across as defiantly fey, Donovan gave the term "flower power" a deeper meaning with tunes that remain beautiful decades later. He was destined to sing convincingly about "rose carmethene," "alizarin crimson" and various other hues on "Wear Your Love Like Heaven"—perhaps his greatest song. The tune was so appealing that it ended up embellishing several commercials for "Eau de Love" and other cosmetics from Menley & James' "Love Cosmetics" firm—a subsidiary of the same Smith, Kline & French Laboratories that also manufactured Thorazine and Dexedrine. Jefferson Airplane recorded commercials for those rough-and-tumble Levi jeans, but only Donovan could get away with endorsing ads for a seductive scent marketed in pretty bottles.

The Menley & James firm was also behind an NBC television show that aired from Los Angeles on the evening of March 19th, 1969, hosted by Andy Williams and called *Andy's Love Concert*. Williams emerged from NBC's Studio-induced mist to introduce Donovan as "the Prince of Magical Mystery." Under a white canopy, held up by a flock of flower-garlanded youths, Donovan led his procession, while Renaissance-style fiddles and flutes ushered him in. More acolytes followed, holding

up a large sign reading "Love"—similar to the ones that the Beatles' entourage exhibited during the worldwide "All You Need is Love" telecast two years before.

Between commercials that exposed living-room spectators to one slick "Love Cosmetics" ad after another, Donovan's image was transmitted into millions of homes. Draped in a virgin-white caftan contrasting with his dark, flowing locks, and in sandals, he resembled a combination of a May Queen, the Maharishi Mahesh Yogi, and a bit of Jesus (who was about to make a comeback thanks in part to such musicals as *Jesus Christ Superstar* and *Godspell*).

Andy's Love Concert lulled many Donovan fans, but as one columnist in the March 19th *Buffalo Courier-Express* described it, the show was "a thinly disguised 60-minute commercial for a new cosmetics line." By 1969, other ad moguls hoped that by adding paisley prints to their ties, growing their hair a bit over their ears, and sporting mutton-chop sideburns, they could neutralize Madison Avenue's powermonger stigma. Likewise, Menley & James sold "Love" as a make-up that did the opposite of its usual function. As its commercials advised, "You've got a complexion worth seeing. You don't need make-ups that blank you out."

Amid the aromatic and cosmetic hype, Donovan made some extra cash while maintaining artistic integrity. He was a realist who was, after all, signed to Epic (a corporate subsidiary

STEREO
LP-12422

IMPERIAL

A PRODUCT OF
LIBERTY RECORDS

THE LES WILLIAMS ORCHESTRA PLAYS
THE COLLECTED WORKS OF DONOVAN

Poor Cow · Jenifer Juniper · Be Not Too Hard · Sunshine Superman · Mellow Yellow · Sunny Goodge Street
Catch The Wind · Skip Along Sam
There Is A Mountain · Wear Your Love Like Heaven · Oh Gosh · Colours

of Columbia Records) and still a component in what Joni Mitchell would later call pop music's "star-maker machinery." Yet his colorful message remained clear as the cosmetics firm sought his melody to bolster Love's look and aroma. Nevertheless, "Wear Your Love Like Heaven" showed up in the Love commercials not as his original recording but as an ethereal studio-group do-over. The commercials sometimes featured Ali MacGraw, about to blossom in *Goodbye Columbus* before wilting as the doomed heroine of *Love Story*, while images of the beautiful bottles full of "Eau De Love" dominated the screen.

As both muse and merchant, Donovan was at peace with his songs as product placement, assured that his melodies of love would seep into the consciousness of the buying public regardless of whether they reached into their wallets or reached out to a neighbor. What a contrast to Jim Morrison who, in the fall of 1968, boosted his lunatic image by threatening to grab a sledgehammer and smash a Buick Opel on stage if the car company continued to air an ad with a refurbished version of "Light My Fire." This sanctimonious adversity to commercials did not stop the Doors from closing the last four notes of "Touch Me" with "Stronger than dirt," the slogan that Ajax used to sell its laundry detergent with the image of a white knight on a white horse, riding from place to place to cleanse a grimy world.

What Donovan referred to as his "song poems" were usually tender enough to please older listeners. He inspired a few adult-oriented vocalists who could fit in with *Billboard*'s Easy-Listening set, but to varying effect. Mel Tormé's "Sunshine Superman," with his incongruous Vegas delivery and big-band funk, is instant fodder for those who get their jollies by snickering at "kitsch." Andy Williams' famous wife Claudine Longet, on the other hand, with her strange whisper of a voice and retiring demeanor, had affection for tunes most other mainstream vocalists ignored. On her 1968 album *Colours*, she sounds nervously intimate while singing "Catch the Wind" and the title song. In 1971, she recorded "Electric Moon," among the less-known of what *Billboard* would describe as Donovan's "shepherd's simple meadow melodies."

More captivating are the tunes and hooks that motivated several like-minded instrumentalists. The Mike Leander Orchestra offered among the first on his 1965 album *The Folk Hits*. With the help of studio reverberation, "Catch the Wind" mixes a slow electric bass with a harpsichord, harp, tambourine, and mostly wordless singing. Likewise, Leander's "Colours" starts with the acoustic guitar picking similar to Donovan's original before the phantom-like harpsichord mixes with a tambourine, giving the melody an outer-space appeal eons from any of folk's so-called "earthy" origins. The chorus breaks its wordless spell by chiming, "Freedom is a word I rarely use." Folk music might have had, as Leander writes, "roots in prisons and warehouses, tobacco fields and saloon bars and amongst fighters of war and fighters of peace," but Leander himself manages to refine such rawness into a refreshing blend of air-conditioned acoustics.

The Mystic Moods Orchestra visits "Sunny Goodge Street" on the 1968 album *Emotions*, as arranger and conductor John Andrews Tartaglia competes with background sounds of revving engines and the ringing signals of an approaching train. He offers a soothing waltz beat with a flute, unassuming drums, and a string orchestra evoking carnival calliopes as another train approaches. The following year, Tartaglia arranged and conducted *Extensions*, another Mystic Moods outing that includes scattered moments of female sirens singing and stammering, children playing, some male spoken-word, and a Jimmy Webb medley where the patter of rain over "MacArthur Park" flows into "The Yard Went on Forever." The grand finale and highlight, however, is "Lalena." The sound of waves intensifies, but strings, an acoustic guitar, a flute, and chimes surface to offer safety from the deluge. The orchestral closing is among the best tributes to this sad ballad about a painted face and a drowning identity.

On the 1971 release *Country Lovin' Folk*, Richard Clements, who had arranged and conducted other Mystic Moods albums including *Love Token* (1969) and *Stormy Weekend* (1970), leads the Orchestra along a more bucolic soundscape of crickets, dogs, frogs, and other organic distractions. Clements' musicians play more in the style of a Nashville studio group, with strings, piano (hinting at Floyd Cramer's slip notes), and tambourine. When the album gets to "Catch the Wind," Donovan's tune escapes the onrushing train and the unforgivable barking dog, but the crickets persist. Soon, a neighing horse and approaching thunder lead to a more assuring mix of trumpet, harpsichord, flute, and an acoustic guitar. As the thunder gets louder, the sea waves get bolder, and the wind trounces the surroundings, the strings rise again to offer Donovan's tune some shelter.

Among Donovan's many psychedelic creations, 1966's "Mellow Yellow" is the easiest to mimic and yet the biggest dare for arrangers trying to avoid improvisational delirium. Actor David McCallum, along with his weekly appearances as Illya Kuryakin on the television series *The Man from U.N.C.L.E.* and his portrayal of a macrocephalic space alien in *The Outer Limits*, took the time to record several instrumental albums on Capitol Records. On his 1968 release *McCallum*, he wraps "Mellow Yellow" in a grand orchestra, arranged by H.B. Barnum (who had worked with the Hollyridge Strings just a few years earlier). The percussive beat is constant, but the horns, flutes, harp, and the mild introduction of strings let the main melody transpire with minimal distractions. With a couple of brief silent breaks as teasers, McCallum finally lets his players tuck in the "e-lec-tri-cal banana" to make way for the next track.

Arranger and conductor Les Williams also had

a Donovan flair. His 1968 album *The Les Williams Orchestra Plays the Collected Songs of Donovan* remains faithful to the composer's melodies but gets creative with the instruments. On "Mellow Yellow," Williams begins with the original's signature drum-and-snare beat before proceeding with flutes, horns, a sneaky electric guitar, a countermelody organ, a brief harp, and what sound like crystals tinkling one moment and splintering the next.

There are times, however, when Williams takes less-innovative short cuts. "Sunshine Superman" is an example that challenges instrumental adapters to break old big-band or jazz habits. Unlike Nelson Riddle's loud and brassy version on his 1968 album *The Riddle of Today*, Williams approaches it with more Easy-Listening nuance by varying the instruments more. The horns approximate that unearthly zing that pops in and out of the original—what Donovan's arranger John Cameron would describe in 2017 to the *Wall Street Journal* as the "meowing guitar line." But Williams also substitutes Donovan's vocal with a blend of high-pitched strings, a restless electric guitar, punchy drums, a harpsichord, and a trumpet that replaces the guitar's meow. Mid-way through, the studio horn and string sections sound cacophonous as they attempt to improvise, but the harpsichord triumphantly returns to forge a more cohesive ending.

Among Williams' best moments is "Wear Your Love Like Heaven." The harpsichord, among Donovan's prized instruments, combines with guitar, flute, and strings. For a layered effect, he allows the harpsichord to be the star of the second verse before flutes take over the third. Where Donovan would ordinarily sing "Lord, kiss me once more," Williams mates the harpsichord with a subtle electric bass, while the flutes befriend a flugelhorn. That same year, Mariano and the Unbelievables proved more intriguing, closing their first album with a "Superman" at war with what initially seem to be such musical foes as a throbbing bass guitar, a bellicose harpsichord, and restless drums. Nevertheless, the instruments somehow make tentative peace with the baroque quartet that softens the mood even as the track fiddles feverishly along. Without Donovan's lyrics, Mariano and his band still convey some kind of a strange place that listeners can enter with just the melody to guide them.

"Jennifer Juniper," one of several blissful singles released during a politically raging spring of 1968, provided another instance of a Top 40 hit courted by its elevator suitor within a month. Donovan's recording peaked at *Billboard*'s #26 on March 9, 1968, and Muzak followed exactly one month later on April 9th with a version by Charles Grean and His Orchestra.

The String-A-Longs, a quartet whose percolating guitars bubbled up to *Billboard*'s #3 Pop listing in January of 1961 with their instrumental "Wheels," provided a fresh interpretation of Donovan's "There is a Mountain." On their 1968 album *World Wide Hits* (produced by Norman Petty at his

150

Clovis, New Mexico studio), the String-A-Longs acclimated to the age of mind-expanding studio maneuvers, providing what the back cover calls "sometimes-soft, sometimes-groovy, velvet-like beautiful happenings in sound." The guitars still percolate and stay on the beat, but thanks to electronic tinkering, some of the instruments exert a semi-raga command.

In April of 1968, bits of information surfaced in *Record World* magazine regarding Donovan, Andy Williams, and English arranger/conductor Vic Lewis. In the April 6 issue, the "London Lowdown" column reported that "London impresario Vic Lewis" was teaming up with the MCA Agency to promote several of Andy Williams' London concerts. The Andy Williams-Donovan connection (supported by Claudine Longet's fondness for Donovan songs) was more apparent when Lewis released an album entitled *The Boy in the Saffron Robe: The Vic Lewis Orchestra Plays the Music of Donovan* (on the U.K.'s NEMS label). The U.S. Epic label called it *Donovan My Way*. Lewis also wrote two tracks: the title song and "A Boy Called Donovan." Considering his more jazz-friendly musical past, Lewis offers welcome surprises with sonically cushioned homages.

Lewis was primarily a British jazz guitarist who, as a teenager, played in a band with George Shearing and grew to admire his British compatriot Ken Thorne. After participating in jazz tours through the 1950s, he gradually retired from performing. He got back into the music game, however, by 1960 when helping to manage the careers of pop singers like Cilla Black. Black was among several English stars under the auspices of Brian Epstein, for whom Lewis also helped organize the Beatles' international tours.

The Donovan tribute was another way for Lewis to get back to recording and be inventive in the process. Even on Donovan compositions that winked at jazz, such as "Mellow Yellow" and "Sunshine Superman," Lewis uses intricate string arrangements that let the songs levitate just in time for the notes to land in their rightful places. John Cameron, the album's arranger, had already arranged and supplied keyboards on some of Donovan's previous work, and on the 1967 *Poor Cow* score for which Donovan also wrote and sang the title song.

"Sunshine Superman," the opening track, succeeds in keeping the song from staggering into the audio clutches fit for a poisonous, smoky nightclub. Regardless of the varying influences that impressed Donovan at the time, this remains what several historians consider the first psychedelic hit (released in July of 1966) to enter *Billboard*'s Pop chart. It is another tune edited from a longer version for Top 40 radio play, but the excision—from over four minutes to a bit over three—is nowhere near as adventurous as the one Paul Rothschild made for the Doors' "Light My Fire."

Hovering above the original record like an

RCA
LSP-4106
VICTOR
STEREO

The Golden Songs of Donovan
PLAYED BY THE JOHNNY ARTHEY ORCHESTRA

astral projection, Cameron's instrumental accolade to "Sunshine Superman" seems to absorb some of Donovan's own misty reflections. Donovan claims he was not thinking of Orange Sunshine but rather the literal daylight coming through his window. He also claims that the "Superman" reference (despite his additional mention of The Green Lantern from DC Comics) refers to the Superman of Friedrich Nietzsche and the supposed higher consciousness touted in *Thus Spoke Zarathustra*.

Donovan's "Superman" is emotionally complex: the braggadocio of a young man comparing himself to superheroes, vowing he will win the love of his life despite secret doubts. This psychological layer is more apparent in Donovan's lyrics, but Lewis and Cameron convey much of this subtext with the right choice of instruments and tempo. The thumping bass and "meowing" remain, albeit altered, but a fusion of plucked strings, a clarinet, and acoustic bass replaces the boastful beat with a lusher mood that avoids swinger delusions.

John Cameron also recalls to the *Wall Street Journal* how much of Donovan's 1966 recording depended on serendipity: "It's a fascinating instrumental texture and style progression. Jimmy Page was brought in later to add the rock guitar solo. From the start, Don wanted a light, trippy backdrop—something quite different then. But the psychedelic sound we created was an accident, really. I had never taken LSD, so I had no idea how

an acid trip would translate into music. We were just shooting for a mystical feel."

Lewis and Cameron had arrayed this "mystical feel" with a more traditional costume when turning "Hurdy Gurdy Man" into a light-classical and light-hearted recital. The baritone strings begin with the original's humming introduction, the strings then go from tenor to soprano as they join a clarinet and harp; some pizzicato adds a bit of tension, but there is no electric sitar within earshot. Instead of a cryptic and possibly malevolent force, their "Hurdy Gurdy Man" arouses images of woodland fairies gamboling about in an English country garden.

However, the album's version of "Lord of the Reedy River" (which Donovan sings in a youth hostel for a rather dour audience in the 1969 movie *If It's Tuesday, This Must Be Belgium*) sounds much more mysterious: a looming flute, a wordless siren's cries, and the somewhat unsettling background strings suggesting a pre-nightmare lullaby. The extraterrestrial effect is similar to the treatment that Billy Vaughn and His Orchestra gave that same year (on the album *The Windmills of Your Mind*) to the Zombies' "Time of the Season." Vaughn's version is as spooky as the original, yet it relieves some of the rougher edges with woodwinds, percussion, piano, electric guitar, and at one point the flash of a softly encroaching vocal chorus.

In the fall of 1968, Donovan introduced "Lalena," his tearful tune suggesting the inner turmoil of a woman of the evening, or as Donovan claims in his autobiography, "the German actress Lotte Lenya and the character she played in the musical *The Threepenny Opera*." The song was nonetheless about conflicting feelings that Lewis and Cameron recapture in their version. The original melody—for which Cameron also arranged Donovan's string quartet—is untouched, but layers of different instruments, including strings (both plucked and strummed), harpsichord, harp, and woodwinds, allow listeners to imagine a sylvan utopia even as the sun sets over a ballad about a troubled mind and world.

Donovan showed his gratitude to Lewis and Cameron when penning the album's back-cover notes: "...it is strange and satisfying to hear the melodies that were spawned in the silence of my own mind being made into orchestrations... All happiness to the world of music lovers. Let it be known that I happily make the pictures of beauty move in the mind. Let it be known that these songs open a new world to my songs, through which I am wandering."

Cameron arranged Donovan songs on other collections as well. On the John Schroder Orchestra's 1967 album *The Dolly Catcher*, he attaches his harpsichord to vibrant drums and a meandering flute on a cover of "Epistle to Dippy." On his 1968 album *Warm and Gentle*, Cameron has adept moments despite getting caught up in some party-time bossa nova with Donovan's otherwise meditative

and somber "Mexico (Sand and Foam)." Still, the consoling cumulus of strings lets enough of the melody survive, and Cameron deserves credit for acknowledging this track from the 1967 *Mellow Yellow* album, for which he also arranged and contributed harpsichord and piano.

A year later, British arranger/conductor Johnny Arthey also presented a Donovan collection. A former pianist for the British military, Arthey became another player amid the European '60s pop circles, arranging for such artists as Sasha Distel, Billy J. Kramer, and (for fans of sweet-vanilla vocals) the Gunter Kallmann Chorus. He also tried his hand at turning some of the most popular songs of the time into string orchestrations with a beat.

Arthey established his knack in 1965 with *Instrumental Performances of the Same Exciting Vocal Versions*, which includes the Beatles' "I Feel Fine" and two Lennon-McCartney tunes they gave to others: Billy J. Kramer's "From a Window" and Peter & Gordon's "A World Without Love." Released just as the psychedelic pop era started, the album focuses more on the innovative accord between string orchestras and electric guitars that resulted in the earlier part of the '60s when surf music and Easy-Listening sometimes drifted together.

His 1969 album *The Golden Songs of Donovan* gets closer to alternately relaxing and energizing instrumental accolades. While Lewis and Cameron's album takes more liberties with Donovan's rhythms by often opting for slower approaches,

Arthey's embellishments are lush and lively. Good examples are "Skip-Along Sam," with its "Penny Lane"-style horn processions, and "Fat Angel," where the rhythm section, an organ, and an electric guitar simulate a sitar. He also includes "Hampstead Incident," another of Donovan's more melancholy and less interpreted compositions, accenting the silky strings with harpsichord, celeste, soft brass, bongos, and a saxophone.

Once again, "Wear Your Love Like Heaven" is the highlight. It is precise with Donovan's melody and rhythm, but gets inventive when layering the woodwinds and violins. The characteristic organ also appears, and the burnished brass adds more energy to the chorus. The harmony between the strings and brass makes this the kind of interpretation that listeners can enjoy as either background music or for active listening—when they take the time to appreciate the combination of instruments that might otherwise clash in the wrong hands.

Among the very best "Wear Your Love Like Heaven" renditions is from David Rose and His Orchestra on the 1970 album *Happy Heart*. Rose, who made his mark back in the '40s, was no stranger to instrumental expertise when adapting to folk and rock. His 1965 album *The Velvet Beat* even tackled the Rolling Stones' "(I Can't Get No) Satisfaction," with a hypnotically slow and highly strung orchestral interpretation supported by guitar and percussion. On "Wear Your Love Like Heaven," Rose deliberates with a mystifying, spacey introduction before gliding into the melody with mellow brass, an electric guitar—and a lavish orchestra that uses conventional means to capture a sense of psychedelic floating.

Were Johnny Arthey's and David Rose's versions of "Wear Your Love Like Heaven" part of a background-music service that programmed songs according to their ascending "stimulus," Rose's somewhat mellower track would likely play in the earlier part of the cycle, leading up to Arthey's more kinetic offering to satisfy that portion of the day requiring a blood-sugar boost. Both tracks are elevating as they tackle a variety of instruments and pop rhythms while traversing boldly into Mantovani country. Time would heal any enmity that might have simmered between Dylan and Donovan back in the mid-'60s, as both song legends got re-engineered into ceiling serenades for dining, relaxing, shopping, and an emotional rescue for those fidgeting in transitory places like airports, hotel lobbies, and of course, dentists' waiting rooms where the din of the drill awaits. ◉

HARD TO BE EASY—DISENTAN HAIR

GLING

"I NEVER EVEN HEARD OF A HIPPIE WHEN I MET THEM."

—GALT MACDERMOT TO *PLAYBILL*

REGARDING GEROME RAGNI AND JAMES RADO

"There's no pop music anymore," Galt MacDermot lamented when appearing on the PBS show *Theater Talk* in May of 2009, just as the "American Tribal Love-Rock Musical" *Hair* was enjoying a Broadway revival. Susan Haskins, the show's host and series director, reminded MacDermot that, despite its free-form celebration of orgies and revolution, *Hair* was the last Broadway extravaganza to conform to that "golden age" when musicals spawned several songs for entertainers like Jack Jones and Barbra Streisand to refurbish and remarket. Decades after *Hair*'s threats of an emerging Aquarian age failed to happen, MacDermot seemed trapped between two worlds: the taboo-buster of yesteryear and the older, wiser composer concerned about his place in the Great American Songbook.

Those behind *Hair* fancied they were spearheading a rebellion that would irrevocably change music and society. Instead, the "hippie musical" ended up at the split-end of a counter-cultural mindset that had been growing for years. It was about the obsession with being "authentic," shocking suburban mores, and defiling the white picket fence that nonconforming conformists of the '60s saw as a symbol of the middle-class "squares" of the '50s. On the surface, *Hair* was dirty, greasy, menacing, and for some, just plain ugly. In time, however, its roots proved to be more embedded in the past than its creators initially realized.

During its previous incarnation, or what MacDermot called its "off-loft Broadway" years, *Hair* was wilder and more unmanageable, especially with James Rado and his partner Gerome Ragni as its sole cultivators. "There were these two characters in search of a composer," Nat Shapiro (who introduced Ragni and Rado to MacDermot) recalled to *Record World* in 1969. "They walked into my office early in 1967, hair all over the place, carrying a withered briefcase filled with notes and drawings on brown paper bags… they began looking for someone to set their words to music."

MacDermot (a clean-cut Canadian) had set out to melodically groom much of the material. In the process, *Hair* ironically retained some of the musical-theater traditions it had aspired to avoid. A restyled *Hair* had its Broadway premiere at the Biltmore Theatre on April 28, 1968. A month later, RCA (which had previously released an off-Broadway version) put out the original-cast Broadway album, destined for a Best Score Grammy. Song-marketing gears started grinding out sheet music while representatives plugged the tunes for potential pop covers, just as they had for *The Sound of Music*, *West Side Story*, and *Thoroughly Modern Millie*.

Several of *Hair*'s numbers retained much of the obscenity, along with the race-baiting and references to "sodomy," while the performers (especially when rising from the audience to mount the stage) still looked fashionably shabby. Yet, somehow in the fickle maw of consumerism, Rado, Ragni, and MacDermot cast mere shadows on the mass-media wall. Their "revolution" was not only televised on talk shows and variety venues but also *lusterized* for "middle-of-the-road" recording artists, kid-friendly pop groups, and perhaps most vital of all, the Easy-Listening instrumentalists, who were masters at operating under the counterculture's radar, teasing out whatever satisfying melodies lay under *Hair*'s frizzy, nappy, oily, and stringy layers. In the summer of 1968, Broadway cast members appeared on *The Tonight Show*. After performing "Let the Sunshine In," they showered the relatively "uptight" Nebraska-bred host Johnny Carson with love beads. This closing number about "facing a dying nation" was engineered to alarm the masses watching from the safety of their living rooms: the same audience that nonetheless continued watching as the cast blared out the same desperate anthem on *The Ed Sullivan Show*.

At the same time, the songs, particularly the less strident ones, were already entering an alternative dimension: a timeless Memory Lane. This was not a mockery of *Hair*'s creative origins but rather a prime example (seen many times before and since) of how, even with the most seditious intent, songs of insurrection, especially when melodic, become palatable even before their fashion fever burns out. Soon, the chanting and the gospel poses associated with such conservative acts as the Young Americans and Up with People took cues

from *Hair*. The late '60s and early '70s onslaught of "Jesus freaks" portended *Jesus Christ, Superstar* and *Godspell*: Biblically inspired musicals deploying similar "Tribal Love-Rock" propaganda to merge popular myths about the noble hippie with myths about the King of Nazareth.

Articles in *Billboard* and other trades reported how *Hair*'s composers were anxious to have their more tuneful numbers introduced to as many venues as possible, such as Top 40 AM. Like a boorish ape, *Hair* beat its chest for the gullible youngsters believing the "fight the power" press releases, while simultaneously acting more entrepreneurial for the musical "establishment" that had the actual power to make the show more vendible. "Music is the medium of today, the medium of revolution," James Rado told the December 28, 1968 issue of *Billboard*. "If any period should be put to music, this is it. Contemporary music is the language of the kids." *Hair* started spreading and shedding all across the pop-music spectrum and into Middle America. In the fall of 1968, "Where Do I Go?" got the attention of the Four Lads, while Julius LaRosa crossed the generational divide a year later by uniting with the Bob Crewe Generation to lend the song his crooner bravado. By March of 1969, record racks contained the Top 40 hit medley of "Aquarius/ Let the Sunshine In" by the Fifth Dimension, and by the end of the same year, there was a choral version by the Ray Conniff Singers—two acts

Good Morning Starshine

Vinnie Bell

GOOD MORNING STARSHINE • AQUARIUS • LOVE ME TONIGHT • LOVE THEME FROM "ROMEO AND JULIET" • BECAUSE OF YOU • HEY, JUDE
LES BICYCLETTES DE BELSIZE • A SINNER KISSED AN ANGEL • I DIDN'T KNOW WHAT TIME IT WAS • IF I ONLY HAD THE TIME • I HEAR A RHAPSODY

that, by the way, had performed at the Nixon White House. In May, "Good Morning Starshine" boasted a Top 40 hit by the genteel Oliver, the same month when the Strawberry Alarm Clock also released it as a pleasurable single, sounding like a glee club chiming in space.

The Cowsills brought out the title song in March of 1969, the Happenings (a vocal quartet from New Jersey who revived "My Mammy" and "I Got Rhythm" two years before) released a medley of "Where Do I Go?/Be-In (Hare Krishna)" in the summer of 1969, as Three Dog Night offered "Easy to Be Hard." Around the same time, Barbra Streisand, Liza Minnelli, and Phyllis Newman covered "Frank Mills." Norman Racusin, who was then the Division VP-General Manager of RCA Records, reminisced in May of 1969 to *Record World*: "Of course, one of the things that sold us on the score was that it would be merchandisable for the buyers who make up much of the record-buying market today."

Shortly after its Broadway debut, several dailies had extreme reactions. John Chapman of the *New York Daily News* called it "cheap, vulgar, foul-mouthed, and tasteless," Clive Barnes of *The New York Times* praised it as "so fresh and so unassuming, even in its pretentions," but Richard Watts of the *New York Post* suggested why the show's more nursery-rhymish numbers would also attract Easy-Listening instrumentalists who specialized in the art of reverse subversion: "MacDer-mot's songs have a pleasant lift to them, and the eager young performers know how they should be put over, which is with zest."

While producing RCA's original Broadway cast album, Andrew Wiswell was also a music director at Muzak, a position that allowed him to morph at least five of the Ragni-Rado-MacDermot songs into elevator-music variations—performed by (according to Muzak's surviving playlist) "Galt MacDermot and His Orchestra." On June 4, 1968, Muzak recorded "Good Morning Starshine," "Where Do I Go?" "Aquarius," "Easy to Be Hard," and "Let the Sunshine In."

Muzak, due to its 24/7 programming demands, did not have the same freedom as commercial Easy-Listening instrumental singles or albums. Their players and programmers avoided overly arranged numbers that proved too distracting. They also had to vary their sequences: too many strings throughout the day slowed the metabolism, while too much brass made people edgy. The instruments and the tempos had to change with each ascending quarter-hour. Still, by the late '60s and into the early '70s, Muzak too altered with the times as more electric guitars and other previously off-limits instruments joined the strings, pianos, harps, and horns. Wiswell helped to rearrange the *Hair* tracks into discrete Stimulus-Progression units to suit Muzak's more modulated palate.

When the company started pressing promotional "Stimulus-Progression" LPs for potential clients, Muzak included Galt MacDermot and His Orchestra's version of "Aquarius" on a 1969 album entitled *Reveille*. The cover alone—a vibrant abstract painting by artist Ray Harrow looking more like a Jackson Pollock than a Peter Max—revealed Muzak's complex goals at that period. The accompanying text describes it as "a visual display that would capture the essence of Muzak's functional program in colors, forms, and values."

The Muzak version of "Aquarius" is one example of how the company arranged its up-tempo rhythms: a friendly clarinet handles the opening verse, followed by a trumpet and an organ, while steady electric guitar strums fill the background. There are no strings this time around, but the melody and rhythm adhere to a simple and accessible formula intended for public concourses, shopping malls, and supermarket aisles.

As with Muzak, many instrumental arrangers and conductors faced the task of arranging some of *Hair*'s tunes to retain MacDermot's blueprints while varying the rhythms with strings, electric guitars, pianos, drums, harpsichords, harps, horns, sitars, synthesizers, and even kazoos. There were such quiet dinnertime offerings as the Midnight String Quartet's "Good Morning Starshine" from the 1968 album, *Rhapsodies for Young Lovers: Volume Three*. Such artists as Ronnie Aldrich, Paul Mauriat, and Raymond Lefevre got more brazen, bringing out a bit of Easy-Listening's id by recording with eccentric twists that, nonetheless,

preserved the main tune and almost always had a reverberating orchestra for support.

Still buzzing a year after his international hit "Love is Blue," Paul Mauriat covered *Hair*'s intense "Let the Sunshine In," but instead of settling for a mellow alternative, he submits it to a competition, making his signature high-pitched and echoing strings more aggressive as they commune with a throbbing bass guitar, the continual cries of a sitar, rhythm-fortifying horns, and a mysterious combination of flutes and a xylophone. Partway into the track, he brings the excitement down a notch by staying faithful to the show and dedicating a short tribute to the sweeter, more sentimental *Hair* piece, "Manchester England."

On his 1969 album *Aquarius*, Franck Pourcel uses a bit of bossa nova with electric guitars, flutes, and percussion while the reverberant strings carry the main melody. Then for "Good Morning Starshine," he adds a flugelhorn and other brass with the busy drums, but once again, the high-pitched violins transmit the gist of the tune. All along, the murmur of an accordion and the spirit of calypso suggest sea shanties, turning Pourcel's "Aquarius" into a potent instrumental goulash.

Meanwhile, musical legends from a distant time were still breathing and wanted to join the action. By May of 1969, Lester Lanin, who played in society ballroom dance bands from the 1930s, tried out the "now sound" and a 45 single release of "Aquarius." As the ad copy running through

NARROWING THE GENERATION GAP

WITH LESTER LANIN AND HIS ORCHESTRA

the trades announced, "This is the dawning of a new age, and one day it dawned on Lester Lanin. He said, 'Let the sunshine in on my orchestra and reflect the change.' So he did, and the result is a dynamic new instrumental version of 'Aquarius,' backed with the 'Love Theme from *Romeo and Juliet*.' Both are happening, and so is Lester." "Aquarius" was one of several selections from his 1969 album *Narrowing the Generation Gap*, for which publicists from Metromedia Records distributed copies to thousands of American disc jockeys.

Violinist Florian Zabach got together with the Nashville Country Strings on a 1969 collection of such hits as "By the Time I Get to Phoenix," "Hey Jude," and "Music to Watch Girls By." "Aquarius" is the album's highlight as it complements and compliments the melody, which (like several others) takes on a life of its own once separated from its "Love-Rock" tribe. Zabach's violin converts sounds that the stage performers might have spontaneously wailed into actual notes that a sight reader could readily identify in the recording studio. Accenting the lavish orchestra with some pizzicato and woodwinds, he also seasons the opening section with electronic effects (hinting of raga) to accompany his gypsy fiddle.

Conductor Nick Perito and arranger Arthur Ferrante give Ferrante & Teicher enough latitude to have fun with *Hair* while fussing with it. Their 1969 album *Midnight Cowboy* pays a nod to "Aquarius," as they tinkle away at the melody, combining the main theme with some playful glissando, while the orchestra lets loose with strings, flutes, and drums. A year later on *Getting Together*, they massage *Hair*'s title song with a somber symphonic opening for the initial verse. Then, as if resorting to the "prepared piano" experiments from their early career, they pound away at their ivories while Mickey-Mousing each note to make "Hair" sound like a tonier revamping of "Chopsticks," even though the strings and brass prevent the dapper duo from going completely bonkers. What a contrast to the more reverent treatment that the Briarcliff Orchestra displays with echoing violin flutters and horns on the 1969 album, *The Briarcliff Orchestra Plays…*

Meanwhile in England, Ronnie Aldrich and his Two Pianos devise a gentler alternative on the 1969 album *Destination Love*. His "Aquarius" combines his moody piano with a combination that had already proven resourceful: strings, horns, harps, an electric guitar, and glissando keyboard strokes that glide across the notes. "Good Morning Starshine" is the more beguiling of the album's two *Hair* tributes, with an introduction of soft, acoustic guitar strums, mellow horns, chimes, a harp, and ascending string echoes. Aldrich's low notes on his studio-enhanced keyboard add a melancholic contrast, but the rest of the instruments make this one of Aldrich's more effervescent offerings.

By October of 1969, critic Gene Lees had all of his prejudices intact when reviewing Percy

Faith and His Orchestra's album, *The Windmills of Your Mind*: "Faith is an imaginative, excellent, and underrated—at least by hippies in the profession—arranger and composer. And the recent albums he's been making of the latest hits have been remarkably good." Lees poisoned his praise, however, with unkind words for the rash of albums instrumentally interpreting popular songs that he did not like: "This month, it's *de rigueur* to record 'Aquarius' and/or 'Galveston,' both miserable but successful songs, and 'The Windmills of Your Mind.'" For Lees, *Hair's* song about Jupiter aligning with Mars joined a hit list of future "chestnuts" that many loved but that snootier ears of the time would not abide.

That same year, Percy Faith, His Orchestra & Chorus did record two *Hair* songs, including Lees' dreaded "Aquarius," on *Love Theme from "Romeo & Juliet."* Faith adapts "Aquarius" and "Good Morning Starshine" as vehicles for his voices to accompany the orchestrations. Like his Columbia Records compère Ray Conniff, Faith helped to establish a trend for choruses (in his case female singers), not just to supply "la-la-la"s but to sing the words. The effect, while exposing the lyrics, allows the vocals to function more as an additional instrument.

In 1970, David Rose and His Orchestra's album *Happy Heart* embellished tunes by the Beatles, Burt Bacharach, Donovan, and MacDermot. "Aquarius" fluctuates from full strings to a harpsichord to an organ, with brass and a mischievous lead guitar weaving in and out. This, like many elevator-music interpretations, has a layered effect: a procession of star instruments, one taking over from another as the track advances.

For those who enjoyed the bells and whistles of horns, feisty drums, and occasional romantic guitars, Edmundo Ros and His Orchestra offered *Hair Goes Latin*, also from 1970, on the Decca Phase 4 label. This album was part of the Latinized Easy-Listening subset—"The Girl from Ipanema," "Summer Samba (So Nice)"—that prompted Julius Wechter and his Baja Marimba Band to add some salsa to the ganja on their 1967 rendition of the Association's "Along Comes Mary." On "Manchester England," Ros' brassy ensemble rumbas along to the Anglo airs. As his trumpets play softly in unison, Ros also manages a good rendition of "Frank Mills," a breathy, baroque-tinted paean to young love that briefly takes the musical into a sweeter direction.

Then there is Mort Garson, who takes "Frank Mills" to another world. Among the talents behind the Hollyridge Strings and their surrealistic "Strawberry Fields Forever," Garson gives the song a pleasing Moog rendition on his 1969 album *Electronic Hair Pieces*—one of Garson's several endeavors to win a place among synthesizer pioneers. While the Moog seems ever-present, there are hints of a genuine harpsichord in the background, making his "Frank Mills" arouse visions of slow dancing inside a futuristic ballroom with roots in the past. This is one example of the link between psychedelia and its "space rock" offspring—maybe even signs of "new age."

Garson's introduction is, of course, "Aquarius"—cosmic baroque with lots of quirky effects but close enough to the original before the multi-layered-dream effects freak out on the fade out. Taking on almost all of the *Hair* tracks, Garson is his astral best on "Good Morning Starshine," as the bizarre keyboard repeats each note of Mac-Dermot's melody to perfection, and the Moog (sounding like a talking robot) provides the kind of background music that might pipe out from the ceiling of that surrealistic lounge from *A Clockwork Orange* or the "Spaceport Cantina" in *Star Wars*.

This mainstreaming of the "Tribal Love-Rock Musical" and the "revolution" in general got more amusing on the 1969 London Records album entitled *Love is All* by the Les Reed Orchestra and the Eddie Lester Singers (which shared both Mantovani's engineer Arthur Lilley and producer Tony D'Amato). They pay light-hearted respects to "Good Morning Starshine," but the showstopper is the opening track, their rendition of Thunderclap Newman's "Something in the Air," the supposed call for insurrection that appeared in both *The Strawberry Statement* and *The Magic Christian*. The drums and a discreet guitar come close to the original, but the string-laden orchestra and the Singers' more traditional on-the-melody choir create an atmosphere that the Weather Underground would have condemned as "counter-revolutionary."

In the 2009 *Theater Talk* show that captured MacDermot in a nostalgic drift, Susan Haskins went on to discuss *Hair*'s major nemesis: the methamphetamine craze. She cited it as "… a dark side to the peace-love hippie movement. And that even in the company of *Hair*, there was a lot of drug abuse backstage, some people had nervous breakdowns… and there were orgies backstage (and that was fine), except people wouldn't make their entrances on time. One member of the cast died of a heroin overdose… there were stories that people didn't even know who was going to sing 'Aquarius' until the curtain went up."

Haskins then attempted to preserve memories of *Hair*'s degenerate "authenticity," reminding MacDermot, the other guests, and the television audience that the real *Hair* was quite a spectacle of grandeur and tragedy. Then, MacDermot succinctly dismissed her wild tales: "I think it's exaggerated… I was playing piano and never heard an orgy." ☾

THE "NEW MUZAK" STEREO

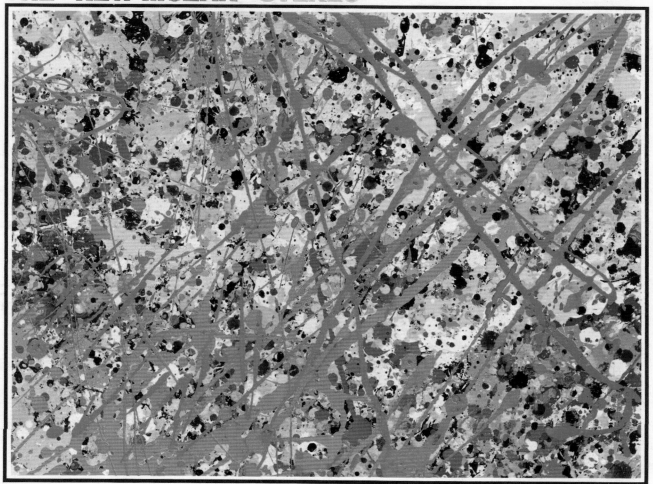

Reveille

MUZAK®—SPECIALISTS IN THE PHYSIOLOGICAL AND PSYCHOLOGICAL APPLICATIONS OF MUSIC

THE "NEW MUZAK"

The assignment was to create a visual display that would capture the essence of MUZAK's functional program in colors, forms, and values.

After probing and interviewing MUZAK psychologists, musicologists and programmers, artist Ray Harrow succeeded in pinpointing two unique qualities that make MUZAK more than music—contemporary arrangements of internationally popular selections, and the functional ascending program.

To represent MUZAK's contemporary international sound, Harrow selected an up-to-date abstract format, and rendered it in oils. He was particularly cautious to avoid painting recognizable shapes. Instead, he took advantage of psychological findings that reveal how colors and shapes affect human behavior. He used these visual tools to evoke carefully calculated physiological and psychological effects, just as MUZAK uses sound.

For example, experiments have shown that people associate mood-tones with definite colors. Psychologist Lois B. Wexner found that exciting or stimulating moods remind many of us of red. On the other hand, calm, peaceful, serene, or soothing moods suggest green and blue. Thus the red tones which dominate this painting not only suggest contemporaneity, but symbolize the music's stimulating psychological effect on listeners.

Since MUZAK programs selections into a rising or ascending order—gradually increasing musical stimulation to offset sagging performance—the left side of the painting begins with more muted colors that suggest calmer moods. As the program continues, toward the right side of the painting, the rising red figure depicts progressively livelier music. These lighter and brighter colors mirror the program's greater stimulation value.

Steeper vertical strokes—and even the painting's "focus"—are keyed to MUZAK's exclusive ascending program. The program begins with soft, fuzzy strokes, progressing smoothly to a sharper, almost crystalline quality as the program gains in stimulation value.

The composition is entitled "Reveille" because it visualizes the wake-up sound of the "New MUZAK"—bright, stimulating, and contemporary, with emphasis on variety, to combat today's ever-increasing boredom, tension, and fatigue.

Reproduced on the other side is the finished painting—actually, a miniature visually-programmed environment, paralleling MUZAK's psychologically programmed environment of sound. Ray Harrow's painting is a capsule definition of the science of MUZAK— functional art, to show you how functional music by MUZAK creates an environment conducive to efficiency and productivity.

William Wokoun, Ph.D.

MUZAK TODAY

THE MUZAK BOARD OF SCIENTIFIC ADVISORS

MUZAK has undergone a striking metamorphosis since its pioneering days in developing concepts of environmental music. Today, as specialists in the physiological and psychological applications of music, MUZAK is concerned with developments in vigilance and human factors research, automobile driver safety, medical and dental studies, noise control, the influence of color and music on emotions and of course, the effects of scientifically planned music on work productivity and efficiency, among others. Professional guidance is provided by the MUZAK Board of Scientific Advisors which consists of distinguished professionals in the field of education, industrial engineering, medicine, psychology and human factors. Under the guidance of the Board, MUZAK aims to make dramatic contributions to the business community through new discoveries in the scientific applications of music.

MUZAK: A TOOL OF MANAGEMENT

Unlike ordinary music or so-called background music, MUZAK is a non-entertainment medium, employing rhythm, tempo, instrumentation, etc., to scientifically-determined specifications. Different types of arrangements and selections are planned for different times of the day to achieve predetermined effects. In work situations, independent studies have documented the effectiveness of MUZAK programs in improving employee attitude, efficiency and productivity. In commercial applications, special MUZAK programs are employed to create environmental conditions conducive to improved customer relations and profits.

MUZAK: INTERNATIONALLY ACCEPTED

The success of MUZAK is manifest in its continued and growing utilization as a management tool by companies large and small throughout the world. Today, MUZAK is represented in Argentina, Australia, Belgium, Brazil, Canada, Colombia, Denmark, Finland, France, Germany, Great Britain, Israel, Japan, Mexico, New Zealand, Norway, Peru, Philippines, Spain, Switzerland, United States and Uruguay. Because it is a non-entertainment medium employing music only as the raw material of its service, MUZAK is universally accepted and effective in all countries in which it operates.

STEREO-33⅓ RPM

Segment A	Segment B
Through The Eyes Of A Child (Un Jour, Un Enfant)	Johnny One Time
En El Rincon Del Alma	The River (Le Colline Sono In Fiore)
Sunshine Wine	Hooked On A Feeling
Jennifer Jennings	Cafe Melody
Aquarius	Boom Bang-A-Bang
Miniskirt	I'm Livin' In Shame

Leading authorities on functional music therapy have found that music design consists of several components which variously affect the listener (e.g. tempo, rhythm, instrumentation and orchestra size). MUZAK continuously screens new compositions published throughout the world. Not every composition is good MUZAK material because certain entertainment devices incorporated into the score, preclude the possibility of adapting the selection to functional music purposes.

The selections you hear on this stereo recording are typical of the selections heard by an estimated 65 million people each day in twenty-two countries and countless cities, ranging alphabetically from Aarhus (Denmark) to Zurich (Switzerland). Also, like the MUZAK program itself, both sides of the record are programmed in an ascending sequence of increasing stimulation.

ARRANGING & RECORDING

MUZAK selects, arranges, and records its own music—specifically and exclusively for functional use. The distracting or irritating musical devices of ordinary entertainment music are avoided. MUZAK tapes new music continuously using top-name arrangers.

TAPING

Programs are recorded on 8-hour reels of tape in elaborate MUZAK studios. Rigid standards are maintained to insure crucial timing and crystal-clear sound. Over 600 quality control checks are made on each MUZAK tape.

TRANSMISSION

MUZAK programs are transmitted from central studios via leased telephone lines or special FM facilities. Precise timing is assured by automated patented MUZAK tape reproducing units, accurate to within two seconds during any 8-hour period. In standard MUZAK operations, central studios play 3285 professional 8-hour tapes, per subscriber, over a three year period. That's 26,289 hours of fresh programs; a fresh **new** program every day.

H-1(1) 79   MUZAK® ©Copyright 1969

SLEEP SAFE AND WARM

CHAPTER 11

"I CONTEND AN ABIDING SENSE OF IRONY OVER ALL I DO."

—JIM MORRISON

With political riots and assassinations, an escalating war in Southeast Asia, the drug culture becoming less peaceful and more dangerous, and the 1967 "Summer of Love" morphing into the 1968 "summer of hate," many Americans accumulated so much emotional debt that they needed a sweet and soothing pop lullaby. Though cloaked in a lovely waltz, this "lullaby" nonetheless conformed to the psychedelic era's *Through the Looking Glass* reversals by getting tangled up in Satanism.

Christopher Komeda's "Lullaby from *Rosemary's Baby*" opened and closed Roman Polanski's 1968 movie about the passive and vulnerable Rosemary Woodhouse who, without her knowledge, succumbs to a plot that her ambitious actor-husband and a coven of witches cook up to have the Devil impregnate her. The movie (as well as Ira Levin's novel) was one more taunt coming from two extremes: Satanists were excited to see the portrayal of their master's Technicolor return, while Godists saw the movie as another warning to an apathetic and immoral society heading toward the "Final Judgment."

The song itself, however, was a charming reminder of those maternal nursery rhymes designed to comfort frightened children. Mia Farrow's Rosemary hums it with diffident "la la la"s—a wordless apology to her misbegotten offspring and a cradle song for withered adults. By August 17th of 1968, its melodic beauty escaped the movie's dark shadow to ascend to #33 on *Billboard*'s Easy-Listening chart, just two pegs down from Paul Mauriat's version of "San Francisco (Be Sure to Wear Flowers in Your Hair)."

In 1967, Scott McKenzie sang about San Francisco as a place full of "gentle people," in keeping with John Phillips' "California Dreamin'" wish to be "safe and warm" in an otherwise hostile world. McKenzie's recording also mentioned "a strange vibration," words that resonated as the "new generation" drifted into murkier corners. But the skies were already starting to show an overcast by the summer of 1965, when the Lettermen used the "safe and warm" refrain on their vocal version of "Theme from *A Summer Place*" with Mack Discant's lyrics.

Larry Kusik and Eddie Snyder added English words to Komeda's "Lullaby," with the alternate title "Sleep Safe and Warm." Claudine Longet, with her occasional penchant for the macabre, also sang it like a terrified child on her 1968 A&M single. The motherly words could easily fool listeners into forgetting about devils: "Sleep safe and warm / From my arms no power can take you / Sleep safe and warm / Till my morning kisses awake you / In the softness of the night / Like a silver-colored kite / All your fears will fly and disappear / By morning's light."

Relaxing and enchanting, "Lullaby from *Rosemary's Baby*" acquired an Easy-Listening life of its own. In 1968, Paramount Pictures' two biggest box office progeny were *Rosemary's Baby* and *The Odd Couple*, both having theme songs popular enough to be among that year's most recorded. Among other instrumental artists to play Rosemary's "Lullaby" were the Brass Ring, Floyd Cramer, Nick De Caro, Leroy Holmes, Enoch Light, the Living Strings, the London Pops Orchestra, Hugo Montenegro, 101 Strings, Billy Vaughn, and Hugo Winterhalter.

In early 1969, fears metastasized. Pre-Woodstock jitters allowed *Billboard*'s Easy-Listening category to reflect some generational bonding as a troubled culture craved sonic relief, even when some of the tunes had daunting overtones. The year kicked off with Glen Campbell's recording of "Wichita Lineman," Jimmy Webb's chilling tale of lost love and stray communications signals, at #7 on *Billboard*'s Easy-Listening chart, and the Larry Page Orchestra's strings-and-brass cover version appearing at #38. At #28 was the Ray Conniff Singers' half-cheerful/half-scary cover of "I've Got My Eyes on You." On the more gleeful side, Roger Williams' rendition of the Glen Campbell hit "Galveston" was further down the roster, along with Hugo Montenegro and His Orchestra and Singers' eccentric salute to the Turtles' "Happy Together."

In March, the New Colony Six entered *Billboard*'s Easy-Listening category with "Things I'd Like to Say," a sad, romantic ballad with a crystal-clear message for those who had altered their minds, survived the "Summer of Love," and lived to remember their unfulfilled dreams. Muzak soon followed with a warm rendition by Dave Terry and His Orchestra, filled with strings, horns, electric guitars, and marimbas—another fine example of Muzak's layered effect that retained the New Colony Six's reflective mood while attempting to prevent workaday listeners from getting depressed. That same month, the Association once again made *Billboard*'s Easy-Listening grade with their puckish title theme to the film *Goodbye Columbus*. Nick De Caro (who had arranged for the Sandpipers) also appeared on the same list with his instrumental version of James Last's "Happy Heart."

A cover story in *Billboard*'s May 31st issue heralded changes: "Pop music is getting softer. There's been a noticeable 'soft sound' creeping into the works of the hard rock groups… Instrumentals, too, are once again getting a share of the pop action. Among the instrumental LPs scoring in the current *Billboard* chart are those by Percy Faith, Ray Conniff, Henry Mancini, Ray Charles [of Ray Charles Singers fame], Roger Williams, Sergio Mendes, Tommy Garrett, Billy Vaughn, Boots Randolph, and Paul Mauriat."

The trend occasionally worked both ways, as some of these instrumental versions revealed how the psychedelic years rubbed off on Easy-Listening audiences, who grew to appreciate bits of the "weird." The Brass Ring's take on Rosemary's "Lullaby" included Vinnie Bell's "water guitar." The middle part of the recording changed to an incongruous brassy and upbeat tempo, with Bell's wah-wah pedal documenting how such trippy touches earned mainstream appeal.

The inter-generational chemistry intensified from May to June. Henry Mancini's "Love Theme from *Romeo & Juliet*," from the Franco Zeffirelli movie that tried to tie in the era's disaffected youth with Shakespeare's alienated lovers, remained at *Billboard*'s Pop and Easy-Listening #1. Mancini's recording of the Nino Rota composition was fraught with seductive piano and strings, but the tone (reflecting Shakespeare's play about impossible romance and inevitable suicide) straddled a fine line between being melancholy and sweetly sentimental. Likewise, Franck Pourcel entered Easy-Listening's May chart with the strings, harpsichord, and a surrealistic choir on a cautionary and downcast instrumental called "The Lonely Season." In contrast, Mason Williams followed up his hit "Classical Gas" with similar guitar flourishes against an orchestra on an update of the traditional English folk tune "Greensleeves," and Sergio Mendes & Brasil '66 sang about a "Pretty World," this time with subtle violins to connote visions of a balloon-filled summertime.

In July of 1969, "Theme from *A Summer Place*," the instrumental favorite that had ushered in the '60s, re-emerged. The Ventures released their electric-surf tribute, while Percy Faith, who had popularized the Max Steiner tune, revived it with a feathery, female chorus. Meanwhile Crosby, Stills & Nash (before adding Young) tried pulling the era into a folksier mode. The same year that the trio admitted to being "scared shitless" at Woodstock during their performance of "Suite: Judy Blue Eyes," Liberace opened his album *A Brand New Me* with a bejeweled interpretation. Joni Mitchell made up for missing out on the festival by attempting to transmute mud into "stardust" on a song called "Woodstock." Ronnie Aldrich, armed with his double-tracked pianos, would be among those revamping her melody with his version on the 1971 album *Love Story*. On July 21, three weeks before the vast swath of America's middle-class youth rollicked in the Woodstock muck, Apollo 11's Neil Armstrong and Buzz Aldrin became the first humans to officially step on the lunar surface. NASA's "giant leap for mankind" was a great accomplishment, but it also left some feeling nervous. Apollo 11 did, after all, inspire Henry Mancini's Orchestra and Chorus to update Beethoven's spine-tingling *Moonlight Sonata*. The Johnny Harris Orchestra released a heavenly yet slightly ominous space-age tribute called "Footprints on the Moon," which Francis Lai and Liberace also recorded.

Another macabre instrumental from 1969 occupied both the Pop and Easy-Listening categories. The Charles Randolph Grean Sounde's recording of "Quentin's Theme" brought Robert Cobert's composition for *Dark Shadows*—a soap opera about people with *real* problems—to a larger audience. By then, *Dark Shadows* had evolved

from its initial gothic melodrama to a full-fledged daytime nightmare engorged with European folklore: ghosts, vampires, werewolves, and a variation on the Frankenstein monster. Grean, once an A&R director for RCA and Dot Records as well as a recurrent Muzak arranger, took Cobert's mesmerizing waltz further out into the stratosphere, set to echoing strings, a still-fashionable harpsichord, and a wordless female chorus to conjure up psychedelic images of skaters suspended on an interdimensional rink.

As the composers and performers of *Hair* continued to wail about America "dying," their messages about an Aquarian redemption were mixed. *Hair* celebrated the end of the Piscean age and the dawning of "harmony and understanding," but others were pulling the youth market into creepier places. "We blew it," Peter Fonda admitted to Dennis Hopper at the end of *Easy Rider*. Rado, Ragni, and MacDermot's "Ripped Open by Metal Explosions" signaled the heavy-metal culture started by Iron Butterfly, Led Zeppelin, and Ozzy Osbourne that became "heavier" as touchy-feely tribes moved over for arena-rock rowdies. Triggering more unease, the Nebraska duo Zager & Evans released the apocalyptic #1 single "In the Year 2525." This did not deter Raymond Lefevre from easing the tune later on, deleting the lyrics and giving the melody a glistening finish on his 1972 album *Oh Happy Day*.

The end of the '60s was not all gloom and counterculture manipulation. A group calling itself the Electric Indian got more playful with "Keem-O-Sabe," a percussion and orchestra allusion to Tonto's nickname for the Lone Ranger. Germany's Bert Kaempfert became prominent in America at the dawn of the '60s with his #1 instrumental "Wonderland by Night" and such subsequent melodies as "Strangers in the Night" and "Moon Over Naples" (which became "Spanish Eyes"), but he took refuge behind a silky string orchestra as his strict-tempo trumpet covered Joe South's "Games People Play." Jimmy Wisner, who arranged the Cowsills' 1967 gem "The Rain, the Park, and Other Things," became the Jimmy Wisner Sound and combined playful harpsichord, tambourine, flute, trumpet, and string pizzicato on the single "Manhattan Safari."

Meanwhile, Ferrante & Teicher's version of John Barry's theme to *Midnight Cowboy*, where Vinnie Bell re-applied his mind-massaging "water guitar," became one of the most popular instrumentals of 1969. In 1970, Bob Dylan's "Lay Lady Lay" would become a *Billboard* Pop smash that showed up simultaneously in the Easy-Listening category. Tinkling away in a parallel world, Ferrante & Teicher rejoined Bell for an up-tempo "water guitar" treatment of "Lay Lady Lay" that summoned more auditory hallucinations than Dylan's original.

When releasing *The Soft Parade* in the summer of 1969, the Doors started to fall out of favor among the "authenticity" police. The Robby Krieger-composed single "Wishful Sinful," despite Morrison-ish lyrics implying Freudian incest or maybe even someone being drowned, is a gorgeous composition—especially when the strings and woodwinds go into a pastoral interlude. Backed by the Los Angeles Philharmonic, its arranger Paul Harris, who supplied the organ and piano for Mama Cass' "Dream a Little Dream of Me" a year before, also led the band into a Vegas-style revue on "Tell All the People" and the more successful single "Touch Me." Even on *The Soft Parade*'s dissonant title song, Morrison (two years from oblivion) intoned, "I can't make it, anymore" and admitted to seeking "soft asylum" and "a place to hide."

With his "abiding sense of irony," Morrison might have enjoyed subverting his marketable bad-boy image by crooning "Wishful Sinful" before a full orchestra, but he was often drugged, drunk, and unpredictable. When Easy-Listening's allure seemed too threatening, he recoiled back to the safer persona of a jazz-happy beat poet or a white bluesman. Some in the underground press were especially harsh during Morrison's desperate hours. Tracks like "Wishful Sinful" prompted *Rolling Stone*'s Alec Dubro to go apoplectic: "While the Doors' *reductio-ad-absurdum* poetry could usually be disguised by invigorating (if not very convincing) emotion, these damn songs stick that idiocy right up front and surround it with the most cliché-ridden sounds this side of the 101 Strings." The affronted Dubro also suggested such alternate album titles as "The Soft Touch."

Despite the winning melody, "Wishful Sinful" got virtually no attention from Easy-Listening instrumentalists—except for America's major elevator-music provider. In the late '60s, when the company still boasted about reinterpreting pop songs shortly after their release, Muzak recorded a version on April 29, 1969 with Sid Bass and His Orchestra, exactly a month after the Doors' record peaked at #44 on *Billboard*'s "Top Pop Singles." Without the weight of the words, the tune alone could be uplifting.

The decade that had evoked so much ecstasy and dread closed with the elevator music still intact. Muzak survived the madness because the company had already braved previous dark scandals, such as when they learned to avoid playing "I've Got a Feeling I'm Falling" on its special jet-plane service. The term "Muzak" had also morphed into a larger concept, usually a prejudicial decree and a pejorative label for any music that seemed insufficiently edgy. In October of 1968, *Rolling Stone* critic Jim Miller described the title track on Pink Floyd's *A Saucerful of Secrets* as "eleven minutes of psychedelic Muzak, hardly electronic music, but hardly creative rock either." In time, the term got more complex, even complimentary, as again in the case of Pink Floyd and their 1971 album *Meddle.* Stuart Shea's book *Pink Floyd FAQ: Everything Left to Know … and More!* cites critic Lynn Van Matre,

who described the group's output as "a sort of psychedelic Muzak," but she also turned the tables by calling the music "Very strange, and very fine."

Despite the calming cadences obscuring its sinister origins, Rosemary's "Lullaby" had acquired new baggage by August of 1969, when life imitated art. Director Roman Polanski's pregnant wife Sharon Tate was found bludgeoned in the infamous slaughter at Cielo Drive in Benedict Canyon. Headlines about the Tate-LaBianca murders and their satanic trappings threw more manna to the feast of fiends. Paranoia struck deep into David Crosby as he armed himself and yelled to a reporter in a telephone interview: "They're killing anyone with property." At the Altamont concert in December, when Mick Jagger pretended to elicit Satan's sympathy but panicked when hell broke loose on his watch, the bedlam threatened to upstage the Winter Solstice.

Amid these crazy coincidences, sinister rites, and soothing music's attempt to relieve some of the pain, the quiet yet queasy "Sleep Safe and Warm," with its glimmer of warmth and tinge of irony, was Easy-Listening balm for those afraid of the approaching '70s. The psychedelic decade's Day-Glo hues were fading into "earth tones"—an appropriate metaphor for the colors of rust and stale blood. ❤

181

"YESTERDAY'S HITS ARE TODAY'S MUZAK, AND TODAY'S HITS ARE TOMORROW'S MUZAK."

—NELSON RIDDLE

Transitioning out of the '60s, cultures clashed and melded. While still in the Hollies, Graham Nash was disturbed by a Diane Arbus photograph of an angry little boy holding a toy grenade. The image struck him as a symbol of a violent culture and inspired him to compose "Teach Your Children," which Crosby, Stills, Nash & Young released in the summer of 1970. It predictably made it to *Billboard*'s Top 40 Pop category but also appeared among its Easy-Listening titles at the same time.

In July of that year, Art Linkletter also had the fate of children on his mind when he continued his anti-drug crusade at *Billboard*'s Annual Radio Programming Forum, warning "half our youngsters will be freaking out within three years if it continues." He also cited LSD as "the most dangerous single drug" and snarled at what he called the "easy familiar, non-shockable" term "acid rock." By 1971, he even served as an adviser to President Nixon, around the time that John Lennon had made it to Nixon's legendary "Enemies List." Linkletter scoffed at the public's relative apathy to Lennon's previous drug bust: "Lennon is an example of how far we have come. It is another callus on top of the sensitivity of young people."Beatles producer George Martin also attended the *Billboard* Forum but tried to deflect. He instead asserted that the pop music industry should not bear the blame for widespread drug use. He did address Linkletter's assault on Beatle lyrics, claiming there were

many times when listeners called in or wrote to his studios to describe double meanings about drugs or sex that were, in his estimation, imaginary. In the meantime, many of those same Beatles tunes inspired "Easy" instrumental spinoffs that wafted into the mainstream.

Despite psychedelic pop's troubled reputation, and Vice President Spiro Agnew's alliance with Linkletter in haranguing the public about the hazards of trippy lyrics, more of the songs that either celebrated or alluded to "turning on" developed Easy-Listening identities. One example is the 1969 album *Contemporary Sound of Nelson Riddle*. Renowned keyboardist Lincoln Mayorga joined a brass and strings section in a tribute to such timely turn-ons as "Light My Fire" and Dino, Desi & Billy's slice of 1968 sunshine-pop, "Tell Someone You Love Them." While Riddle supplemented his strings with fits of cosmetic jazz, the album stood comfortably in the "Easy-Listening" bin, ignored or disdained by "purists." Morgan Ames nearly had a conniption when reviewing it in *High Fidelity*: "What has this entire computerized, drab, supermarket rock to do with one of our finest arrangers?" But Riddle, liberated from the aesthetic fetters that critics tried to impose on him, had no apologies in the early 1980s, when he spent several days at Muzak's studios, re-recording much of his previous work for the company's background purposes.

Like Riddle, other accomplished instrumentalists coasted along the Easy-Listening melody track, with varying results. On his 1970 album *Franck Pourcel Meets the Beatles*, the distinguished French arranger offered enigmatic re-entries into "Penny Lane" and "Here, There, and Everywhere." He then reshaped the Beatles' hard-rocking "I Me Mine" into finger-sandwich servings of strings and other quaint embellishments. The English-teatime effect intensified just when listeners feared Pourcel might ruin the mood by rocking out at the song's bridge, when the Beatles repeat "I-I-me-me-mine" as if on speed or singing in tongues. Pourcel's orchestra instead pulled a complete reversal, adding a romantic flamenco guitar for a softer, more seductive atmosphere. Despite this gentle treatment, his version never swayed from the core tune hiding beneath George Harrison's rollicking rhythm. Those familiar with the track, from the Beatles' swansong album *Let It Be*, would still recognize it, even after Pourcel reconstructed it to an extreme.

Also in 1970, a group of Philadelphia studio musicians became the Assembled Multitude and entered the Top 40 with their "Overture from *Tommy*," a stately tribute to the Who's rock opera about "a deaf, dumb, and blind kid" who, at one point, seeks a cure from an "Acid Queen." With the single, they also released an album that continued using strings, brass, and electric guitar to interpret songs already evoking psychedelic nostalgia. They included "MacArthur Park" and "Woodstock," as well as the Beatles' "While My Guitar Gently Weeps" and "I Want You (She's So Heavy)."

The Assembled Multitude's unexpected highlight was their version of Crosby, Stills, Nash & Young's "Ohio." The Kent State shootings occurred on May 4 of that year, CSNY's "Ohio" came out on Atlantic a month later, and the Multitude's instrumental arrived on the same label shortly thereafter. The Multitude recreated it with drums, horns, sitar, and the contrast of soothing violins reminiscent of a movie score. This schizoid merger between the song's protest origins and the Multitude's studio maneuvers was another example of how a beguiling melody and beat could ultimately override topical politics, no matter how tragic. CSNY's dissident Top 40 hit raised some timely ire, but it too was destined to become another "classic rock" commodity.

Already sanctified by the London Festival Orchestra on *Days of Future Passed*, the Moody Blues were familiar with pop's more ornate side. Peter Knight's gorgeously arranged "Nights in White Satin," after bubbling under in 1968 as a single the first time, got re-released in 1972 to greater success when reaching *Billboard*'s #2. Its dirge-like reflection on people espousing "thoughts they cannot defend" apparently had a greater impact on early '70s America, with continued radio play into the summer of 1973. By then, as the Watergate scandal loomed, feelings of cynicism and impending dread overshadowed any remaining fascination with '60s ideals.

The Moody Blues elicited several Easy-Listening tributes. Franck Pourcel's "Nights in White

STEREO/SP 44204

A MYSTIC PORTRAIT OF THE MOODY BLUES

WERNER MÜLLER
and the London Festival Orchestra and Chorus

PHASE 4 STEREO

Satin" was one of the best, as it captured the original's plaintive cries with deep, dark strings. On his 1971 album *El Condor Pasa*, Paul Mauriat got mixed results on "Melancholy Man" when he merged his strings, horns, and guitar to a beat that is harsher than the more contemplative original from the 1970 Moody Blues LP *A Question of Balance*. The 1973 album *New Songs of the Seventies*, by the Sounds of the Seventies Orchestra, included four-channel Quadraphonic salutes to both "Nights in White Satin" and, from the 1972 album *Seventh Sojourn*, "Isn't Life Strange." Focusing on English psychedelia, the Sounds of the Seventies Orchestra also adapted "A Whiter Shade of Pale" and provided another tribute to the "*Tommy* Overture."

Other Moody melodies like "Tuesday Afternoon," from *Days of Future Passed*, and "The Story in Your Eyes," from the 1971 album *Every Good Boy Deserves Favour*, got renewed attention in 1974, when German composer and conductor Werner Müller joined the London Festival Orchestra and Chorus for *A Mystic Portrait of the Moody Blues*. The vigorous symphonic sweeps seemed at times grandiose, but the accompanying acoustic guitars, drums, horns, and woodwinds helped to smooth any tension. The vocal chorus, however, apparently influenced by the kind of gospel singing that caught on in musicals like *Hair* and *Godspell*, distracted from what would have survived better as instrumentals.

Ronnie Aldrich played it Moody as early as 1969 on his album *It's Happening Now*, adding comical, bouncy effects on an interpretation of "Ride My See-Saw" from the 1968 release *In Search of the Lost Chord*—the same Moody Blues album featuring "Legend of a Mind," which proclaims, "Timothy Leary's dead / No, n-n-no he's outside looking in." Ten years later, Aldrich's *Tomorrow's Yesterdays* used the "two pianos" technique on "Nights in White Satin." The orchestra's cello and bass guitar sulked along to Aldrich's mournful keys. On the same album, Aldrich also reintroduced "The Fool on the Hill" with the original Beatles arrangement: again, using the piano and orchestra to bring out more of its intended sorrow and wonder. Aldrich closed *Tomorrow's Yesterdays* with appropriate space-age effects, blending his piano with the strings and a chorus (called "The Ladybirds") in a flashback to "Lucy in the Sky with Diamonds."

Reader's Digest, that bastion of middle-class decorum, released two multi-album volumes that reflected and also respected pop's changing soundscape: one in 1969 called *Love is Blue: Music in a Mellow Mood* and another the following year called *Happiness Is… Up-Up and Away with the Happy Hits of Today*. Featuring top-notch orchestrations, and an assortment of both distinguished and obscure names, these collections kept the psychedelic elevator running.

Tributes included "All You Need is Love" (Norman Percival), "A Day in the Life" (Ken

Thorne), "Here, There, and Everywhere" (Peter King), "Mr. Tambourine Man" (Johnny Harris), "Jennifer Juniper" and "The Mighty Quinn" (Arthur Greenslade), and "Norwegian Wood," "For What It's Worth," and "A Whiter Shade of Pale" (Perry Botkin, Jr.). The most surprising of all was Les Reed and His Orchestra's strings-and-brass accolade to Jefferson Airplane's "Somebody to Love." Here, violins play behind the same beat that previously had Grace Slick's laser-beam voice lamenting "When the truth is found to be lies…"

As Easy-Listening FM (or "Beautiful Music") stations multiplied in the '70s, they provided additional sources of elevator psychedelia. An airwave paragon was WPAT, which operated in Paterson, New Jersey but served the greater New York area. Its instrumental programming goes back to the '50s with its AM broadcast "Gaslight Revue," but in time the station added FM and advanced stereo, with LP tracks by the likes of Caravelli, Percy Faith, Henry Mancini, Paul Mauriat, Franck Pourcel, and Roger Williams. In 1970, WPAT was among those helping Caravelli acquire additional fame with his cover of Bob Dylan's "Wigwam," around the time when Dylan's own version showed up on *Billboard*'s Easy-Listening chart in August of that same year.

Easy-Listening FM attained a reputation for being disciplined. It had limited commercials but such a growing audience that it nonetheless drew in advertisers satisfied with trading time for more exposure. The two major FM syndicators in this category were Bonneville Broadcast Consultants and Stereo Radio Productions (or simply SRP). SRP founder Jim Schulke supposedly coined the term "Beautiful Music" for this format, but with beauty being in the ear of the beholder, "Easy-Listening" survived as the better label. Marlin Taylor, who became one of the "Easy" FM pioneers in 1963 with WDVR in Philadelphia, once described the ideal combination: "90% to 95% instrumental, and the one or two vocals that played in an hour were what you'd call 'choral,' in that they were groups of singers such as the Johnny Mann Singers and the Ray Conniff Singers."

The Ray Conniff Singers' version of "If You Could Read My Mind" was a staple on several of these channels and is an example of an "Easy" FM tune that could affect audiences in different ways. Even when attempting to sound cheerier by changing the line "But heroes often fail" into "But heroes never die," they inadvertently made Gordon Lightfoot's quasi-psychedelic love plaint (already rife with flashbacks of dark castles, old-time movies, and wishing-well ghosts) sound spookier.

These stations eventually faced a challenge. They had early warnings around 1973, when Easy-Listening instrumental titles began to disappear among *Billboard*'s lists of Top Pop Albums. Surely, those who purchased these LPs up till then did not suddenly stop buying or spontaneously combust. Perhaps *Billboard* simply reflected problems that the record companies experienced when distributing these albums, or the agenda of a new generation of editors and surveyors trying to erase these titles from the future by ignoring them. Many of the artists continued to record, but radio programmers had to look beyond *Billboard* for the latest releases. Despite decades of albums to keep them afloat, they eventually sought new material to freshen their 24/7 repertoires.

"Easy" FM started to commission and play custom-made tracks, recorded in both London and Los Angeles. By the early '70s, SRP and Bonneville got reputable arrangers and conductors like Leroy Holmes to record strictly for their stations. One of those who worked at SRP was Jim Schlichting, who also operated a store in Sherman Oaks, California called The Easy-Listening Den. There, he sold albums that by then had limited circulation.

Among the commercially available Percy Faith, Ferrante & Teicher, and Paul Mauriat LPs that he sold when other stores failed to stock them, Schlichting encountered many patrons who raved about the new slew of custom-made tracks playing on the FM dials. This inspired him to create his own production company called Starborne, through which he commissioned additional custom recordings that he licensed to similar "Easy" stations.

To help launch this endeavor, Schlichting sought out Britain's Frank Chacksfield to conduct additional sessions and help organize the music library. Chacksfield, who gained American fame in 1953 with one of the best-known instrumental versions of "Ebb Tide" and continued to record albums on the Decca/London label through the '60s and '70s, was Starborne's first Musical Director, overseeing recordings from his home in England. Soon another distinguished name joined the Starborne circuit: Sven Libaek, the former Norse sailor who grew to be a movie composer and a Muzak contributor—the one who made that nice elevator version of "Light My Fire." Libaek arranged and recorded additional Starborne tracks from his adopted home of Sydney, Australia.

Along with his "Light My Fire," Libaek provided interpretations of "The Fool on the Hill" and "Catch the Wind." Tommy Deering and His Strings added more layers of luster to "Penny Lane" and "Nights in White Satin," while Peter Murray and His Orchestra covered "Strawberry Fields Forever" and "A Day in the Life." Frank Chacksfield re-contoured Tommy James & the Shondells' "Crystal Blue Persuasion" and arranged a soothing-yet-haunting take on Bobby Vee's pre-psychedelic paean to love and paranoia, "The Night Has a Thousand Eyes."

Tallying up the custom-made releases from SRP, Bonneville, and Starborne, Easy-Listening psychedelia enjoyed a renaissance. The Nick Ingman Orchestra adorned "Hello Goodbye" with tingly strings, piano, horns, and electric bass. John Fox and His Orchestra maintained the harmonium-inspired beat that the Beatles used in "Straw-

phase **4** stereo

SP 44127
LONDON

IT'S HAPPENING NOW

RONNIE ALDRICH
AND HIS TWO PIANOS
with
THE LONDON FESTIVAL ORCHESTRA

HEY JUDE
RIDE MY SEE-SAW
CONCIERTO DE ARANJUEZ
LIGHT MY FIRE
SCARBOROUGH FAIR
BOTH SIDES NOW
THEME FROM "ELVIRA MADIGAN"
SOULFUL STRUT
THE NATURE OF LOVE
I'VE GOTTA BE ME
LITTLE GREEN APPLES
FOR ONCE IN MY LIFE

berry Fields Forever," while violins and cellos contrasted with acoustic guitar, drums, and a combination of flute and flugelhorn. Fox's Orchestra combined massed strings, harps, fluttering woodwinds, and percussion on "Lucy in the Sky with Diamonds," while Ronnie Aldrich showed up with his elegiac piano to join crying violins, a harp, and some moody brass on "California Dreamin.'"

Lex De Azevedo was another significant "Easy" FM figure. The son of Alyce King of the King Sisters, he went on to forge his own musical mark, producing, among other releases, the 1968 hit "Nobody But Me" by the Human Beinz. As a musical director, he worked for *The Sonny & Cher Show*, the Jackson Five, and the Osmonds. For the "Beautiful Music" format, he got a bit more up-tempo with flute, acoustic guitar, and soprano strings on "Norwegian Wood," while a bouncing piano, embellished by violins and drums, replaced the Association's choirboy vocals on "Never My Love." Strings, horns, a surf-style bass guitar, and a synthesized approximation of the theremin filled out "Good Vibrations."

At the same time, a post-psychedelic malaise set in, as several '70s Top 40 hits seemed to be infused with sad acid flashbacks. The continual presence of strings on many of these songs made the Easy-Listening adaptors' tasks less daunting in their quest to create instrumental companions to these often-lonesome tunes. Chacksfield saluted Kansas' "Dust in the Wind." John Fox and His Or-

chestra covered America's "Lonely People," while Pat Valentino and His Orchestra helped teary eyes sparkle on a version of the Carpenters' "Rainy Days and Mondays."

Among Starborne's most impressive players was Arthur Greenslade, a well-known English arranger-conductor who had previously worked with Vic Lewis and Cyril Stapleton but moved on to make elaborate string arrangements for Chris Farlowe's 1967 version of the Jagger-Richards song "Out of Time." He arranged several of David Bowie's 1967 recordings, such as "When I Live My Dream." Greenslade also lent his lush style to French chanteuses Françoise Hardy and Sylvie Vartan, as well as the risqué 1969 Serge Gainsbourg-Jane Birkin duet "Je T'Aime ... Moi Non Plus." Through Starborne, on recordings which also made it to Muzak, Greenslade did outstanding instrumental versions of C.W. McCall's "Convoy" and Gordon Lightfoot's "Rainy Day People."

Fans of custom-made "Beautiful Music" were not alone. In the late '70s, the Canadian-American sportsman and business tycoon Jack Kent Cooke, then-chairman and chief executive of the Tele-PrompTer Corporation that also owned Muzak, liked what he heard on several "Easy" FM channels and arranged with Schlichting to license over $1.5 million worth of Starborne recordings for Muzak's library. Easy-Listening FM and the standard elevator music from Muzak were formally united. All of those stories, based on actual Otis Elevator Company advertisements from decades past, about Muzak's "lilting melody" for elevators were again proven to be more than just an urban legend.

The synthesis of Easy-Listening FM and Muzak had a healing effect on John Lennon during his final days in New York City, living with Yoko in the Dakota. Lennon had previously attempted to mock McCartney's work as "Muzak to my ears" on the 1971 song "How Do You Sleep?" but by 1980, he was humming differently. In an extensive *Playboy* interview not long before his assassination, Lennon gave a surprising answer when asked about his favorite listening choices: "Muzak or classical. I don't purchase records. I do enjoy listening to things like Japanese folk music or Indian music. My tastes are very broad. When I was a housewife, I just had Muzak on, background music, 'cuz it relaxes you."

Fortunately, the folklore growing around Muzak and other forms of elevator music was not always negative. Sometimes it came across as fascinating, mysterious, and even mind-altering. As early as 1966, Thomas Pynchon gave it sci-fi charisma. A character in *The Crying of Lot 49* is (after routine LSD doses) capable of listening to the Music by Muzak in a restaurant and figuring out, amid "all strings, reeds, and muted brass," the exact number of violins in a tune, aspiring to eventually intuit the musician's musculature and personality.

Underground filmmaker Todd Rutt recalled being astounded when hearing an instrumental ver-sion of Iron Butterfly's "In-A-Gadda-Da-Vida" at a Mr. Steak restaurant in Grand Junction, Colorado. This got him to thinking about how such ceiling serenades occupy a different and rarefied aesthetic law: "Strip away something original with orchestral strings and what you have is something so far re-moved from the real thing it assumes a new reality."

The listening might have been "Easy" all those years ago, but the circumstances got tougher. Though continually reporting on Easy-Listening FM's success, *Billboard* made its fateful decision in April of 1979 to change "Easy-Listening" to "Adult Contemporary." In a way, this alteration deterred previous confusion as Adult Contemporary (or AC) became the star vocalists' medium, leaving possible leeway for Easy-Listening to regain its instrumental prowess.

Billboard's name change also portended more trouble for those FM stations once dedicated almost entirely to what WDBN, an "Easy" chan-nel in Ohio, had described as a "Quiet Island in radio's sea of noise." Into the '80s, more and more Easy-Listening stations caught the AC bug, feeling pressure from advertisers and sponsors. The late ac-tor Robert Urich became an Adult Contemporary attaché, appearing in television ads urging people to go back to the Easy-Listening dial but to "forget what they used to play." And so the enigmatic instrumental mood faded.

Under the Adult Contemporary dictates, supermarket shoppers, instead of encountering an orchestral version of "Mellow Yellow," would likely hear the actual Donovan singing over the bananas. Donovan's mesmerizing voice, while sounding scrumptious on the home stereo, was likely less appetizing in the produce aisle.

By the late '80s and early '90s, fans of the Beatles, Donovan, or the Doors heard in public places what they could already access on their car radios, home stereos, and mix tapes. But what was the point of hearing the exact same renditions at a department store? What happened to the art of the instrumental revision and the subtle power of background music? What about the wisdom behind the idea that music has a *civic* as well as a *private* function? All of that got sacrificed in favor of a sluggish, patchwork alternative. Foregrounding drained songs of their shadow identities and forced the original recordings to stand naked and alone in a dystopian Foreground Flatland.

As late as 1989, the psychedelic side of "Easy" re-emerged, thanks to Ted Nugent—the heavy-metal badass and outspoken Muzak-hater. He offered to buy the company for $10 million just for the sadistic pleasure of wiping all of the tapes. Muzak responded by having the Jim Devlin Orchestra—one of its regular contributors—make an elevator-music version of a song that Nugent performed with the '60s Detroit band the Amboy Dukes.

"Journey to the Center of the Mind," a hit from 1968, was all that it was supposed to be: catchy, threatening, and sounding like what many imagined or dreaded as the ultimate acid trip. Its distorted guitar, disorienting rhythms, and electronically altered voices made the lead singer John Drake sound all the more "out there." Drake invited listeners to "Come along if you care / Come along if you dare." He also warned, "You might not come back," just before Nugent's mind-jerking guitar spasm.

Though "Journey" was not the most melodic of '60s entries and harder-edged than what Muzak was used to adapting, the mere fact that Muzak recorded it, and so cleverly, remains a marvel. The company could have simply gone the lethargic route and used a guitar or a saxophone to approximate the original's loud and aggressive style. Instead, they reversed the psychology, preserving the kernels of the original tune but substituting woodwinds and sonic meadows of strings to lift the song from a lysergic nightmare into a pastoral reverie. The Muzak version proves that, even without Nugent's riffs, the re-contoured variation could still arouse thoughts of a strange, but less menacing, passage.

The Jim Devlin Orchestra's "Journey to the Center of the Mind" is, in many ways, the perfect Muzak recording, sending hard rock into an altered state while keeping the shards of melody and even the beat. Unfortunately, Muzak never used the recording on its program. It was not a music rights issue but a company choice. In an effort to seem "tasteful," Muzak decided not to stray from the original recordings. Up till then, one of the most fascinating factors of Muzak—and Easy-Listening in general—was how an orchestra could maintain the melody but retain a free hand with the arrangements and often-novel instrument replacements.

Into the '90s, as the original Muzak started to fade away, the tenacious Timothy Leary defied the wrath of Art Linkletter's god, focusing less on drugs and more on the mind-shaping potential of software technology. However, with virtual reality touted as the new altered state, those seduced by such ideas journeyed so far into their own minds that they got increasingly atomized. By then, the old psychedelic notion about the right "set and setting" catered more to a bunker mentality.

Sensational talk shows made life seem even more hazardous with topics like the "Satanic Panic," stressing how the back-masking effects that once made for great psychedelia now became evidence against metal bands that allegedly sent subliminal messages instructing impressionable fans to worship the devil and to kill themselves.

LSD, still available long after many hippies traded their love beads for BMWs, often got repackaged into smaller doses, usually on blotter paper, and sometimes emblazoned with images of the *Peanuts* comic-strip character Woodstock. By then, those tripping with the hope of finding philosophical meanings in the variegations on a leaf might have been demoralized to find those around them fantasizing about owning swimming pools. Into the 21st century, CEOs from places like Silicon Valley lauded the supposed advantages of "micro-dosing," ingesting much smaller LSD hits to get more creative, focused, and productive at work.

As denizens of the new millennium fed their heads with new ideas, they were often at odds about choosing the right soundtracks to their lives. Businesses obsessed with "branding" used music to reinforce an image, piping out anything from classic rock, current pop, dance, trance, varieties of "ambient" and the mutating styles of "new age." For some, Easy-Listening took on a new allure: an inverted taboo. Its relative lack of pretense and its often outlandish ways of reinterpreting pop favorites made it sound more mystifying, especially as it became less accessible in daily life. In the late '80s, CD collections, mostly from Europe, still appeared with psychedelic re-interpretations. The highly synthesized Wallis Blue Orchestra, for example, provided spectral renditions of "San Francisco (Be Sure to Wear Flowers in Your Hair)," "Good Vibrations," "Nights in White Satin," and a quasi-psychedelic tune from 1969 that got recognized only a bit later as a "glitter" anthem: David Bowie's "Space Oddity."

Now, members of an emergent subculture, seeking alternatives to increasingly medicated, microchipped, and surveilled surroundings, are keen to turn the "truth" on its head. For them, the sounds that academia and media groupthink

195

accused of being manipulative have become an ironic escape from the "foreground" tyranny and its false freedoms of choice. When not searching through old-record bins at garage sales, those who wish to hear "classic" elevator music can also opt for streaming services. As vintage tapes and vinyl from Muzak and other background music companies like Seeburg and 3M Sound Products show up on the Internet, some refurbished psychedelic gems are bound to rematerialize.

The psychedelic era from the mid- to late '60s offered fluorescent promises of love and expanded consciousness, but it also unleashed darker moments of uncertainty and even violence. For many, the strobe light's beam calculated to ignite cosmic energy also morphed into bleak, hypnotic triggers that prompted others to surrender to psycho messiahs or to self-destruct. A healthy portion of psychedelic pop, however, offered a safety net for those who cherished the "trippy" production novelties but wanted to avoid oblivion, inspiring elevator-music maestros to extract more method out of the madness. Through it all, elevator music in its various forms had softened the edges of the visionary yet perilous days of the psychedelic '60s and their ensuing aftershocks.

These were the most challenging and most creative years for Easy-Listening, resulting in sonic adventures that even the composers, arrangers, players, conductors, and producers might not have fully anticipated. The recordings might not offer the grandiose perks that acid gurus had promised with their drug culture, but the elevator variations can help listeners keep some perspective, even a sense of being protected, as the world around them gets blurry, brittle, and more than slightly out of tune. Nothing feels and sounds sweeter than an Easy-Listening Acid Trip—but be sure to guard the "set and setting" against buzz-killing invaders that stalk the periphery. ◎

50

PSYCHEDELIC FAVORITES REFURBISHED

(BY RECORDING ARTIST AND CHRONOLOGY)

THE MYSTIC MOODS ORCHESTRA

EXTENSIONS

STEREO PHS 600-301
PLAYABLE ON MODERN MONAURAL EQUIPMENT

PHILIPS

STEREO
LST-7567

LIBERTY

A PRODUCT OF
LIBERTY RECORDS

TOMORROW'S STANDARDS
THE MARBLE ARCH ORCHESTRA

Baby, Now That I've Found You
Daydream Believer
Your Mother Should Know
Massachusetts
Judy In Disguise (With Glasses)
Hello Goodbye
Whiter Shade Of Pale
It Must Be Him
Zabadak
Thank U Very Much
Up-Up And Away
Everlasting Love

1. ALL YOU NEED IS LOVE

Ferrante & Teicher *In the Heat of the Night* United Artists UAS-6624S (1967)

Hollyridge Strings *Play Magical Mystery Tour: The Beatles Song Book Vol. 5* Capitol ST-2876 (1968)

101 Strings *Play the Hits Written by the Beatles* Alshire S-5111 (1968)

Astromusical House of Aquarius GWP ASTRO-1011 (1969)

Norman Percival and His Orchestra *Love is Blue: Music in a Mellow World* Reader's Digest RDA-77-A [4-LP Box Set] (1969)

Living Strings Play Songs of the Swingin' Sixties RCA Camden CAS-2397 (1970)

Norman Percival and His Orchestra *Happiness Is… Up Up and Away* Reader's Digest RDA-106-A [9-LP Box Set] (1970)

London Starlight Orchestra *20 Beatles Greatest Hits* Star Inc. Music CD-86021 Netherlands (1988)

Christian Colombier and His Orchestra *A Tribute to the Beatles* Reader's Digest Association ULC-035-3675 (Canada) (2009)

2. AQUARIUS

"Galt MacDermot & His Orchestra" Muzak Session June 4, 1968

Don Tweedy and His Orchestra *The Honey Touch* United Artists UAS-6661 (1968)

Astromusical House of Aquarius GWP Records ASTRO-1011 (1969)

Briarcliff Orchestra *The Briarcliff Orchestra Plays…* Harmony HS-11364 (1969)

Ronnie Aldrich & His Two Pianos (with the London Festival Orchestra) *Destination Love* London SP-44135 (1969)

Vinnie Bell *Good Morning, Starshine* Decca DL-75138 (1969)

Ray Conniff and the Singers *Jean* Columbia CS-9920 (1969)

Percy Faith, His Orchestra & Chorus *Love Theme from "Romeo & Juliet"* Columbia CS-9906 (1969)

Ferrante & Teicher *Midnight Cowboy* United Artists UAS-6725 (1969)

Enoch Light & the Brass Menagerie, Vol. II Project 3 Records PR 5042 SD (1969)

Mort Garson *Electronic Hair Pieces* A&M Records SP-4209 (1969)

Jack Gold Orchestra & Chorus *It Hurts to Say Goodbye* Columbia CS-9851 (1969)

Mike Leander Orchestra *Migration* MCA MUPS-383 (1969)

Mike Leander Orchestra *A Time for Young Love* Decca DL-75144 (1969)

Mike Leander Orchestra *Together* MCA Records CKPS-1003 U.K. (1969)

"Galt MacDermot & His Orchestra" *Reveille* Muzak Corporation H-1(1) 35-B (1969)

Mantovani *The World of Mantovani* London PS-565 (1969)

Paul Mauriat and His Orchestra *L.O.V.E.* Philips PHS-600-320 (1969)

Peter Nero *Hits From "Hair" To Hollywood* Columbia CS-9907 (1969)

101 Strings *Gold Award Hits* Alshire International S-5161 (1969)

Franck Pourcel *Aquarius* ATCO Records SD 33-299 (1969)

John Andrews Tartaglia *Good Morning Starshine* Capitol ST-280 (1969)

Terry Baxter and His Orchestra *What the World Needs Now is Love* Columbia Special Products C8SPS 1005 [8-LP box set] Canada (1970)

Big Ben Hawaiian Band *Hit Me Hawaiian* Polydor 583084 U.K. (1970)

Joe Reisman and His Orchestra *Happiness Is… Up Up and Away* Reader's Digest RDA 106-A [9-LP Box Set] (1970)

Edmundo Ros *Hair Goes Latin* London Phase 4 SP-44134 (1970)

David Rose & His Orchestra *Happy Heart* Capitol ST-393 (1970)

Sounds Orchestral *Good Morning Starshine* Pye Records NSPL-18333 U.K. (1970)

Florian Zabach *Florian Zabach and the Nashville Country Strings* Swampfire SF-205 (1970)

Helmut Zacharias *The Sensational Sound of Zacharias* Columbia TWO-298 U.K. (1970)

Klaus Wunderlich, Jerry Wilton and His Orchestra *Super Star Sound Hammond Gala* Ace Of Clubs SSS-1001 (1972)

Norrie Paramor and the Midland Radio Orchestra *Silver Serenade* BBC Records REB-272 U.K. (1977)

3. AS TEARS GO BY

Frank Chacksfield *1st Hits of 1965* Decca SKL-4666 U.K. (1965)

Mike Leander Orchestra *The Folk Hits* London PS-453 (1965)

Ray Martin and His Orchestra *Michelle, Going for Baroque* RCA Camden CAS-976 (1966)

Andrew Loog Oldham Orchestra *The Rolling Stones Songbook* London Records PS-457 (1966)

Cyril Stapleton *The Late Night Sound of Golden Hits* Pye Records NSPL-18152 U.K. (1966)

Mariano and the Unbelievables (self-titled) Capitol ST-2831 (1968)

Astromusical House of Pisces GWP Records ASTRO-1012 (1969)

Hank Levine and His Orchestra *Happiness Is… Up Up and Away* Reader's Digest RDA-106-A [9-LP Box Set] (1970)

Mike Batt Orchestra *Portrait of the Rolling Stones* DJM Silverline DJSL-005 U.K. (1971)

phase **4** stereo

SP 44142
LONDON

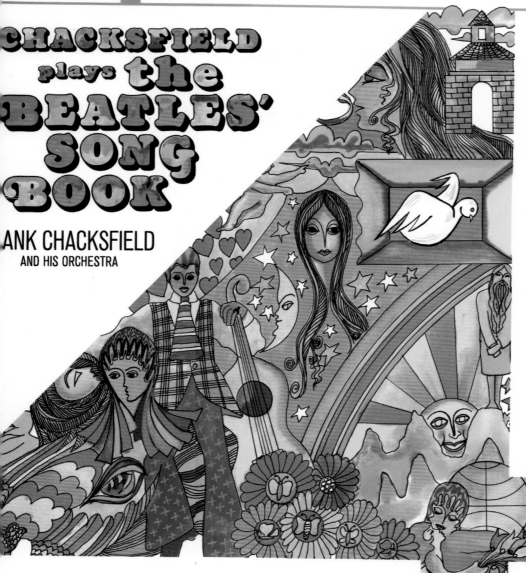

CHACKSFIELD plays the BEATLES' SONG BOOK

ANK CHACKSFIELD
AND HIS ORCHESTRA

GET BACK
MICHELLE
GOT TO GET YOU
    INTO MY LIFE
YESTERDAY
SOMETHING
HEY JUDE
A HARD DAY'S NIGHT
NORWEGIAN WOOD
TICKET TO RIDE
THE FOOL ON THE HILL
COME TOGETHER
OB-LA-DI, OB-LA-DA

SP 44136

phase **4** stereo

LONDON

Love is all
Les Reed
and his Orchestra with
THE EDDIE LESTER SINGERS

SOMETHING IN THE AIR
GOOD MORNING STARSHINE
SPINNING WHEEL
I'LL FIND MY LOVE
SPARTACUS (THE SPARTANS)
MY CHERIE AMOUR
SWEET CAROLINE
CRYSTAL BLUE PERSUASION
A WAY OF LIFE
SUGAR PIE
ON DAYS LIKE THESE
LOVE IS ALL

4. CALIFORNIA DREAMIN'

Trombones Unlimited *These Bones are Made for Walkin'* Liberty LST-7449 (1966)

The Brass Ring *The Disadvantages of You* Dunhill D-50017 (1967)

101 Strings *Sounds of Today* Alshire S-5078 (1967)

David McCallum *McCallum* Capitol ST-2748 (1968)

Enoch Light and the Brass Menagerie (self-titled) Project 3 Total Sound PR-5036-SD (1969)

Mystic Moods Orchestra *Extensions* Philips PHS-600-301 (1969)

Terry Baxter and His Orchestra *What the World Needs Now is Love* Columbia Special Products C8SPS 1005 [8-LP box set] Canada (1970)

Ronnie Aldrich *The Radio Recordings Collection* Surrey House Music CD-7001 (2011)

5. CATCH THE WIND

Mike Leander Orchestra *The Folk Hits* London PS-453 (1965)

Billy Strange *Billy Strange Plays the Hits* GNP Crescendo GNP-2012 (1965)

Vic Lewis Orchestra *The Boy in the Saffron Robe: The Vic Lewis Orchestra Plays the Music of Donovan* NEMS 6-63388 (U.K.), also as *Donovan, My Way* Epic BN-26418 (1968)

Nirvana Sitar and String Group *Sitar and Strings* Mr. G 8001 (1968)

Johnny Arthey Orchestra *The Golden Songs of Donovan* RCA Victor LSP-4106 (1969)

Mystic Moods Orchestra *Country Lovin' Folk* Philips PHS-600-351 (1971)

Sven Libaek Orchestra *Nadia's Theme* Starborne Productions (2011)

6. COLOURS

Mike Leander Orchestra *The Folk Hits* London PS-453 (1965)

Billy Strange *The Big Sound of Billy Strange and His Guitar: Folk Rock Hits* GNP Crescendo GNP-S2016 (1965)

The Les Williams Orchestra *Plays the Collected Songs of Donovan* Imperial LP-12422 (1968)

Johnny Arthey Orchestra *The Golden Songs of Donovan* RCA Victor LSP-4106 (1969)

Percy Faith, His Orchestra & Chorus *Leaving on a Jet Plane* Columbia CS-9983 (1970)

7. A DAY IN THE LIFE

Peter Knight Orchestra *Instrumental Beatles Themes from Sgt. Pepper's Lonely Hearts Club Band* Mercury SR-61132 (1967)

Gabor Szabo *Wind, Sky, & Diamonds* Impulse AS-9151 (1967)

Hollyridge Strings *Play Magical Mystery Tour: The Beatles Song Book Vol. 5* Capitol ST-2876 (1968)

John Andrews Tartaglia *Good Morning Starshine* Capitol ST-280 (1969)

Ken Thorne and His Orchestra *Happiness Is... Up Up and Away* Reader's Digest RDA-106-A [9-LP Box Set] (1970)

London Starlight Orchestra *20 Beatles Greatest Hits* Star Inc. Music CD-86021 Netherlands (1988)

Peter Murray Orchestra *Starborne Limited Edition #45* Starborne Productions (2011)

Al Di Meola *All Your Life (A Tribute To The Beatles Recorded At Abbey Road Studios, London)* Valiana VSR-169128 CD, Album, Digipak (2013)

8. DAYDREAM BELIEVER

Charles Grean and His Orchestra Muzak Session S-2451 (1967)

Marble Arch Orchestra *Tomorrow's Standards* Liberty LST-7567 (1968)

Horst Fischer/Werner Muller and His Orchestra *Trumpet for Lovers* London PS-549 (1968)

Big Jim Sullivan *Lord Sitar* Capitol ST-2916 (1968)

Pat Valentino and His Orchestra *The Radio Recording Collection, Vol. 1* Surrey House CD-7041 (2011)

Lex de Azevedo and His Orchestra *The Radio Recordings Collection, Vol. 16* Surrey House CD-7036 (2011)

9. ELEANOR RIGBY

The Baroque Inevitable (self-titled) Columbia CS-9387 (1966)

Chim Kothari *Sound of Sitar* Deram DES 18001 (1966)

George Martin *Instrumentally Salutes the Beatle Girls* United Artists UAS-6539 (1966)

Vinnie Bell *Pop Goes the Electric Sitar* Decca DL-74938 (1967)

Morton Gould *Morton Gould Makes the Scene* RCA LSP-3771 (1967)

Hollyridge Strings *The Beatles Songbook Vol. 4* Capitol ST-2656 (1967)

Kai Winding *Penny Lane & Time* Verve V6-8691 (1967)

Al Hirt *In Love with You* RCA LSP-4020 (1968)

The Mystic Moods
  Orchestra *Emotions*
  Philips PHS-600-277
  (1968)

101 Strings *Play Hits
  Written by the Beatles*
  Alshire S-5111 (1968)

Big Jim Sullivan *Lord Sitar*
  Capitol ST-2916 (1968)

The Waikikis *Midnight
  Luau* Kapp KS-3575
  (1968)

Paul Mauriat *Prevailing
  Airs* Philips PHS-600-
  280 (1969)

Mike Melvoin *The Plastic
  Cow Goes Mooooog*
  Dot Records DLP-
  25961 (1969)

Percy Faith Strings
  The Beatles Album
  Columbia C-30097
  (1970)

Franck Pourcel *Franck
  Pourcel Meets the
  Beatles* Studio 2 TWO-
  371 U.K. (1970)

Enoch Light and His
  Orchestra *Beatles
  Classics* Project 3 Total
  Sound PR4C-5084
  (1974)

Pat Valentino *Valentino's
  Morningsong* Pianolight
  PM-9702-33 (1997)

Pat Valentino and His
  Orchestra *The Radio
  Recordings Collection, Vol.
  7* Surrey House CD-
  7047 (2011)

10. EVERYONE'S GONE TO THE MOON

Percy Faith and His
  Orchestra *Themes
  for the "In" Crowd*
  Columbia CS-9241
  (1966)

Larry Page Orchestra
  Executive Suite Page
  One POLS-002 U.K.
  (1967)

Ivor Raymonde
  Orchestra and Chorus
  It's Lovely Up There
  Decca SKL-4944 U.K.
  (1968)

John Andrews Tartaglia
  Good Morning Starshine
  Capitol ST-280 (1969)

Nick Ingman Orchestra
  *Midnight Train to
  Georgia* Starborne
  Productions (2012)

Sven Libaek Orchestra
  From Russia with Love
  Starborne Productions
  (2012)

11. FOOL ON THE HILL

Groovin' Strings & Things
  Cub Records CUS-
  80,000 (1968)

Hollyridge Strings *Play
  Magical Mystery Tour:
  The Beatles Song Book
  Vol. 5* Capitol ST-2876
  (1968)

Jack Pleis and His
  Orchestra *The Sounds
  of Our Times Play Hey
  Jude* Capitol ST-117
  (1968)

Alan Tew Orchestra *Rosie*
  Columbia ELS-332
  (1968)

Astromusical House
    of Aquarius GWP
    ASTRO-1011 (1969)

Xavier Cugat and
    His Orchestra *The
    Beautiful New Sound
    of Strings* Musicor
    Records M2S-3179
    (1969)

Marty Gold *Moog Plays
    The Beatles* AVCO
    Embassy AVE-33003
    (1969)

Andre Kostelanetz and
    His Orchestra *Traces*
    Columbia CS-9823
    (1969)

Mike Leander Orchestra
    Migration MCA MUPS-
    383 (1969)

Mike Leander Orchestra
    A Time for Young Love
    Decca DL-75144
    (1969)

*Enoch Light and the Brass
    Menagerie* (self-titled)
    Project 3 Total Sound
    PR-5036-SD (1969)

Mario Said *Ev'rybody's
    Talkin'* Liberty LST-
    7601 (1969)

Cyril Stapleton Choir &
    Orchestra *Panoramic
    Lennon & McCartney*
    Pye NSPL-18274
    (1969)

Frank Chacksfield
    and His Orchestra
    *Chacksfield Plays the
    Beatles' Song Book*
    London Phase 4 SP-
    44142 (1970)

Percy Faith Strings
    The Beatles Album
    Columbia C-30097
    (1970)

Percy Faith, His
    Orchestra, and Chorus
    Those Were the Days
    Columbia CS-9762
    (1970)

Frank Hunter and His
    Orchestra Muzak
    Session S-2960

Joe Reisman and His
    Orchestra *Happiness
    Is… Up Up and Away*
    Reader's Digest RDA-
    106-A [9-LP Box Set]
    (1970)

Ronnie Aldrich *Yesterday's
    Tomorrows* Decca SKL-
    5305 U.K. (1979)

Fantastic Strings
    My Favorites Vol. 4
    Laserlight Digital 15-
    065 (1988)

London Starlight
    Orchestra *20 Beatles
    Greatest Hits* Star Inc.
    Music CD-86021
    Netherlands (1988)

*Romantic Harmonica
    Melodies* CD BMC-
    87121 France (1989)

Sven Libaek Orchestra
    Starborne Vol. #2
    Starborne Productions
    (2009)

12. GOOD MORNING, STARSHINE

"Galt MacDermot & His
    Orchestra" Muzak
    Session June 4, 1968

Midnight String Quartet
    *Rhapsodies for Young
    Lovers, Volume 3* Viva
    V-36022 (1968)

Ronnie Aldrich and His
    Two Pianos (with
    the London Festival
    Orchestra) *Destination
    Love* London SP-44135
    (1969)

Vinnie Bell *Good Morning
    Starshine* Decca DL-
    75138 (1969)

Percy Faith, His
    Orchestra & Chorus
    *Love Theme from
    "Romeo & Juliet"*
    Columbia CS-9906
    (1969)

Mort Garson *Electronic
    Hair Pieces* A&M
    Records SP-4209
    (1969)

*Enoch Light & the Brass
    Menagerie, Vol. II* Project
    3 Records PR 5042 SD
    (1969)

STEREO PS 453

THE MIKE LEANDER ORCHESTRA

MR. TAMBOURINE MAN	IT AIN'T ME BABE
AS TEARS GO BY	CATCH THE WIND
THE TIMES THEY ARE A CHANGIN'	THERE BUT FOR FORTUNE
COME AND STAY WITH ME	THIS LITTLE BIRD
I'LL NEVER FIND ANOTHER YOU	A WORLD OF OUR OWN
CONCRETE AND CLAY	COLOURS

LE GRAND ORCHESTRE DE

Paul Mauriat

GRAVURE UNIVERSELL
stéréo/mono   844 735

PHILIPS

rain and tears

alouett

ma maison et la riviè

dis-moi ce qui ne va pas

le ruisseau de mon enfance

tous les arbres sont en fleur

après tou

una canzone

mrs. robinson

eleanor rigby

oh! oui, je suis bien...

lady madonna

Peter Nero *Hits From "Hair" To Hollywood* Columbia CS-9907 (1969)

Franck Pourcel *Aquarius* ATCO Records SD 33-299 (1969)

Les Reed and His Orchestra with the Eddie Lester Singers *Love is All* London Records SP-44136 (1969)

John Andrews Tartaglia *Good Morning Starshine* Capitol ST-280 (1969)

Terry Baxter and His Orchestra *What the World Needs Now is Love* Columbia Special Products C8SPS 1005 [8-LP box set] Canada (1970)

Big Ben Hawaiian Band *Hit Me Hawaiian* Polydor 583084 U.K. (1970)

Ferrante & Teicher *Getting Together* United Artists UAS-5501 (1970)

Benny Goodman and His Orchestra *Happiness Is… Up Up and Away* Reader's Digest RDA-106-A [9-LP Box Set] (1970)

Mantovani *Mantovani Today* London PS-572 (1970)

Hugo Montenegro *Colours of Love* RCA LSP-4273 (1970)

Edmundo Ros *Hair Goes Latin* London Phase 4 SP-44134 (1970)

Sounds Orchestral *Good Morning Starshine* Pye Records NSPL-18333 U.K. (1970)

Moonlight Moods Orchestra *Themes & Dreams* Pickwick CD-PWK013 U.K. (1987)

Fantastic Strings *My Favorites Vol. 4* Laserlight Digital 15-065 (1988)

13. GOOD VIBRATIONS

Floyd Cramer *Here's What's Happening!* RCA LSP-3746 (1967)

Hollyridge Strings *Play the Beach Boys Song Book, Vol. 2* Capitol ST-2749 (1967)

Peter Knight Singers *Voices in the Night* Deram SML-702 (1967)

Steve Douglas *Reflections in a Golden Horn* Mercury SR-61217 (1969)

Hugo Montenegro *Good Vibrations* RCA LSP-4104 (1969)

Jean Michel De France *Golden Sixties* Delphine 818 894-1 France (1984)

Wallis Blue Orchestra *Digital Melodies* Cocktail Hour Series CHC-8105 France (1989)

Alan Tew Orchestra *Starborne Limited Edition #23* Starborne Productions (2011)

Lex De Azevedo *The Radio Recordings Collection, Vol. 10* Surrey House CD-7030 (2011)

14. GREEN TAMBOURINE

Terry Baxter and His Orchestra *The Best of '68* Columbia Musical Treasuries DS-414 (1968)

The Beautiful People "Green Tambourine" 7" single Roulette R-7001 (1968)

Lennon Sisters *The Lennon Sisters Today!!* Mercury SR-61164 (1968)

Enoch Light Singers *12 Smash Hits* Project 3 Total Sound PR-5021-SD (1968)

Mariano and the Unbelievables *The 25th Hour* Capitol ST-2875 (1968)

Earl Sheldon and His Orchestra [Muzak Session S-2461] (March 1968)

Sir Julian *Love is Blue* United Artists MS-21029 (1968)

Sounds Orchestral *Words* Pye Records (UK release) NSPL-18224 (1968)

Trombones Unlimited *One of Those Songs* Liberty LST-7549 (1968)

Lawrence Welk "Green Tambourine" Ranwood R-801 45 RPM 7" single (1968)

Lawrence Welk *Love is Blue* Ranwood RLP-8003 (1968)

The Young Lovers *Love Is Blue - Green Tambourine - Love Theme of Elvira Madigan* Design Records DLP-285 (1968)

Living Percussion *The Beat Goes On* RCA-Camden CAS-2255 (1969)

15. HAIR

Briarcliff Orchestra *The Briarcliff Orchestra Plays…* Harmony HS-11364 (1969)

Enoch Light & the Brass Menagerie, Vol. II Project 3 Records PR 5042 SD (1969)

Peter Nero *Hits From "Hair" To Hollywood* Columbia CS-9907 (1969)

101 Strings *Gold Award Hits* Alshire International S-5161 (1969)

Terry Baxter and His Orchestra *What the World Needs Now is Love* Columbia Special Products C8SPS 1005 [8-LP box set] Canada (1970)

Ferrante & Teicher *Getting Together* United Artists 5501 (1970)

Edmundo Ros *Hair Goes Latin* London Phase 4 SP-44134 (1970)

16. HELLO GOODBYE

The Baroque Brass (self-titled) Fontana SRF-67582 (1968)

Hollyridge Strings *Play Magical Mystery Tour: The Beatles Song Book Vol. 5* Capitol ST-2876 (1968)

Marble Arch Orchestra *Tomorrow's Standards* Liberty LST-7567 (1968)

Mariano and the Unbelievables *The 25th Hour* Capitol ST-2875 (1968)

Baker Street Philharmonic *Yesterday's Dreams* Universal Summit SRA250.093 (1970)

Enoch Light and His Orchestra *Beatles Classics* Project 3 Total Sound PR4C-5084 (1974)

101 Strings *Best of the Beatles* Madacy Records CD 628261054022 (2004)

Nick Ingman Orchestra *The Radio Recordings Collection, Vol. 4* Surrey House CD-7014 (2011)

---

17. HERE, THERE, AND EVERYWHERE

George Martin *Instrumentally Salutes the Beatle Girls* United Artists UAS-6539 (1966)

Cyril Stapleton *The Late Night Sound of Golden Hits* Pye Records NSPL-18152 U.K. (1966)

Kai Winding *Penny Lane & Time* Verve V6-8691 (1967)

The Baroque Brass (self-titled) Fontana SRF-67582 (1968)

John Cameron and His Orchestra *Warm and Gentle* Studio 2 Stereo TWO-197 (1968)

Manny Kellem, His Orchestra & Voices *Love is Blue* Epic BN-26367 (1968)

The Waikikis *Midnight Luau* Kapp KS-3575 (1968)

Julius Wechter & the Baja Marimba Band *Those Were the Days* A&M SP-4167 (1968)

Astromusical House of Gemini GWP Records ASTRO-1003 (1969)

Mike Leander Orchestra *Migration* MCA MUPS-383 (1969)

Mike Leander Orchestra *A Time for Young Love* Decca DL-75144 (1969)

Percy Faith Strings *The Beatles Album* Columbia C-30097 (1970)

Liberace *A Brand New Me* Warner Bros. Records WS-1847 (1970)

Franck Pourcel *Franck Pourcel Meets the Beatles* Studio 2 TWO-371 U.K. (1970)

Baker Street Philharmonic *Yesterday's Dreams* Pye Records PKL-4401 U.K. (1971)

Mystic Moods Orchestra *English Muffins* Philips PHS-600-349 (1971)

John Fox Orchestra *Here, There, and Everywhere* BBC Records REB-168 U.K. (1974)

Chet Atkins with Cam Mullins and His Orchestra *Masters of Melody* Reader's Digest RDS-10486 8-LP set Germany (1987)

Lex De Azevedo and His Orchestra *The Radio Recordings Collection, Vol. 7* Surrey House CD-7027 (2011)

18. HURDY GURDY MAN

Ray Davies and the Button-Down Brass *This Guy's in Love* Fontana LPS-16258 (1968)

Vic Lewis Orchestra *The Boy in the Saffron Robe: The Vic Lewis Orchestra Plays the Music of Donovan* NEMS 6-63388 (U.K.), also as *Donovan, My Way* Epic BN-26418 (1968)

Johnny Arthey Orchestra *The Golden Songs of Donovan* RCA Victor LSP-4106 (1969)

Helmut Zacharias *Zacharias Plays the Hits* Capitol ST-150 (1969)

19. I AM THE WALRUS

Hollyridge Strings *Play Magical Mystery Tour: The Beatles Song Book Vol. 5* Capitol ST-2876 (1968)

George Martin *London By George!* United Artists UAS-6647 (1968)

Big Jim Sullivan *Lord Sitar* Capitol ST-2916 (1968)

John Andrews Tartaglia *Tartaglian Theorem* Capitol ST-166 (1968)

The Royal Philharmonic Orchestra *A Tribute to the Beatles* Reader's Digest Association ULC-035-3675 Canada (2009)

Al Di Meola *All Your Life (A Tribute To The Beatles Recorded At Abbey Road Studios, London)* Valiana VSR-169128 CD, Album, Digipak (2013)

20. INCENSE AND PEPPERMINTS

Charles Grean and His Orchestra [Muzak Session S-2451] (1967)

Martin Denny *A Taste of India* Liberty LST-7550 (1968)

21. JENNIFER JUNIPER

Vic Lewis Orchestra *The Boy in the Saffron Robe: The Vic Lewis Orchestra Plays the Music of Donovan* NEMS 6-63388 (U.K.), also as *Donovan, My Way* Epic BN-26418 (1968)

Sounds Orchestral *Words* Pye Records NSPL-18224 U.K. (1968)

Alan Tew Orchestra *Rosie* Columbia ELS-332 (1968)

Don Tweedy and His Orchestra *The Honey Touch* United Artists Records UAS-6661 (1968)

The Les Williams Orchestra *Plays the Collected Songs of Donovan* Imperial LP-12422 (1968)

Johnny Arthey Orchestra *The Golden Songs of Donovan* RCA Victor LSP-4106 (1969)

Arthur Greenslade and His Orchestra *Happiness Is… Up Up and Away* Reader's Digest RDA-106-A [9-LP Box Set] (1970)

22. LALENA

Vic Lewis Orchestra *The Boy in the Saffron Robe: The Vic Lewis Orchestra Plays the Music of Donovan* NEMS 6-63388 (U.K.), also as *Donovan, My Way* Epic BN-26418 (1968)

Mystic Moods Orchestra *Extensions* Philips PHS-600-301 (1969)

Waldo de los Rios *El Sonido Magico De Waldo De Los Rios y su Orquesta* Hispavox HHS-11-167 Spain (1969)

23. LET THE SUNSHINE IN

"Galt MacDermot & His Orchestra" Muzak Session [June 4, 1968]

Astromusical House of Aquarius GWP Records ASTRO-1011 (1969)

Briarcliff Orchestra *The Briarcliff Orchestra Plays…* Harmony HS-11364 (1969)

Ray Conniff and the Singers *Jean* Columbia CS-9920 (1969)

Mike Leander Orchestra *Migration* MCA MUPS-383 (1969)

Peter Nero *Hits From "Hair" To Hollywood* Columbia CS-9907 (1969)

Big Ben Hawaiian Band *Hit Me Hawaiian* Polydor 583084 U.K. (1970)

Paul Mauriat *Let the Sunshine In/Midnight Cowboy/And Other Goodies* Philips PHS-600-337 (1970)

24. LIGHT MY FIRE

Enoch Light Singers *Whoever You Are, I Love You* Project 3 Total Sound PR-5030-SD (1968)

Jack Pleis and His Orchestra *The Sounds of Our Times Play "Hey Jude"* Capitol ST-117 (1968)

Nelson Riddle *Contemporary Sound of Nelson Riddle* United Artists UAS-6670 (1968)

Astromusical House of Aries GWP Records ASTRO-1001 (1969)

Ronnie Aldrich and His Two Pianos *It's Happening Now* London Phase 4 SP-44127 (1969)

Mike Curb & the Waterfall *The Doors Songbook* Forward Records ST-F-1020 (1969)

Enoch Light and Glittering Guitars Project 3 Total Sound PR-5030-SD (1969)

Helmut Zacharias *Zacharias Plays the Hits* Capitol ST-150 (1969)

Terry Baxter and His Orchestra *What the World Needs Now is Love* Columbia Special Products C8SPS 1005 [8-LP box set] Canada (1970)

Johnny Gregory *Cascading Strings* Philips 6308016 U.K. (1970)

Ananda Shankar (self-titled) Reprise RS-6398 (1970)

Sven Libaek Orchestra [Muzak Session S-3047]

Sven Libaek Orchestra *Sven Libaek Conducts His 38 Piece Orchestra* Festival Records L-35419 Australia (1975)

Lex De Azevedo and His Orchestra *The Radio Recordings Collection, Vol. 2* Surrey House CD-7024 (2011)

Sven Libaek Orchestra *Starborne Limited Edition #30* Starborne Productions (2011)

Nick Ingman Orchestra *Mister Bojangles* Starborne Productions CD (2012)

25. LUCY IN THE SKY WITH DIAMONDS

Peter Knight Orchestra *Instrumental Beatles Themes from Sgt. Pepper's Lonely Hearts Club Band* Mercury SR-61132 (1967)

Alan Lorber Orchestra *The Lotus Palace* Verve V-8711 (1967)

John Schroeder Orchestra *The Dolly Catcher* Piccadilly NPL-38036 UK (1967)

Gabor Szabo *Wind, Sky, & Diamonds* Impulse AS-9151 (1967)

Marty Gold *Moog Plays The Beatles* AVCO Embassy AVE-33003 (1969)

Richard Hayman and His Orchestra *Cinemagic Sounds* Command-941S (1969)

Percy Faith Strings *The Beatles Album* Columbia C-30097 (1970)

Enoch Light and His Orchestra *Beatles Classics* Project 3 Total Sound PR4C-5084 (1974)

John Keating *Space Experience 2* EMI SM-11635 (1975)

101 Strings *101 Strings Orchestra Play & Sing the Songs Made Famous by Elton John, Featuring The Alshire Singers* Alshire S-5329 (1976)

Ronnie Aldrich *Yesterday's Tomorrows* Decca SKL-5305 U.K. (1979)

London Starlight Orchestra *20 Beatles Greatest Hits* Star Inc. Music CD-86021 Netherlands (1988)

John Fox Orchestra *The Radio Recordings Collection, Vol. 2* Surrey House CD-7062 (2011)

Simon Park and His Orchestra *The Radio Recordings Collection, Vol. 2* Surrey House CD-7082 (2011)

26. LULLABY FROM ROSEMARY'S BABY ("SLEEP SAFE AND WARM")

Chet Atkins *Solid Gold '68* RCA LSP-4061 (1968)

Floyd Cramer *Floyd Cramer Plays "MacArthur Park"* RCA LSP-4070 (1968)

Mia Farrow 45 RPM 7" single Dot 17126 (1968)

Enoch Light and the Light Brigade 45 RPM single Project 3 Total Sound PR-1339 (1968)

Enoch Light and the Light Brigade *The Best Of Hollywood - Movie Hits '68-'69* Project 3 Total Sound PR-5027-SD (1968)

Living Marimbas *Plus Strings MacArthur Park and Other Favorites* RCA Camden CAS-2283 (1968)

101 Strings *Million Seller Hits of Today* Alshire S-5112 (1968)

Hugo Winterhalter and His Orchestra *Classical Gas* Musicor MS-3170 (1968)

Nick De Caro and Orchestra *Happy Heart* A&M SP-4176 (1969)

Raymond Lefevre and His Orchestra *Volume Four* Major Minor SMLP-45 (1969)

Hugo Montenegro *Good Vibrations* RCA LSP-4101 (1969)

Roger Williams *Happy Heart* Kapp KS-3595 (1969)

27. MACARTHUR PARK

Ronnie Aldrich and His Two Pianos *This Way "In"* London Phase 4 SP-44116 (1968)

Floyd Cramer *Floyd Cramer Plays "MacArthur Park"* RCA LSP-4070 (1968)

Martin Denny *Exotic Love* Liberty LST-7585 (1968)

Percy Faith, His Orchestra, and Chorus *Angel of the Morning* Columbia CS-9706 (1968)

Ferrante & Teicher *A Bouquet of Hits* United Artists UAS-6659 (1968)

Midnight String Quartet *"The Look Of Love" and Other Rhapsodies for Young Lovers* Viva V36015 (1968)

Raymonde Singers Etcetera *Feelin'* London Phase 4 SP 44111 (1968)

Doc Severinsen & Strings (self-titled) Command Records RS-937-SD (1968)

Hugo Winterhalter and His Orchestra *Classical Gas* Musicor MS-3170 (1968)

Raymond Lefevre and His Orchestra *Volume Four* Major Minor SMLP-45 (1969)

Mystic Moods Orchestra *Extensions* Philips PHS-600-301 (1969)

101 Strings *Play Million Seller Hits Composed by Jimmy Webb and Burt Bacharach* Alshire S-5162 (1969)

Assembled Multitude (Self-Titled) Atlantic SD-8262 (1970)

Terry Baxter and His Orchestra *What the World Needs Now is Love* Columbia Special Products C8SPS 1005 [8-LP box set] Canada (1970)

Frank Chacksfield and His Orchestra *Chacksfield Plays Simon & Garfunkel & Jim Webb* London SP-44151 (1970)

Liberace *A Brand New Me* Warner Bros. WS-1847 (1970)

Francis Lai *More Love Themes* Kapp KS-3646 (1971)

28. MELLOW YELLOW

Vic Lewis Orchestra *The Boy in the Saffron Robe: The Vic Lewis Orchestra Plays the Music of Donovan* NEMS 6-63388 (UK), also as *Donovan, My Way* Epic BN-26418 (1968)

David McCallum *McCallum* Capitol ST-2748 (1968)

The Les Williams Orchestra *Plays the Collected Songs of Donovan* Imperial LP-12422 (1968)

Johnny Arthey Orchestra *The Golden Songs of Donovan* RCA Victor LSP-4106 (1969)

BILLY VAUGHN **THE WINDMILLS OF YOUR MIND**

THE WINDMILLS OF YOUR MIND • HEAVEN
SOULFUL STRUT • WICHITA LINEMAN
TRACES • YOU GAVE ME A MOUNTAIN
TRACI'S TRACKS • GLAD SHE'S A WOMAN
THE WAY THAT I LIVE • TIME OF THE SEASON
PROMISES, PROMISES • HELP YOURSELF

DOT RECORDS
STEREO
DLP 25937

29. MR. TAMBOURINE MAN

Golden Gate Strings *Bob Dylan Song Book* Epic BN-26158 (1965)

James Last Orchestra *Beat in Sweet* Polydor PD-249002 Germany (1965)

Mike Leander Orchestra *The Folk Hits* London PS-453 (1965)

David Rose *The Velvet Beat* MGM SE-4307 (1965)

Billy Strange *Billy Strange Plays the Hits!* GNP Crescendo GNP-2012 (1965)

Lester Lanin *At the Country Club* Philips PHS-600-192 (1966)

Johnny Harris and His Orchestra *Love is Blue: Music in a Mellow World* Reader's Digest RDA-77-A 4-LP Box Set (1969)

Johnny Harris Orchestra *Happiness Is... Up Up and Away* Reader's Digest RDA-106-A [9-LP Box Set] (1970)

30. NEVER MY LOVE

Johnny Mann Singers *Don't Look Back* Liberty LST-7535 (1967)

101 Strings *Sounds of Today* Alshire S-5078 (1967)

Floyd Cramer *Class of '68* RCA LSP-4025 (1968)

Percy Faith, His Orchestra & Chorus *For Those in Love* Columbia CS-9610 (1968)

Midnight String Quartet *Love Rhapsodies* Viva V-36013 (1968)

Nirvana Sitar and String Group *Sitar and Strings* Mr. G 8001 (1968)

Roger Williams *More Than a Miracle* Kapp KS-3550 (1968)

Xavier Cugat and His Orchestra *The Beautiful New Sound of Strings* Musicor Records M2S-3179 (1969)

Steve Douglas *Reflections in a Golden Horn* Mercury SR-61217 (1969)

Mario Said *Ev'rybody's Talkin'* Liberty LST-7601 (1969)

Bert Kaempfert *6 Plus 6* Decca DL-75322 (1972)

Henry Mancini & Doc Severinsen *Brass on Ivory* RCA LSP-4629 (1972)

Peter Nero *Summer of '42* Columbia C-31105 (1972)

Acker Bilk *The Magic Clarinet of Acker Bilk* K-Tel CD-6513 (1986)

Perry La Marca Orchestra *Hopelessly Romantic* Parfait Records CD-1 (2002)

Lex de Azevedo and His Orchestra *The Radio Recordings Collection, Vol. 2* Surrey House CD-7024 (2011)

31. NIGHTS IN WHITE SATIN

Franck Pourcel *The Franck Pourcel Sound* Columbia TWO 202 U.K. (1968)

Claude Denjean and the Moog Synthesizer *Electronic Experience* London Phase 4 SP-44155 (1970)

Percy Faith *Clair* Columbia KC-32164 (1973)

Sounds of the Seventies Orchestra *New Songs of the Seventies* Capitol (Special Markets) QL-6876 (1973)

Werner Muller *A Mystic Portrait of the Moody Blues* London Phase 4 SP-44204 (1974)

Norman Candler and His Magic Strings *Romantic Moods* Telefunken 6.24641 AS Germany (1978)

Ronnie Aldrich *Tomorrow's Yesterdays* Decca SKL-5305 U.K. (1979)

Francis Goya *Goya by Candlelight — 20 Romantic Hits* Arcade ADE H-50 (Holland) 1979

Studio London Orchestra and Singers *Feelings* Laser CD-2668022 Holland (1985)

Richard Clayderman *A Little Night Music: 12 Classic Love Songs* Decca 828-125-1 U.K. (1988)

Wallis Blue Orchestra *Late Night Melodies* Cocktail Hour Series CHC-8108 CD France (1988)

Northern Lights Orchestra *Hits of the '60s* SMS-32 CD U.K. (1990)

James Last and His Orchestra *Pop Symphonies* Polydor 849-429-2 Canada (1991)

Gino Marinello Orchestra *Golden Love Instrumentals* NCN-038 CD (1995)

Alain Morisod *20 Melodies to Dream By Vol. 3* Shangali CD-BIB081 (2002)

Acker Bilk *Stranger on the Shore* Music Digital CD-6818 U.K. (2010)

Tommy Deering and Strings *Starborne Limited Edition #49* Starborne Productions (2011)

---

32. NORWEGIAN WOOD

Hollyridge Strings *The New Beatles Song Book* Capitol ST-2429 (1966)

The Paul Horn Quintet *Monday, Monday* RCA LSP-3613 (1966)

Marty Gold *Moog Plays The Beatles* AVCO Embassy AVE-33003 (1969)

Mystic Moods Orchestra *Extensions* Philips PHS-600-301 (1969)

Perry Botkin, Jr. *Happiness Is... Up Up and Away* Reader's Digest RDA-106-A [9-LP Box Set] (1970)

Frank Chacksfield and His Orchestra *Chacksfield Plays the Beatles' Song Book* London Phase 4 SP-44142 (1970)

Percy Faith Strings *The Beatles Album* Columbia C-30097 (1970)

Enoch Light and His Orchestra *Beatles Classics* Project 3 Total Sound PR4C-5084 (1974)

Lex de Azevedo and His Orchestra *The Radio Recordings Collection, Vol. 13* Surrey House CD-7033 (2011)

33. PENNY LANE

Hollyridge Strings *The Beatles Songbook Vol. 4* Capitol ST-2656 (1967)

Paul Mauriat and His Orchestra *Blooming Hits* Philips PHS-600-248 (1967)

Franck Pourcel *The French Touch* Imperial LP-12357 (1967)

Kai Winding *Penny Lane & Time* Verve V6-8691 (1967)

Alan Tew Orchestra *This is My Scene* Decca Phase 4 PFS-4120 (1967)

The Four Score Pianos (self-titled) Ranwood RLP-18001 (1968)

David McCallum *McCallum* Capitol ST-2748 (1968)

101 Strings *Play the Hits Written by the Beatles* Alshire S-5111 (1968)

Marty Gold *Moog Plays The Beatles* AVCO Embassy AVE-33003 (1969)

Franck Pourcel *Franck Pourcel Meets the Beatles* Studio 2 TWO-371 U.K. (1970)

Enoch Light and His Orchestra *Beatles Classics* Project 3 Total Sound PR4C-5084 (1974)

London Starlight Orchestra *20 Beatles Greatest Hits* Star Inc. Music CD 86021 Netherlands (1988)

Ralph Benatar and His Orchestra *A Tribute to the Beatles* Reader's Digest Association ULC-035-3675 Canada (2009)

34. SAN FRANCISCO (BE SURE TO WEAR FLOWERS IN YOUR HAIR)

101 Strings *Sounds of Today* Alshire S-5078 (1967)

Fausto Papetti 7" single Durium Ld A-7536 (1967)

John Schroeder Orchestra *The Dolly Catcher* Piccadilly NPL-38036 U.K. (1967)

Sounds of Our Times *Music of the Flower Children* (Jack Pleis, arranger/conductor) Capitol ST-2817 (1967)

Big Ben Hawaiian Band *Hawaiian Styled* Columbia EMI STUDIO 2 TWO-205 (1968)

Caravelli and His Magnificent Strings *La, La, La A'la Caravelli* Columbia CS-9690 (1968)

Raymond Lefevre *La, La, La (He Gives Me Love)* 4 Corners of the World FCS-4250 (1968)

Living Guitars *San Franciscan Nights* RCA Camden CAS-2192 (1968)

Paul Mauriat *Mauriat Magic* Philips PHS-600-270 (1968)

Fausto Papetti *8a Raccolta* Durium MS A-77189 Italy (1968)

Franck Pourcel *Love is Blue* Imperial LP-12383 (1968)

Miguel Ramos *Organo Hammond y Orquesta, Volumen 3* Hispavox HH 11-136 Spain (1968)

Roger Bennet and
His Magic Clarinet
Tanzparty à Gogo SR
International 92-373
(3-album box set)
Germany (1970)

Roger Bennet, His
Clarinet, and His
Orchestra *What a
Wonderful World* ABC/
Dunhill DS-50043
(1970)

Anthony Ventura
Orchestra *Je T'Aime
Vol. 2* RCA PPL-1-4045
(1975)

Fausto Papetti *Petite
Fleur - 20 Melodien für
zärtliche Stunden* Hansa
International 34-275-8
(1979)

Bruno Bertone
Orchestra *Melodien
zum Träumen* Delta
DA-2026 (1980)

Jean Michel De France
Golden Sixties Delphine
818-894-1 France
(1984)

Bruno Bertone
Orchestra *Love Letters*
LaserLight Digital CD
15-054 (1988)

Wallis Blue Orchestra
Magic Melodies
Cocktail Music Series
CHC-8109 France
(1989)

Gino Marinello
Orchestra *Magic Light*
Laserlight CD DGC-
1022 Holland (2008)

35. SCARBOROUGH FAIR/ CANTICLE

Don Costa *Instrumental
Versions of Simon and
Garfunkel* Mercury SR-
61177 (1968)

Percy Faith, His
Orchestra & Chorus
Angel of the Morning
Columbia CS-9706
(1968)

Al Hirt *Al Hirt Now!* RCA
LSP-4101 (1968)

Hollyridge Strings *Play
the Hits of Simon and
Garfunkel* Capitol ST-
2998 (1968)

Andre Kostelanetz
*"Scarborough Fair" and
Other Great Movie Hits*
Columbia CS-9623
(1968)

Tony Mottola (with The
Free Design as "The
Groovies") *Warm, Wild,
and Wonderful* Project
3 Total Sound PR-
5025-SD (1968)

Mystic Moods Orchestra
Emotions Philips
PHS600-277 (1968)

Mario Said *Sensational!*
Liberty LST-7562
(1968)

Don Tweedy and His
Orchestra *The Honey
Touch* United Artists
UAS-6661 (1968)

Briarcliff Strings *Music
from the Movies*
Harmony HS-11315
(1969)

Ray Conniff & The
Singers *I Love How You
Love Me* Columbia CS-
9777 (1969)

Ferrante & Teicher
Midnight Cowboy
United Artists UAS
6725 (1969)

101 Strings *101 Strings
Play Million Seller Hits
Of Today* Alshire S-5156
(1969)

The Current Event *Hits
of Simon & Garfunkel*
Ambassador S-98094
(1970)

Frank Chacksfield
and His Orchestra
*Chacksfield Plays Simon
& Garfunkel and Jim
Webb* London Phase
4 Stereo SP 44151
(1971)

Midnight String Quartet
*Chamber Music for
Lovers* Viva V36024
(1971)

Peter Nero *Love Story*
Columbia C-30586
(1971)

Santo & Johnny *Il Padrino
E Altri Famosi Temi Da
Films* CAN-LPS 710
Italy (1972)

36. SGT. PEPPER'S LONELY HEARTS CLUB BAND

Peter Knight Orchestra *Instrumental Beatles Themes from Sgt. Pepper's Lonely Hearts Club Band* Mercury SR-61132 (1967)

Hollyridge Strings *Play Magical Mystery Tour: The Beatles Song Book Vol. 5* Capitol ST-2876 (1968)

George Martin *London By George!* United Artists UAS-6647 (1968)

Andre Kostelanetz *Plays "Murder on the Orient Express" and Other Great Themes* Columbia PC-33437 (1975)

101 Strings *Best of the Beatles* Madacy Records CD 628261054022 (2004)

37. SHE'S LEAVING HOME

Peter Knight Orchestra *Instrumental Beatles Themes from Sgt. Pepper's Lonely Hearts Club Band* Mercury SR-61132 (1967)

Big Jim Sullivan *Sitar Beat* Mercury SR-61137 (1967)

Hollyridge Strings *Play Magical Mystery Tour: The Beatles Song Book Vol. 5* Capitol ST-2876 (1968)

Julius Wechter & the Baja Marimba Band *Fowl Play* A&M SP-4136 (1968)

London Starlight Orchestra *20 Beatles Greatest Hits* Star Inc. Music CD-86021 Netherlands (1988)

38. SOMEBODY TO LOVE

Living Guitars *San Franciscan Nights* RCA Camden CAS-2192 (1968)

Les Reed *Love is Blue: Music in a Mellow World* Reader's Digest RDA-77-A [4-LP Box Set] (1969)

39. STRAWBERRY FIELDS FOREVER

Hollyridge Strings *The Beatles Songbook Vol. 4* Capitol ST-2656 (1967)

The Ventures *Super Psychedelics* Liberty LST-8052 (1967)

David McCallum *McCallum* Capitol ST-2748 (1968)

Astromusical House of Sagittarius GWP Records ASTRO-1009 (1969)

John Fox and His London Studio Orchestra *The Radio Recordings Collection*, Vol. 7 Surrey House Music CD-7067 (1988)

Gino Marinello Orchestra *Romantic Nights* DGR DGC-1032 CD Netherlands (1988)

101 Strings *Best of the Beatles* Madacy Records CD 628261054022 (2004)

Christian Colombier and His Orchestra *A Tribute to the Beatles* Reader's Digest Association ULC-035-3675 Canada (2009)

Peter Murray Orchestra *Starborne Limited Edition #26* Starborne Productions (2011)

40. SUNDAY WILL NEVER BE THE SAME

The Billy Vaughn Singers *I Love You* Dot Records DLP-25813 (1967)

Mariano and the Unbelievables (self-titled) Capitol ST-2831 (1968)

Nirvana Sitar and String Group *Sitar and Strings* Mr. G 8001 (1968)

Charles Grean and His Orchestra [Muzak session] *Muzak: New Dimensions* H-1(1)35 (1969)

Nick Ingman and His Orchestra *The Radio Recordings Collection from Surrey House Music*, Vol. 1 CD-7011 (1984)

41. SUNSHINE SUPERMAN

Enoch Light's Action *It's Happening... So Let's Dance!* Project 3 Total Sound PR-5004-SD (1967)

Big Jim Sullivan *Sitar Beat* Mercury SR-61137 (1967)

Vic Lewis Orchestra *The Boy in the Saffron Robe: The Vic Lewis Orchestra Plays the Music of Donovan* NEMS 6-63388 (U.K.), also as *Donovan, My Way* Epic BN-26418 (1968)

Mariano and the Unbelievables (self-titled) Capitol ST-2831 (1968)

Nelson Riddle *The Riddle of Today* Liberty LST-7532 (1968)

The Les Williams Orchestra *Plays the Collected Songs of Donovan* Imperial LP-12422 (1968)

Johnny Arthey Orchestra *The Golden Songs of Donovan* RCA Victor LSP-4106 (1969)

42. THERE IS A MOUNTAIN

Vic Lewis Orchestra *The Boy in the Saffron Robe: The Vic Lewis Orchestra Plays the Music of Donovan* NEMS 6-63388 (UK), also as *Donovan, My Way* Epic BN-26418 (1968)

The String-A-Longs *Wide World Hits* Atco SD-33-241 (1968)

The Les Williams Orchestra *Plays the Collected Songs of Donovan* Imperial LP-12422 (1968)

Johnny Arthey Orchestra *The Golden Songs of Donovan* RCA Victor LSP-4106 (1969)

Bones and Fifes *There is a Mountain* Starborne CD SLD-1119 (2011)

43. WEAR YOUR LOVE LIKE HEAVEN

The Les Williams Orchestra *Plays the Collected Songs of Donovan* Imperial LP-12422 (1968)

Johnny Arthey Orchestra *The Golden Songs of Donovan* RCA Victor LSP-4106 (1969)

Steve Douglas *Reflections in a Golden Horn* Mercury SR-61217 (1969)

David Rose and His Orchestra *Happy Heart* Capitol ST-393 (1970)

44. WHEN I'M SIXTY-FOUR

Peter Knight Orchestra *Instrumental Beatles Themes from Sgt. Pepper's Lonely Hearts Club Band* Mercury SR-61132 (1967)

Hollyridge Strings *Play Magical Mystery Tour: The Beatles Song Book Vol. 5* Capitol ST-2876 (1968)

Cyril Stapleton Choir & Orchestra *Panoramic Lennon and McCartney* Pye NSPL-18274 (1969)

Austria Pop Symphony Orchestra *Best of the Beatles* ZYX Classics CD CLS-4121 Germany (1990)

London Starlight Orchestra *20 Beatles Greatest Hits* Star Inc. Music CD 86021 Netherlands (1988)

101 Strings *Best of the Beatles* Madacy Records CD 628261054022 (2004)

Nick Ingman and His Orchestra *The Radio Recordings Collection, Vol. 1* Surrey House CD-7011 (2011)

Simon Park and His Orchestra *The Radio Recordings Collection from Surrey House Music, Vol. 1* Surrey House CD-7082 (2011)

THE SOUNDS OF OUR TIMES PLAY HEY JUDE

STEREO
PLAYABLE ON STEREO
& MONO PHONOGRAPHS

Capitol
RECORDS

Harper Valley P.T.A.
To Wait for Love
Light My Fire
The Fool on the Hill
Windmills of My Mind
Who Is Gonna Love Me?
"Zorba" (from the Broadway Musical "Zorba")
The Sounds of Silence
Love Theme from "Elvira Madigan" (In the Days of Splendor)
Arranged and Conducted by Jack Pleis

45. A WHITER SHADE OF PALE

Ronnie Aldrich *Two Pianos – Today!* London SP- SP 44100 (1967)

Peter Knight Singers *Voices in the Night* Deram SML-702 (1967)

Raymond Lefevre and His Orchestra *Soul Coaxing (Ame Caline)* 4 Corners of the World FCS-4244 (1967)

Peter Nero *Nero-ing in on the Hits* RCA LSP-3871 (1967)

101 Strings *Sounds of Today* Alshire S-5078 (1967)

Big Jim Sullivan *Sitar Beat* Mercury SR-61137 (1967)

Big Ben Hawaiian Band *Hawaiian Styled* Columbia EMI STUDIO 2 TWO-205 U.K. (1968)

Living Guitars *San Franciscan Nights* RCA Camden CAS-2192 (1968)

Marble Arch Orchestra *Tomorrow's Standards* Liberty LST-7567 (1968)

George Martin and His Orchestra *London By George!* United Artists UAS-6647 (1968)

Nirvana Sitar and String Group (self-titled) Mr. G 8001 (1968)

Astromusical House of Pisces GWP Records ASTRO-1012 (1969)

Perry Botkin, Jr. and His Orchestra *Love is Blue: Music in a Mellow World* Reader's Digest RDA-77-A 4-LP set (1969)

Anthony Ventura and His Orchestra *Je T'Aime Vol. 1* RCA PPL1-4010 Germany (1973)

Bruno Bertone Orchestra *Melodien zum Träumen* Delta DA-2026 Germany (1980)

Gino Marinello Orchestra *Magic Light* Laserlight CD DGC-1022 Holland (2008)

Acker Bilk *Stranger on the Shore* Music Digital CD-6818 U.K. (2010)

Sven Libaek Orchestra *Starborne Limited Edition #56* Starborne Productions (2012)

46. WITH A LITTLE HELP FROM MY FRIENDS

Peter Knight Orchestra *Instrumental Beatles Themes from Sgt. Pepper's Lonely Hearts Club Band* Mercury SR-61132 (1967)

Tony Mottola (with The Free Design as "The Groovies") *Warm, Wild, and Wonderful* Project 3 Total Sound PR-5025-SD (1968)

Cyril Stapleton Choir & Orchestra *Panoramic Lennon and McCartney* Pye NSPL-18274 (1969)

Enoch Light and His Orchestra *Beatles Classics* Project 3 Total Sound PR4C-5084 (1974)

Francis Moore Orchestra *Memories, Volume 2* Bridge CD 100.016-2 Switzerland (1985)

London Starlight Orchestra *20 Beatles Greatest Hits* Star Inc. Music CD-86021 Netherlands (1988)

Arthur Greenslade and His Orchestra *A Tribute to the Beatles* Reader's Digest Association ULC-035-3675 (Canada) (2009)

Lex De Azevedo and His Orchestra *The Radio Recordings Collection, Vol. 6* Surrey House CD-7026 (2011)

47. WITHIN YOU, WITHOUT YOU

Peter Knight Orchestra *Instrumental Beatles Themes from Sgt. Pepper's Lonely Hearts Club Band* Mercury SR-61132 (1967)

Alan Lorber Orchestra *The Lotus Palace* Verve V-8711 (1967)

Big Jim Sullivan *Sitar Beat* Mercury SR-61137 (1967)

Soulful Strings *Groovin' with the Soulful Strings* Cadet Records LPS-796 (1967)

Clebanoff Strings *Once Upon a Summertime* Decca DL-74956 (1968)

John Andrews Tartaglia *Good Morning Starshine* Capitol ST-280 (1969)

48. WOODSTOCK

Assembled Multitude (Self-Titled) Atlantic SD-8262 (1970)

Ronnie Aldrich and His Two Pianos *Love Story* London SP-44162 (1971)

Baker Street Philharmonic *Yesterday's Dreams* Pye Records PKL-4401 U.K. (1971)

Alan Tew Orchestra *These I Like* CBS-64424 (1971)

49. YELLOW SUBMARINE

The Baroque Inevitable (self-titled) Columbia CS-9387 (1966)

Caravelli *Canción De Lara / Un Hombre Y Una Mujer / El Submarino Amarillo / Monday Monday* CBS – EP 6174 7" 45 RPM Spain (1966)

George Martin *Instrumentally Salutes the Beatle Girls* United Artists UAS-6539 (1966)

Hollyridge Strings *The Beatles Songbook Vol. 4* Capitol ST-2656 (1967)

Enoch Light's Action *It's Happening… So Let's Dance!* Project 3 Total Sound PR-5004-SD (1967)

Ferrante & Teicher *Listen to the Movies* United Artists UAS-6701 (1969)

50. YOUR MOTHER SHOULD KNOW

Hollyridge Strings *Play Magical Mystery Tour: The Beatles Song Book Vol. 5* Capitol ST-2876 (1968)

Marble Arch Orchestra *Tomorrow's Standards* Liberty LST-7567 (1968)

Raymonde Singers Etcetera *Feelin'* London Phase 4 SP 44111 (1968)

INDEX

231

R

Rado, James 159–60, 163, 178
Ragni, Gerome 160, 163, 164, 178
Rajput & the Sepoy Mutiny 98
Raymonde, Ivor 85
Reed, Les 168, 189
Riddle, Nelson 50, 150, 185
Rimbaud, Arthur 24
Rolling Stones, the 29, 50, 63, 73, 93, 97, 100, 125, 127, 155
Ros, Edmundo 62, 167
Rose, David 26–29, 155, 167
Rothschild, Paul 59, 151
Rowan & Martin's Laugh-In 145

S

Sandals, the 40
Santo & Johnny 36
Schlichting, Jim 190, 192
Schroeder, John 113
Schulke, Jim 189
Seeburg 196
Selvin, Ben 20, 21
Severinsen, Doc 140
Shadows, the 36
Shakespeare, John (pseudonym: John Carter) 50, 113

Shankar, Ananda 63
Shankar, Ravi 63, 93, 94, 102, 108
Shepherd, Bill 53, 54
Simon & Garfunkel 97
Sinatra, Frank 27, 60, 81
Nancy 97, 116
Slick, Grace 27, 49, 98, 189
Small Faces, the 29, 49, 94
Sopwith Camel, the 56
Soulful Strings 100
Sousa, John Philip 122
Spanky and Our Gang 54, 78, 121, 125
Spector, Phil 39
Spice, Irv 124–25, 134
SRP (Stereo Radio Productions) 189–90
Stanley, Augustus Owsley 108
Stapleton, Cyril 30, 81, 82, 192
Starborne Productions 190–92
Steiner, Max 36, 177
Stigwood, Robert 52, 53
Strawberry Alarm Clock 27, 94, 163
Szabo, Gabor 82, 83, 98

T

Tartaglia, John Andrews 149
Taylor, Marlin 189
Tew, Alan 50
Thorne, Ken 151, 189
Tiny Tim 56, 58, 125
Tonight Show, the 160
Turtles, the 27, 54, 176

U

Urich, Robert 193
Usher, Gary 42

V

Valentino, Pat 192
Vallee, Rudy 50, 77
Vaughn, Billy 31, 50, 153, 176–77
Ventures, the 36, 40, 60, 177
Vickers, Mike 78, 101
Voormann, Klaus 52

W

Wallis Blue Orchestra 195
WDBN (Ohio) 193
WDVR (Philadelphia) 189
Webb, Jimmy 138–39, 149, 176
Wechter, Julius 167
Weill, Kurt 57
Welch, Bruce 36
Welk, Lawrence 16, 18, 35, 50, 77, 135
Weston, Paul 18, 20, 101
Whisky a Go Go 57, 124
Williams, Andy 56, 146, 148, 150–51
Williams, Les 150–52
Williams, Mason 121, 177
Williams, Roger 21, 56, 62, 77, 176–77, 189
Wilson, Brian 40–45, 126
Wilson, Murry 45
Winterhalter, Hugo 140, 176
Wisner, Jimmy 179
WPAT (Paterson, N.J.) 189

Z

Zabach, Florian 166
Zacharias, Helmut 62
Zombies, the 31, 153

233

ENDNOTES

CHAPTER 1. STROBE LIGHTS AND SWEET MUSIC

Cardinell, R.L. "The Nature and Development of Work Music," "Selection of Equipment," and "Principles of Programming." Three-part monograph. *Music in Industry*. New York: ASCAP Monograph, No. 3, 1944: 3–9.

Conniff, Ray, quoted in "The New Ray Conniff Story," by Serge Elhaik. S'Conniff: The Ray Conniff Newsletter #3 (1991): 8. This is also quoted in *Elevator Music: A Surreal History of Muzak, Easy Listening, and Other Moodsong: Revised and Expanded Edition*, by Joseph Lanza. Ann Arbor: University of Michigan Press, 2004: 104.

Faith, Percy, quoted in "Percy Faith Dead at 67; Conductor and Arranger," by Robert McG. Thomas, Jr. *The New York Times*, 10 February 1976.

Gleason, Jackie, quoted in *The Great One: The Life and Legend of Jackie Gleason*, by William A. Henry III. New York: Doubleday, 1992.

Gould, Glenn. "The Prospects of Recording." *The Glenn Gould Reader* (ed. Tim Page). New York: Vintage Books, 1990: 350.

Gould, Morton quoted in *Elevator Music: A Surreal History of Muzak, Easy Listening, and Other Moodsong: Revised and Expanded Edition*, by Joseph Lanza. Ann Arbor: University of Michigan Press, 2004: 34.

Hofmann, Albert. *LSD: My Problem Child* (trans. Jonathan Ott). Los Angeles: J.P. Tarcher, Inc., 1983: 17–18.

Lee, Martin A., and Bruce Shlain. *Acid Dreams*. New York: Grove Press, 1992: 55, 253–54. [Includes the origin of the term "psychedelic."]

McDermott, Jeanne. "If It's to Be Heard but Not Listened to, It Must Be Muzak." *Smithsonian*, January 1990: 74.

Mantovani quoted in *The Best of the Music Makers*, by George T. Simon (and Friends). Garden City, NY: Doubleday, 1979: 381.

Monroe, Keith. "Paul Weston: Master of Mood Music." *Coronet*, February 1950, Vol. 27, No. 4.

Schumach, Murray. "The Music Between." *High Fidelity*, February 1957: 89.

Selvin, Ben. "Programming Music for Industry." *Journal of the Acoustical Society of America*, Vol. 15 No. 4, April 1943, American Institute of Physics for the Acoustical Society of America: 131–2.

Sullivan, Robert. "This is Not a Bob Dylan Movie." *The New York Times*, 7 October 2007: 658. www.nytimes.com/2007/10/07/magazine/07Haynes.html

Tiomkin, Dimitri, quoted in *Film Score: The Art & Craft of Movie Music*, by Tony Thomas. Burbank, CA: Riverwood Press, 1991: 127.

"Top 40 Chart by *Billboard*." Billboard, 5 June 1965: 1, 4. [*Billboard* introduces its first 40-song "Easy-Listening" chart.]

CHAPTER 2. FIXING A HOLE WHERE THE WAVES CRASH IN

"The Beat, Beat of Surf Music." *Billboard*, 29 June 1963: 26. [Murry Wilson interviewed]

Beautiful Dreamer: Brian Wilson and the Story of "Smile." Dir. David Leaf. 2004 Showtime Networks.

Jackson, Andrew Grant. *1965: The Most Revolutionary Year in Music*. New York: Thomas Dunne Books, St. Martin's Press, 2015: 68.

Kutner, John, and Spencer Leigh. *1000 UK Number One Hits*. London: Omnibus Press, 2005.

Larsen, Peter. "Orange County surf rock pioneer and 'Pipeline' guitarist Brian Carman of the Chantays dies at 69." *Orange County Register*, 4 March 2015. www.ocregister.com/2015/03/04/orange-county-surf-rock-pioneer-and-pipeline-guitarist-brian-carman-of-the-chantays-dies-at-69/

Lee, Martin A., and Bruce Shlain. *Acid Dreams*. New York: Grove Press, 1992: 130.

Phillips, Stu, quoted in *Elevator Music: A Surreal History of Muzak, Easy Listening, and Other Moodsong: Revised and Expanded Edition*, by Joseph Lanza. Ann Arbor: University of Michigan Press, 2004: 200–1.

Williams, Richard. "Jack Nitzsche." *The Guardian*, 30 August 2000. www.theguardian.com/news/2000aug/31/guardianobituaries.richardwilliams

Zhito, Lee. "Surfing Craze Ready to Splash Across Country to East's Youth." *Billboard*, 29 June 1963: 26, 31.

CHAPTER 3. WE SKIPPED THE LIGHT FANDANGO INTO A FUNERAL PYRE

Clash, Jim. "Part 4: Doors Drummer John Densmore Talks About Preserving Band's Legacy." Forbes.com, 5 February 2015. www.forbes.com/sites/jimclash/2015/02/05/part-4-doors-drummer-john-densmore-talks-about-preserving-bands-legacy/#6107af15291c

Davis, Stephen. *Jim Morrison: Life, Death, Legend*. New York: Gotham Books, 2004: 104, 126, 211.

Flans, Robyn. "John Densmore—Reflections." *Modern Drummer*, December 1982. www.moderndrummer.com/article/december-1982-john-densmore-reflections/

Mann, Johnny, quoted in *Vanilla Pop: Sweet Sounds from Frankie Avalon to ABBA*, by Joseph Lanza. Chicago: Chicago Review Press, 2005: 154–5.

Manzarek, Ray, quoted in "An Archival Interview with Ray Manzarek, Keyboardist for The Doors." *Fresh Air*, NPR 28 July 2017 (original broadcast from 1998). www.npr.org/2017/07/28/539989187/an-archival-interview-with-ray-manzarek-keyboardist-for-the-doors

"Reviews and Ratings of New Popular Album [*Music for Two Sleepy People*]." *Billboard*, 3 November 1958: 40.

Runtagh, Jordan. "Unhinged: Doors Drummer John Densmore Puts Bandmates on Trial to Preserve Jim Morrison's Legacy." VH1.Com, 1 May 2013. www.vh1.com/news/50717/doors-john-densmore-lawsuit-unhinged/

CHAPTER 4. SHADOWS OVER SGT. PEPPER

Agnew, Spiro, quoted in "The Second Coming of 'Sgt. Pepper,'" by Mary Stevens. *Chicago Tribune*, 29 May 1987. www.chicagotribune.com/news/ct-xpm-1987-05-29-8702090656-story.html

Ames, Morgan. Review of *Percy Faith Strings: The Beatles Album*. *High Fidelity*, November 1970: 128.

Christgau, Robert. "Sgt. Pepper, the Monkees, the Candymen, Frank Zappa, miscellaneous." *Esquire*, December 1967. www.robertchristgau.com/xg/bk-aow/column2.php

Fonda, Peter. *Don't Tell Dad: A Memoir*. New York: Hyperion, 1998: 208.

Hofmann, Albert. *LSD: My Problem Child* (trans. Jonathan Ott). Los Angeles: J.P. Tarcher, Inc., 1983: 198.

King, Stephen. *The Shining*. New York: Anchor Books, 1977, 2012: 388.

Leary, Timothy, quoted in *Rock, Counterculture and the Avant-Garde, 1966–1970: How the Beatles, Frank Zappa and the Velvet Underground Defined an Era*, by Doyle Green. Jefferson, NC: McFarland, 2016: 25.

Lee, Martin, and Bruce Shlain. *Acid Dreams*. New York: Grove, 1992: xx, xxiv, 47, 101, 180.

Lees, Gene. "Beatles, Op. 15." *High Fidelity*, August 1967: 94.

Lees, Gene. "Rock, Raga, and the Cop-Out." *High Fidelity*, July 1967: 82–3.

Naphtali, Wagner. "The Beatles' Psychoclassical Synthesis: Psychedelic Classicism and Classical Psychedelia in *Sgt. Pepper*." *Sgt. Pepper and the Beatles: It Was Forty Years Ago Today* (ed. Julien, Olivier). Ashgate, 2008: 76, 89–90.

Norman, Philip, quoted in "The Second Coming of 'Sgt. Pepper,'" by Mary Stevens. *Chicago Tribune*, 29 May 1987. www.chicagotribune.com/news/ct-xpm-1987-05-29-8702090656-story.html

Phillips, Stu, quoted in *Elevator Music: A Surreal History of Muzak, Easy-Listening, and Other Moodsong: Revised and Expanded Edition*, by Joseph Lanza. Ann Arbor: University of Michigan Press, 2004: 200.

Shaw, Arnold. "Rocks in Their Heads: What Will the Protest Generation Listen to Now That the Professors Have Taken Over Rock?" *High Fidelity*, April 1969: 49–51.

Stevens, Mary. "The Second Coming of 'Sgt. Pepper.'" *Chicago Tribune*, 29 May 1987. www.chicagotribune.com/news/ct-xpm-1987-05-29-8702090656-story.html

CHAPTER 5. A WAIL OF ILLUSION

Ballard, J.G. *Vermilion Sands*. Frogmore, St. Albans, Herts.: Panther, 1975: 112–23.

"Command Will Launch Electronic Music LPs." *Billboard*, 5 April 1969: 3.

Lees, Gene. "Rock, Raga, and the Cop-Out." *High Fidelity*, July 1967: 82–3.

Tiegel, Eliot. "U.S. Digs East Music: Shankar." *Billboard*, 24 February 1968: 1, 6.

Wilson, John S. Review of *Paint It Black*, by the Soulful Strings. *High Fidelity*, June 1967: 106.

CHAPTER 6. SAN FRANCISCO – AND THE FLOWERS ARE BLUE

Harris, Mark. "The Flowering of the Hippies." *Atlantic Monthly*, September 1967. www.theatlantic.com/magazine/archive/1967/09/the-flowering-of-the-hippies/306619/

Hennessey, Mike. "'Blue' Strikes Up the Band." *Billboard*, 24 February 1968: 1, 6.

Legrand, Emmanuel. "Still Touring and Recording at 70, Mauriat is Anything but Blue." *Billboard*, 20 January 1996: P3 & P-5. www.grandorchestras.com/mauriat/misc/-mauriat-interview-billboard1996.html

McAlester, Keven. "1967 | San Francisco (Be Sure to Wear Some Flowers in Your Hair) by Scott McKenzie: How a Commercial Became an Anthem." PBS.org, 16 June 2017. www.pbs.org/wgbh/americanexperience/features/Songs-of-the-summer-1967/

"New Instrumental Sounds Top Chart." *Billboard*, 3 August 1968: 1, 54, 65.

Savage, Jon. "Scott McKenzie's San Francisco was a Hippy Anthem with a Life of Its Own." TheGuardian.com, 20 August 2012. www.theguardian.com/music/musicblog/-2012/aug/20/scott-mckenzie-san-francisco-anthem

Smith, Alan. "Parents 'Built Up' Son Paul So He Could Play." *New Musical Express*, 13 April 1968: 2. [Profile of Paul Mauriat]

"'Soul' Riviera Stereo Single." *Billboard*, 13 April 1968: 53. [Re: Raymond Lefevre's single "Soul Coaxing"]

"Two States in West Ban Sale of LSD; California and Nevada Act to Control Illegal Use." *The New York Times*, 31 May 1966: 1.

Way, Michael. "Strictly Instrumental." *Billboard*, 8 July 1972: F.4.

CHAPTER 7. LOVE AND "THE INTERNAL-MUZAK DENIAL MOVE"

Echols, Johnny, quoted in "Love—Forever Changes | Johnny Echols Interview." *Vinyl Rewind*, 10 January 2016. IMDb. www.imdb.com/title/tt5963052/?ref_=fn_al_tt_1

Einarson, John. *Forever Changes: Arthur Lee and the Book of Love*. New York: Jawbone Press, 2010.

Hultkrans, Andrew. "Forever Changes." *33 1/3 Greatest Hits, Vol. 1* (ed. David Barker). New York: Continuum, 2006: 20. [re: Sandy Pearlman's "Internal-Muzak Denial Move"]

Lee, Arthur quoted in a '70s interview with Lenny Kaye from *33 1/3 Greatest Hits, Volume 1*. "Forever Changes," by Andrew Hultkrans (ed. David Barker). New York: The Continuum International Publishing Group, Inc., 2006.

Loew, Steven. Review of *Forever Changes*. *High Fidelity*, March 1968: 118.

Rosen, Jody. "Good Love: Remembering the Psychedelic Folk Rocker Arthur Lee." *Slate*, 10 August 2006. slate.com/news-and-politics/2006/08/remembering-the-psychedelic-folk-rocker-arthur-lee.html

CHAPTER 8. A SEA OF GREEN TAMBOURINES

"Enoch Light Singers Debut." *Billboard*, 23 March 1968: 6.

"'Green Tambourine' (Newest Releases)." *Billboard*, 1 June 1968: 17.

Kennedy, Rick. "Off the Charts." Cincinnatimagazine.com, 11 May 2011. www.cincinnatimagazine.com/citywiseblog/off-the-charts3/

"Leka and Pinz Author Spot for Job Corps." *Billboard*, 30 December 1967: 3.

Simpson, Dave. "How We Made MacArthur Park." *The Guardian*, 11 November 2013. www.theguardian.com/culture/2013/nov/11/how-we-made-macarthur-park

Tuyl, Ian Van, and Owen Grover. *Popstrology*. New York: Bloomsbury, 2004: 205.

Varias, Chris. "50 years later: Relive the Summer of Love." *The Enquirer*, 8 August 2017. www.cincinnati.com/story/entertainment/music/2017/08/08/50-years-later-relive-summer-love/549092001/

CHAPTER 9. DONOVAN'S BRAIN AND THE CEILIING REFRAIN

Altham, Keith. "India Inspires Donovan to Compose." *New Musical Express*. 30 March 1968: 12.

"Donovan: 'Guruvy' Song Spinner." *Billboard*, 9 November 1968: 14.

"'Goodtime Hour' Rated Tonight's Best Show." *Buffalo Courier-Express*, 18 March 1969: 59.

Griffiths, Jean. "London Lowdown." *Record World*, 6 April 1968: 20.

Leitch, Donovan. *The Autobiography of Donovan: The Hurdy Gurdy Man*. New York: St. Martin's Press, 2005: 11, 195, 239.

"Menley & James Turns To Love 1969 Style." *New York Times*, 26 January 1969, Page F16.

Myers, Marc. "The Story Behind Donovan's 'Sunshine Superman': How Donovan came up with 'Sunshine Superman,' the first psychedelic hit to top *Billboard*'s pop chart." WallStreetJournal.com, 9 April 2017: www.wsj.com/articles/the-story-behind-donovans-sunshine-superman-1491735610

"Mystic Moods Going Mod." *Billboard*, 5 October 1968: 4.

Rolling Stone Interviews: 1967–1980 (ed. Peter Herbst). New York: St. Martin's Press/Rolling Stone Press, 1981: 5–8. [Reprint of John Carpenter's November 9, 1967 interview with Donovan]

CHAPTER 10. HARD TO BE EASY

Barnes, Clive. "Theater: 'Hair'—It's Fresh and Frank; Likable Rock Musical Moves to Broadway." *The New York Times*, 30 April 1968: 40.

Finkle, Dave. "'Hair' Composer Galt Mac-Dermot: The Muse Grooves on Staten Island." *Record World*, 17 May 1969, Section II: 13.

Chapman, John. "'Hair' is Itchy, Twitchy, & Dirty: The Company Dance with Zest." *New York Daily News*, 30 April 1968: 48.

Gross, Mike. "'Hair' Scraggly; Bare of Form, Not Forms." *Billboard*, 11 May 1968: 14.

"Here's What Dailies Said." *Billboard*, 11 May 1968: 14. [Brief synopsis of some *Hair* critiques.]

Lee, Martin A., and Bruce Shlain. *Acid Dreams*. New York: Grove Press, 1985, 1992: 228, 258.

Lees, Gene. Review of *"The Windmills of Your Mind": Percy Faith and His Orchestra Play the Academy Award Winner and Other Great Movie Themes*. High Fidelity, October 1969: 130–31.

Peikert, Mark. "Galt MacDermot, Composer of *Hair*, Dead at 89." Playbill.com, 17 December 2018. www.playbill.com/article/galt-macdermot-composer-of-hair-dead-at-89

Rado, James, quoted in "'Hair' Songs Too Hot to Handle, Authors Claim." *Billboard*, 28 December 1968: 56.

"RCA Will Give 'Hair' New Cut." *Billboard*, 4 May 1968: 71.

"RCA's Racusin Recalls: 'Hair' in Class By Itself Right from the Start." *Record World*, 17 May 1969, Section II: 5.

Reich, Charles A. *The Greening of America*. New York: Bantam, 1971: 3, 195, 255, 289–90, 429.

Shapiro, Nat. "The 'Hair' Story and How It Grew." *Record World*, 17 May 1969, Section II: 3.

Theater Talk, 16 May 2009, PBS [Susan Haskins interviews with Galt MacDermot, James Rado, and Gavin Creel]

Watts, Jr., Richard. "Music of the American Tribe." *New York Post*, 30 April 1968. www.orlok.com/hair/holding/articles/HairArticles/NYPost4-30-68.html

CHAPTER 11. SLEEP SAFE AND WARM

Crosby, David, quoted in *Jim Morrison: Life, Death, Legend*, by Stephen Davis. New York: Gotham Books, 2004: 347.

Davis, Stephen. *Jim Morrison: Life, Death, Legend*. New York: Gotham Books, 2004: xi, 347–8.

Dubro, Alec. Review of *The Soft Parade*. Rolling Stone, 23 August 1969. www.rollingstone.com/music/music-album-reviews/the-soft-parade-206183/

Gross, Mike. "Pop Speaks Soft, Carries Big Stick." *Billboard*, 31 May 1969: 1, 4.

"Letters to the Editor." *Billboard*, 8 November 1969: 22.

Miller, Jim. Review of Pink Floyd's *A Saucerful of Secrets*. Rolling Stone 26 October 1968. www.rollingstone.com/music/music-album-reviews/a-saucerful-of-secrets-184964/

"Percy Faith Cuts New 'Summer Place.'" *Billboard*, 5 July 1969: 34.

"'Rosemary,' 'Odd Couple' Much-Waxed." *Record World*, 9 November 1969: 36.

Shea, Stuart. *Pink Floyd FAQ: Everything Left to Know … and More!* Lanham, MD: Backbeat, 2009.

CHAPTER 12. YOU MIGHT NOT COME BACK

Ames, Morgan. Review of *Contemporary Sound of Nelson Riddle*. High Fidelity, May 1969: 124.

"Beautiful Music Boom is Cited." *Billboard*, 3 August 1968: 14.

"Bonneville Binder for Fox, Sammes." *Billboard*, 10 November 1979: 28.

"Linkletter Raps Drug Risks." *Billboard*, 11 July 1970: 33.

Martin, George, quoted in "Program Directors Share Burden of Improving Disks." *Billboard*, 11 July 1970: 34.

Pynchon, Thomas. *The Crying of Lot 49*. London: Vintage Books, 1966: 98-9.

Riddle, Nelson, quoted in *September in the Rain: The Life of Nelson Riddle*, by Peter J. Levinson. Lanham, MD: Taylor Trade Publishing, 2005: 260.

Ross, Sean. "Fallen on Hard Times, Easy Moves Toward Soft AC." *Billboard*, 26 May 1990: 1, 89.

Rutt, Todd quoted in *Elevator Music: A Surreal History of Muzak, Easy Listening, and Other Moodsong: Revised and Expanded Edition*, by Joseph Lanza. Ann Arbor: University of Michigan Press, 2004: 196–7.

Schlichting, Jim, author telephone interview, 1 October 2019.

Sheff, David. "Interview with John Lennon and Yoko Ono." (Interview in September of 1980) *Playboy* January 1981. www.beatlesinterviews.org/db1980.jlpb.beatles.html

Taylor, Marlin R. *Radio: My Love, My Passion*. Herndon, VA: Mascot Books, 2018: 107.